Topographic Mapping
of the
Americas, Australia, and New Zealand

TOPOGRAPHIC MAPPING
OF THE
AMERICAS, AUSTRALIA, AND
NEW ZEALAND

Mary Lynette Larsgaard

1984

Libraries Unlimited, Inc.   Littleton, Colorado

LIBRARIES UNLIMITED, INC.
P.O. Box 263
Littleton, Colorado 80160-0263

Library of Congress Cataloging in Publication Data

Larsgaard, Mary Lynette, 1946-
  Topographic mapping of the Americas, Australia, and New Zealand.

  Bibliography: p. 113
  1. Topographic maps. 2. North America--Maps, Topographic. 3. Latin America--Maps, Topographic. 4. Australia--Maps, Topographic. 5. New Zealand--Maps, Topographic. I. Title.
GA125.L37 1984   912   84-3874
ISBN 0-87287-276-9.

Libraries Unlimited books are bound with Type II nonwoven material that meets and exceeds National Association of State Textbook Administrators' Type II nonwoven material specifications Class A through E.

For

Dr. William Loy
thesis advisor *extraordinaire*

TABLE OF CONTENTS

List of Maps and Figures. ix

Preface xi

Part I
Topographic Maps and Mapping

1   Topographic Maps: What They Are. 3

    Definitions. 3
    Methods of Relief Depiction 9
    Problems in Relief Depiction 12
    Conclusion. 13

2   History of Relief Portrayal on Maps 14

    The Sixteenth Century. 14
    The Seventeenth Century 15
    The Eighteenth Century 15
    The Nineteenth Century. 17
    The Twentieth Century 18

3   Topographic Surveys: Methodology, Fifteenth Century
    through Twentieth Century. 19

    The Geodetic Basis of Topographic Surveying. 19
    The Fifteenth and Sixteenth Centuries 20
    The Seventeenth Century 21
    The Eighteenth Century 22
    The Nineteenth Century. 22
    The Twentieth Century 23

Part II
Topographic Mapping of Australia and New Zealand

4   Australia 35

5   New Zealand 41

Part III
Topographic Mapping of Latin America

6 Introduction and Overview 49

7 Mexico 53

8 Central America 57

   Belize 57
   Costa Rica 57
   El Salvador. 58
   Guatemala 59
   Honduras. 59
   Nicaragua. 60
   Panama 61

9 South America 63

   Argentina. 63
   Bolivia. 65
   Brazil 66
   Chile. 69
   Colombia. 70
   Ecuador. 71
   Guyanas 72
   Paraguay 73
   Peru 74
   Uruguay 75
   Venezuela 76

Part IV
Topographic Mapping of North America

10 Greenland 83

11 Canada 84

12 United States 92

Part V
Bibliography

Bibliography. 113

Index 171

LIST OF
MAPS AND FIGURES

MAPS

Map of Australia and New Zealand:
Topographic Mapping, 1900-1970
(1:250,000 and more detailed). 44

Map of South America:
Topographic Mapping, 1900-1970
(1:250,000 and more detailed). 78

Map of North and Central America:
Topographic Mapping, 1900-1970
(1:250,000 and more detailed). 109

FIGURE

Argentinian Topographic Map Issuance, 1900-1940 .64

PREFACE

Topographic Mapping of the Americas, Australia, and New Zealand provides an overview of the history and current status of topographic mapping in twenty-four countries.

The need for this book became apparent to me during fifteen years as a map librarian. Working as I was in a relatively small collection, I repeatedly discovered that I needed to find out about detailed topographic mapping of various land areas outside of the United States. Citations to such information, while copious, were often listed only in esoteric bibliographies, and the publications which they described were often held by no more than five or ten libraries in the entire country. Considering that topographic sheets form the bulk of the 85,000 to 100,000 maps published every year and are, moreover, the most frequently used maps in almost any map collection (Hagen 1977, p. 202), the above is an unfortunate situation which this reference tool is intended to alleviate.

The first section of the book looks at the history of the topographic map, tracing the evolution of the tools and methods of mapping, from the rudimentary surveying devices of the fifteenth century to the satellites and computers of the twentieth.

These introductory chapters are followed by chapters devoted to the maps and mapping history of North, Central, and South America, Australia, and New Zealand. Mapping conducted during these countries' colonial eras, as well as their own national mapping efforts, are covered.

The maps included in this survey are restricted to official, publicly available, civilian (or military, if that is all that is available) contoured maps. Each must be part of a series intended to cover an entire nation, and must be at a scale of 1:250,000 or more detailed. Sheets issued as recently as the early 1980s have been included.

Twentieth-century maps included in this study use contours as the major method of showing relief, as contours have been widely considered in this century to be the most accurate method of depicting landforms. The scale—1:250,000 or more detailed—was chosen because there is a consensus that it represents the upper limit at which contours may be effectively used to depict relief. Generally only those series issued by a country for its own territory and colonies were considered; if no coverage is available, foreign mapping is noted.

The numerous references scattered through the text serve to direct the reader to the extensive bibliography of topographical mapping that comprises the last third of the book. The reader will note that in many cases a number of references have been supplied for a given statement. The literature of cartography can be esoteric; as many relevant citations as could be found are included here in the hope that the user will have access to at least one.

Certainly it would have been ideal to have samples of the various topographic series discussed accompanying the text; unfortunately, such illustrations would make the book both impossibly bulky and prohibitively expensive. Three maps depicting topographic coverage over the years have been included, along with lists of the sources used to compile them.

I could not have accomplished this project without the help and encouragement of my good friends in the library world. My heartfelt thanks to Fred Stair, reference librarian at the Arthur Lakes Library of the Colorado School of Mines, who heroically sent out literally hundreds of interlibrary forms for me. Thanks also to those libraries that generously loaned so many items and to those libraries that allowed me to use their collections even though I was neither student, faculty, nor (except in Colorado) taxpayer—the University of Colorado at Boulder; the Denver Public Library; the University of Minnesota; and the University of Illinois at Urbana-Champaign. A special thanks to Mai Treude in the Map Room at Minnesota for providing tea to sweep the dust from my throat, and to David Cobb at Illinois for checking on items beforehand and having them pulled for me. The section on New Zealand could not have been written without the able assistance of P. L. Barton, map librarian at the National Library of New Zealand. The Library of Congress served magnificently as my court of last resort; I shall always cherish a fondness for the summer coolness of the marble floors of the stacks in the main building.

Dr. William Loy, whom I was fortunate enough to have as my thesis advisor in geography, merits thanks not only for his superb and tactful job of editing but especially for treating my thesis (from which this book has evolved) as if it were very important not just to me but to him also.

This work could never have been completed without the support and trust of Hartley K. Phinney, Jr., director of the Arthur Lakes Library, Colorado School of Mines, where I was employed while I labored away at this tome. Hart gave me time away from the Map Room reference desk to research and to write, time without which I doubt I could have completed this work.

Thanks go to my sister and brother-in-law and their family for letting me be such a boring three-week house guest during my stay in St. Paul. And thanks to my parents for everything—a thanks that I am afraid all too often goes without saying.

M. L. L.

Part I
TOPOGRAPHIC MAPS
AND MAPPING

1
TOPOGRAPHIC MAPS:
What They Are

The supreme achievement of the modern age of cartography is undoubtedly the topographical map.

—Jervis 1938, p. 171

A book could be written about the topographic map.

—Mitchell 1925, p. 222

DEFINITIONS

There is a lack of unanimity as to the definition of a topographic map. In the original Greek, topography means topos (place) + graphia (style of drawing or description) therefore—description of a place (Sylvester 1952, p. 3; Skelton 1952, p. 10.). In this volume, a topographic map is considered to be a map showing both cultural and natural features, the latter predominately by the use of contour lines. However, in order to demonstrate the variety of definitions that have been used in the mapping literature, a selection is provided here, as follows:

- graphic representation of the physical features of a portion of the Earth's surface, plotted to scale on a flat sheet; depicts relief, water features, vegetation, and works of man, thereby portraying cumulative effects of the forces of nature and man (Thompson and Speert 1964, p. 30)

- includes geodetic controls, all stable constructional features, lakes and selected rivers, administrative boundaries and topographic details (UN 1974b, p. 32)

- graphic representation of natural features and many man-made features on a particular part of the Earth's surface (Cobb 1971, p. 272)

- graphic representation of selected man-made and natural features of a part of the Earth's surface plotted to a definite scale to portray shape and elevation of terrain (United States. General Accounting Office 1968, p. 1)

- a reasonably large-scale map with contours (Simonpietri 1947, p. 86)

- delineation of all natural and artificial physical features together with a system of contours depicting the third dimension of relief (L. Fitz-Gerald 1951b, p. 244)

- fairly large scale (1:63,360) map depicting landforms and all other objects and aspects both of natural or human origin (F. J. Monkhouse. 1965. *A dictionary of geography.* London: Edward Arnold, p. 311)

- "la que está confecionada mediante de un levantamiento regular que incluye la topografía y los accidentes artificiales, permitando facilmente la determinación de altura" (that [map] which is made during a regular survey, including topography and artificial roughness, and easily permitting the determination of altitude); a planimetric map with the addition of altitude information (Pan American Consultation on Cartography 1954, p. 28)

- map portraying terrain, usually by contours (lines connecting points of equal elevation) or hachures (short wedge-shaped marks radiating from high elevations and following the direction of slope to low land) (Ehrenberg 1982, p. 56)

- map based on actual survey of position and leveled in the field, in sufficient detail to allow of portraying, with reasonable accuracy to a scale of 1:500,000 (or more detailed) and with contours at least 500 feet apart, most natural physical features and artifical features, such as railroads, roads, towns, reservoirs, aerodromes, etc. (A. D. Lewis 1938, p. 3)

- a graphic representation of the Earth's surface depicting primarily the hypsography and the planimetry of a given area, usually published in multicolours; the hypsography, or relief, is generally indicated by contour lines at definite intervals, while in certain cases spot elevations, formlines, hachures and shading are also used, either separately or in combination with contour lines; planimetric details include water features or drainage, and other natural or cultural (man-made) features (UN. Secretariat 1957, p. 3)

- only those maps at scales larger than 1:100,000, which show by signs and symbols all the major and many of the minor features of scenery, generally at a scale of 1:10,000 to 1:500,000, and typically at a scale of about 1:63,360 (Jervis 1938, p. 18)

- a map which presents the vertical position of features in measurable form as well as their horizontal positions (Defense Mapping Agency 1973, p. 253)

- large-scale, general purpose map of a relatively small portion of the Earth's surface; key point is that it shows not only correct planimetric (horizontal) relationships but hypsometric (vertical) as well (*Great international atlas*. 1981. Englewood Cliffs, N.J.: Prentice-Hall, p. xxiii)

- representation on paper that is designed to portray certain selected features of a section of the Earth's surface plotted on some form of projection and to a certain scale; it primarily depicts the relief of the country mapped, but also shows its drainage and cultural features, and delineates all parts in a rigidly correct relative position (Thiele 1938, p. 122)

- shows location of hills, valleys, streams, lakes, and other features contributing to land forms and cultural features; in addition to showing horizontal position of land forms and cultural features, also shows vertical relationships (relief) (Stephenson 1949, p. 1)

- a map whose principal purpose is to portray and identify the features of the Earth's surface as faithfully as possible within the limitations imposed by scale (*Multilingual dictionary of technical terms in cartography*. 1973. Wiesbaden: Franz Steiner, p. 278)

- a map intermediate between a general map and a plan, on a scale large enough to show roads, plans of towns, and contour lines (*Webster's third international dictionary*, p. 2411)

- a map that represents the horizontal and vertical positions of the feature represented; uses contours or comparable symbols to show mountains, valleys and plains (United Nations. Dept. of Economic and Social Affairs. 1970. "A guide to standard technological specifications for aerial photographs." *World cartography* 10:97-113)

- a map on sufficiently large scale to show detailed surface features of an area, including its relief (usually by means of contours), and such physical features as forests, rivers, and lakes, and such artificial features as roads, railroads, and canals (W. G. Moore. 1967. *A dictionary of geography, definitions and explanations of terms used in physical geography*. New York: Praeger, p. 222)

- a systematic representation of a small part of the land surface showing physical features and cultural features; large-scale map presenting both vertical and horizontal features in measurable form (Thrower 1972, p. 174)

- presents both the horizontal and vertical detail in measurable form, so that distances, azimuths, and elevations may be accurately determined from the map by the map user (United States. Dept. of the Army 1970, p. 1-1)

- map giving a detailed description of a portion of the Earth's surface, representing a three-dimensional land surface; arrangement of features in physical space at a certain time (Biddle, Milne and Shortle 1974, pp. 10, 53, 94)

- large-scale map that conveys shape and pattern of landscape by selected features in a standardized form set in a framework at uniform scale (Harvey 1980, p. 9)

- concise record of the surface features of a piece of country (Sylvester 1952, p. 3)

There is also no consensus of opinion on what constitutes "large-scale," "medium-scale," and "small-scale" topographic maps, as the following list indicates:

- scales between 1:25,000 and 1:250,000 (Arden-Close 1905, p. 633)

- scales greater than 1:500,000 (F. J. Monkhouse. 1965. *A dictionary of geography*. London: Edward Arnold, p. 311)

- scales greater than 1:75,000 as being large-scale (Thrower 1972, p. 171)

- scales 1:250,000 to 1:10,000 (Harris 1970, p. 104)

- scales of 1:254,000 to 1:25,000 (Duncan Johnston 1909, p. 508)

- small-scale, to 1:63,360; medium-scale, 1:25,000 to 1:10,560; large-scale, 1:2,500 to 1:1,056 (Great Britain. Ordnance Survey 1949, p. 1, 2; UN. Secretariat 1957, p. 22; Winterbotham 1932, p. 20; Great Britain. Ordnance Survey 1954, p. 1)

- scales of 1:10,000 to 1:25,000 as large-scale (France. Institut 1950, p. 34)

- 1:200,000 and larger as large-scale (in Russia) (Polezhayev 1962, p. 75)

- 1:2,500 to 1:5,000 as large-scale (UN 1974b, p. 49)

- 1:50,000 as medium-scale (in Japan) (Kakisita 1963, p. 192)

- 1:100,000 as small-scale (in Israel) (Israel 1970, p. I/9)

- only those maps at scales larger than 1:1,000,000 as topographic; large-scale as larger than 1:25,000, medium-scale as 1:25,000-1:75,000 (UN. Secretariat 1957, p. 3)

- small-scale as smaller than 1:500,000; intermediate-scale as 1:50,000 to 1:500,000; large-scale as larger than 1:50,000 (Floyd F. Sabins, 1978. *Remote sensing: principles and interpret..tion.* San Francisco: W.H. Freeman. p. 7)

- small-scale as smaller than 1:200,000 (Imhof 1982, p. 115)

- large-scale as 1:100,000 and larger; medium-scale as 1:100,000 to 1:1,000,000; small-scale as 1:1,000,000 (Short 1982, p. 486)

- large-scale as 1:25,000, medium-scale as 1:250,000, and small-scale as 1:1,000,000 (L. FitzGerald 1980, p. xi)

- large-scale plans as 1:2,500 and larger, small-scale maps as 1:250,000 to 1:2,500,000 (Lawrence 1971, p. 7)

- 1:250,000 to 1:10,000 as topographic maps; smaller scale maps as geographic maps (Harris 1970, p. 104)

- 1:250,000 as small scale (in the United States) (Fry 1975, p. 338)

- usually 1:20,000-scale to 1:200,000-scale; medium-scale maps as 1:200,000 to 1:1,000,000, and small-scale as 1:100,000 on up; a topographic map as being a large-scale map only (Marschner 1943, pp. 209, 212)

- large-scale as 1:24,000, and intermediate-scale as 1:50,000 to 1:100,000 (United States. Geological Survey 1979, p. 48)

- medium- and large-scale as 1:31,680, and larger; medium-scale as 1:25,000 to 1:50,000; small- and medium-scale as 1:1,000,000, 1:250,000, 1:100,000, 1:50,000, and 1:25,000 (Lambert 1969, pp. 517, 524)

- large-scale as 1:25,000 to 1:50,000 (Simonpietri 1947, p. 87)

- large-scale as 1:50,000 to 1:25,000; small-scale as 1:500,000 to 1:200,000 (Martinson 1975, p. 10)

- large-scale as 1:75,000 and larger; medium-scale as 1:75,000 to 1:600,000 (United States. Dept. of the Army 1963, p. 272)

- 1:25,000 to 1:50,000 (1:100,000-scale and smaller are geographic maps); large-scale in the United States as 1:20,000 to 1:62,500; in Chile, 1:25,000 to 1:100,000 (Consultation on Geodesy 1945, pp. 142, 145, 148)

- 1:10,000 to 1:500,000; best scales as 1:10,000 to 1:1,000,000, and very best scales as 1:63,360, 1:50,000, and 1:100,000 (Jervis 1938, p. 174)

- small-scale as 1:50,000 and smaller; medium-scale as ·1:20,000 to 1:50,000; large-scale as 1:10,000 and larger (UN 1966b, p. 315)

- small-scale as 1:250,000 to 1:25,000; medium-scale as 1:25,000 to 1:10,000; and large-scale as 1:10,000 to 1:500 (in Cambodia) (UN 1966b, p. 26)

- large-scale as greater than 1:40,000; medium-scale as 1:40,000 to 1:300,000; and small-scale as smaller than 1:300,000 (Ewing and Marcus, 1966, p. 764)

- large-scale as 1:63,360 and larger; medium-scale as 1:63,361 to 1:126,760; small-scale as 1:126,761 to 1:253,440 (Platt 1945, p. 175)

- small-scale as 1:100,000 to 1:1,000,000; medium-scale as 1:25,000 to 1:100,000; small-scale maps as showing relief, drainage and culture highly generalized; medium-scale maps as showing relief and drainage well and to scale, with drainage conventionalized; large-scale maps as depicting all three in true shape and to scale (O'Brien 1970, p. 154)

- large-scale as 1:250,000 or larger (Jáuregui 1968, pp. 5-6)

- not larger than 1:10,000 or smaller than 1:10,000,000 (Scientific Council 1955, p. 9)

- 1:500,000 or smaller; reliable large-scale as 1:63,360 and larger; secondary large-scale as 1:63,360 to 1:126,720; medium-scale as 1:126,720 to 1:500,000 (Karo 1955, plate II)

- small-scale as 1:200,000 to 1:2,000,000 (UN 1979, p. 254)

- 1:200,000 and larger (Meine 1972, p. 182)

- larger than 1:125,000; large-scale as 1:2,500 to 1:1,250 (Harris 1964, p. 229)

- large-scale as 1:6,000 to 1:120; small- and intermediate-scale as 1:96,000 to 1:6,000 (Low 1952, pp. 107, 168)

- scales from 1:2,500 to 1:500,000 (Frenzel 1962, p. 295)

- small-scale as 1:250,000 to 1:100,000; medium-scale as 1:50,000 to 1:25,000; large-scale as 1:5,000 to 1:500 (Boaga 1952, p. 86)

- 1:10,000 to 1:200,000 (Pan American Consultation on Cartography 1948, pp. 97-98)

It all seems to be a relative matter, depending upon the range of scales at which a country is mapped.

Despite the lack of agreement regarding the precise definition and scale of topographic maps, they are the most frequently used of all types of maps. They are also among the most exacting of all maps to make, largely because of the difficulties and expense of the field work and because of the problem of depicting relief, "showing the three-dimensional ground surface by two-dimensional means" (Biddle, Milne and Shortle 1974, p. 43). In addition to this, the perfect topographic map should not merely indicate relief but actually convey an expressive representation of landforms, correctly indicate the measure of relief, faithfully delineate the true shape and size of each topographic unit, and be reliable as to the relative position and orientation of such units (Matthes 1908, p. 893). Not only must a topographic map give a visual impression of relief, it must also supply precise values (Lawrence 1971, p. 14).

Topographic maps are usually issued in series by the national surveys. Individual parts of these series are called "sheets"; the series as a whole is referred to as a map. Each sheet is usually oblong and of a "manageable size," that is to say, no more than 36 inches wide (Sylvester 1952, p. 5; Janicot 1969, p. 66). The total number of sheets in a series may change for any number of reasons, such as a decision to change the sheet lines (which determine what size and location of area will be shown on each sheet); these changes are reflected in the final drawing of the index map. Each sheet depicts physical and cultural features of a relatively small section of the Earth's surface, using a method of representing relief that gives an accurate picture of the Earth's surface. Scales chosen are usually from about 1:20,000 to 1:100,000.

This work restricts its discussion of topographic maps to those using contour lines to show relief. National official topographic sheets issued in the twentieth century have used contours almost exclusively. Nevertheless contour lines have not always been the premier method of depicting relief, and to understand why it is helpful to study the various methods available, and the history of relief depiction.

METHODS OF RELIEF DEPICTION

There are many different methods used to depict relief. These include hachuring, hill shading and shaded relief, contour lines, formlines, hypsometric tints, hill and mountain profiles, physiographic sketching, spot elevations, cliff drawing and rock drawing, almost any combination of the aforementioned, and three-dimensional methods such as embossing or raised relief. Each has its merits and demerits and "drawn battles have been fought over every known method" (Hotine 1956, p. 271). As will be seen, the prime difficulty is "arriving at a compromise between nature and mathematics.... Relief can be portrayed with picturesque naturalness, or it can be represented with mathematical precision. To combine the two and yet show other detail with satisfactory clarity seems well-nigh impossible" (Jervis 1938, p. 57)—but the Swiss, among others, have certainly made a sporting try.

Hachuring

Hachuring is a system in which light is assumed to fall in vertical rays upon slopes, the illumination received by each slope varying in proportion to its divergence from the plane of the horizontal. Vertical rays of light falling on a plane inclined at an angle of 45° are reflected horizontally; such a plane is represented by complete black on the "scale of shade." A horizontal plane that reflects all light rays upward is thus white. The intermediate slopes are divided into nine parts, each comprising 5°, with the proportion of black to white varying with the slope (Wallis 1976, p. 29). It was very popular in Europe in the nineteenth century, but it is heavily dependent upon the manual skill of the draftsperson. Large series that are hachured may lack uniformity from sheet to sheet, and on steep slopes such thick lines are required that detail is obscured—the ruling principle being that the steeper the slope, the closer together, darker, and shorter are the hachures (Sylvester 1952, p. 25; Romer 1930; Imhof 1958, p. 11; Wallis 1976, p. 29). While much less accurate than contours, since there is no numerical altitudinal value attached to a hachure, they can give a more realistic representation (when skillfully done) than do contours (Stephenson 1949, p. 3).

Hill Shading

Hill shading (of which hachuring is occasionally considered to be a form) involves coloring slopes in rough proportion to the intensity of the slope. It is unsuitable for showing detail, but can give an excellent plastic effect, particularly when shaded relief, a similar system, is used in combination with contour lines. Hill shading works well on less detailed maps, such as those of states, nations, and continents (Dake 1925, pp. 6-10). The use of shaded relief significantly increases the cost of producing the map (UN 1966b, p. 483) in that it may involve complicated procedures (e.g., constructing a three-dimensional model, illuminating that model obliquely, and then photographing it) (Davis 1924, p. 326).

Contours and Formlines

Contour lines are curves produced by the intersection of imaginary horizontal planes at a selected interval with the three-dimensional shape of the terrain (Richardus 1973, p. 81). Formlines, usually shown as a dashed contour line, are contour lines that have been sketched in through general observation rather than instrumentally determined by exact measurement (Biddle, Milne and Shortle 1974, p. 61).

The size of the interval between contours ("contour interval" or "CI") depends on the scale of the map and on the steepness of the terrain; the interval is large when the scale is small and when the relief is steep. Although CI would, in a perfect cartographic world, be the same not only on a given sheet (as indeed it is) but on all sheets in a series, in practice it often varies from sheet to sheet, depending upon the terrain depicted. For example, in Great Britain's 1:63,360 series, CI varies from 50 feet to 1,000 feet, depending upon whether land shown by the map is, respectively, flat or mountainous (Duncan Johnston 1909, p. 515).

Contour lines are presently the most important form of cartographic relief portrayal; they represent form relatively well and give a numerical altitudinal value to a large number of points, the latter being the quality that gives them the edge over other methods (Imhof 1982, p. 111). Contour lines are not generally suitable for the representation of glaciers, steep cliffs, and deserts. Generalization begins at a scale of 1:25,000; at less detailed scales the line is so thick that it may obscure detail; detail between lines is of course lost; and, most tellingly, "the general public is apt to misunderstand contours" (Cluerg 1933, p. 122). Users must be educated before a contoured map will mean anything to them (Lyons 1914, pp. 236-38; UN 1968, p. 468; Imhof 1951, p. 85; Jenks 1971; Winters 1922; Wood 1977 and 1978).

Hypsometric Tints

Hypsometric tints give a good overall effect of relief; they illustrate contour lines for the inexperienced user, and they show absolute height with clarity. It is difficult, however, to provide enough tints to represent great variations in elevation because of the eye's inability to differentiate between a large array of tints. Other problems that arise with the use of hypsometric tints to depict relief include: CIs are so large that important surface features may be missed completely; unless reproduction work is well done the map may have a stepped appearance; the use of tints makes the use of overlays almost impossible; and darker tints may obscure detail (UN 1968, pp. 468-69; Pannekoek 1949, p. 136; Sylvester 1952, p. 24; Leo Roberts 1924, p. 67).

The conventions of hypsometric, or layer, tints are in some ways problematic; traditionally, green is used for low ground and reds and browns for mountains, which can lead the unwary to suppose the Dead Sea and Death Valley are covered with lush vegetation. Possibly the only way to deal with this is to realize that relief is a single characteristic, and should be represented by shades of a single color.

Tints do give an attractive overall effect of relief, and since they are actually a combination of contours and color, there is an altitudinal value provided, which the use of color alone (in which method green, for example, slowly fades into brown as elevation increases) does not (Carmichael 1969; Yoéli 1959 and 1964; Leo Roberts 1924, p. 67). The use of tints is generally appropriate on smaller scale maps. In the early part of this century this method was more popular in Europe than in the United States (Lee Roberts 1924, p. 67).

Other Methods and Combinations of Methods

Hills and mountains drawn in profile are relatively easy to do but they are inexact and can hide other physical features behind them. Physiographic sketching, as epitomized by the work of Raisz and Lobeck, gives an excellent effect but no information about elevation; it is actually a sophisticated version of hill and mountain profiling (Raisz 1931, pp. 297, 303).

Spot elevations have proven themselves to be almost indispensable when used in combination with other methods, such as contouring and hachuring. Alone they are not enough. The same may be said of cliff drawing and rock drawing.

Three-dimensional methods, while producing maps that are excellent for the young or inexperienced map user, incorporate considerable vertical exaggeration (the circumference and size of the Earth being such that if true altitude relative to area were shown, the "raised" relief would be scarcely perceptible). Such maps are also far more expensive to produce than are standard maps (Field and Stetson 1942; Imhof 1982; Matthews 1908; Meux 1960; Tanaka 1974; Upton 1970; Joseph Williams 1952).

The most popular combination is that of contours, shaded relief, and spot heights, which supplies accuracy and specific numerical value while giving a vivid plastic effect. It may also be helpful in teaching new map users how contour lines work (Huber 1962, p. 130). The United States Geological Survey has issued some of its sheets in both a standard contour version and a combined-method version.

PROBLEMS IN RELIEF DEPICTION

Certain types of landforms (such as steep cliffs and broken, rocky ground; deserts; and glaciers) are especially difficult to represent on a map (A. M. L. Phillips 1915). The problem with the first is that change occurs so quickly in a short distance that it is impossible to show exactly on a reduced plan. With deserts and glaciers, the difficulty is the changeability over relatively short periods of time of the surface mapped.

Deserts are usually represented by a dot pattern (a convention dating at least from Martini's *Novus Atlas Sinensis* of 1655 and possibly of Chinese origin), or by the use of such words as "dunes," the latter doubtless showing the desperation of the cartographer (Unno 1978, p. [1]).

Mapping snow and ice, specifically mapping Antarctica and Greenland, is mainly a twentieth-century concern. The problem of mapping snow-covered areas begins even before pen is set to paper (or, today, before scribing instrument is set to Mylar)–with the interpretation of aerial photographs: What is ice? What is perennial snow? What is seasonal snow? (Henoch 1969, p. 19). The high albedo (the fraction of light, impinging on a surface, that is reflected by that surface) of snow-covered areas obscures landforms and makes contour plotting difficult or impossible; the smoother the texture of the snow and the greater the height of the airplane from which the photographs are being taken, the greater the chance for error (Henoch and Croizet 1976, p. 71).

It is often impossible even to obtain stereographic effects (essential for compiling maps from aerial photographs) from photographs of firn areas (areas of partially compacted, granular snow, also called névé); one way to circumvent this, and to dispose of the which-is-the-seasonal-snow problem, is to take photographs in the late summer, when the seasonal snow has melted and when dust and so forth have been deposited on the snow. Dye on the snow–if permitted in these environmentally conscious times–will also work (Henoch 1969, p. 121). When the relatively permanent snow has thus been identified, shaded relief used with blue contour lines on white seems to be the most easily interpreted method of relief depiction (Henoch 1969, p. 123; Ewing and Marcus 1966, p. 762).

If the decision is made to portray perennial snow, it can be done, although obviously such maps represent only the conditions at the time of the mapping far more than do the maps of permanent snow. If desired, mapping snow on such areas can be completely ignored, and the relief of the bedrock underlying the ice cap represented instead (Henoch 1969, p. 122; Espenshade and Schytt 1956; Symposium on Glacier Mapping 1966).

CONCLUSION

No one system is a panacea. The most effective form of relief portrayal for any given map or map series is dependent upon the scale, the purpose of the map, the means at the disposal of the cartographer, and the habits and aptitudes of the cartographer.

Contour lines may be used to best advantage at scales up to 1:500,000, although at scales of 1:250,000 and smaller they should be used in combination with other methods, such as shaded relief (Maugenest 1950, pp. 129, 135; Imhof 1951, p. 84; Lyons 1914, pp. 235, 397-98; Sylvester 1952, p. 22). For topographic maps of scales from 1:10,000 to 1:25,000 contours are always the most satisfactory of methods (Lyons 1914, p. 235; Maugenest 1950, p. 129).

Hachures are most effectively used on maps from 1:50,000 scale to 1:100,000 scale, while hypsometric tints are best for maps from 1:150,000 scale to 1:1,000,000 scale (Lyons 1914, p. 397). Overall, the contour line is the best method for depicting relief on detailed maps.

2
HISTORY OF
RELIEF PORTRAYAL ON MAPS

Maps are symbols, which talk to us in a secret code.
—Oscar Peschel (1826-1875)
German geographer
(Imhof 1958, p. 11)

The oldest examples of human efforts to describe landform relief (excepting the pictographic cave paintings of prehistoric man) are probably the Babylonian clay tablets of approximately 3800 B.C., where fish scale designs were used to represent valleys and mountains (Baldock 1971, p. 75; Hodgkiss 1981, p. 39). This type of relief portrayal continued for many centuries. Highlands were marked off from lowlands and filled in with color (frequently ochre or sepia), or hills and mountains were shown in profile (an early tradition, especially popular up to A.D. 1500), or the two methods were combined (Dainville 1970, and 1964, p. 167; Crone 1968, p. 66; Hodgkiss 1981, pp. 39-62; see Imhof 1982, pp. 1-8 for an excellent account of this time period).

Between A.D. 1500 and 1800, the representation of relief continued to be a problem for cartographers. In the sixteenth century the maturity of copper plate engraving led to a refinement and elaboration of the method of hill and mountain profiling, with a greater variety of mountains, especially conical sugarloafs, aligned in ranges and shaded in the east and southeast (the latter convention due to engravers working with light from the left) (Dainville 1964, pp. 196-98; Skelton 1952, p. 11). Possibly the reduction of these symbols to molehills, "the almost meaningless convention current before the introduction of modern hachures and contours," may be laid at the door of the great cartographers of the Dutch and Flemish schools. Many maps made by earlier cartographers, in the late fifteenth and sixteenth centuries, "give a vivid, if rough, interpretation of the relief of the land, such as is entirely wanting in a map of Ortelius or Mercator" (Taylor 1928, p. 474).

THE SIXTEENTH CENTURY

In 1581 Thomas Digges made reference to the heights of fourteen points above sea level in his plan of Dover Harbor. In the same decade, in 1584, lines connecting points of equal elevation—albeit of land under water—were first used, displayed as isobaths (lines on a map connecting all land points of the same depth underneath the surface of a body of water) on European river charts (Crone 1948 p. 228; Ehrenberg 1977, p. 141; Wallis 1976, p. 33; Hodgkiss 1981, p. 154).

THE SEVENTEENTH CENTURY

At the beginning of the seventeenth century, the topographic map had begun to take on a distinct and characteristic form, separate from the geographic (that is planimetric) map (Larned 1907, p. 18). While the maps of the seventeenth and for that matter the eighteenth centuries were characterized by a pictorial rather than a conventional symbol quality, and by relief information of considerable detail but limited realism, the period 1600 to 1700 was marked by the cartographers' realization—especially among those who were military engineers—that making molehills out of mountains had the inconvenient trait of hiding other features by covering the area where the other features were located.

The practice of drawing relief features as if seen from directly above, beginning with vertical shading on each slope and more dense shading on steeper slopes, thus came as an important new convention. It was used effectively late in the century by Hans Konrad Gyger in his Swiss cantonal maps. His superb 1667 map of the canton of Zurich is the first true "relief," (that is, showing landforms in a plan view, as if looking down on the land from directly above) map that has come down to us. It was considered a military secret, just as very detailed maps are often considered to be today (Imhof 1982, pp. 5, 7; Skelton 1952, p. 12; Dainville 1964, p. 168; Crone 1968, p. 126).

Hachures, introduced about 1675, were an important innovation of the seventeenth century. Hachures are a modified version of the pictographic method of hatching, which had employed oblique shading as if the object were illuminated from the northwest (Leo Roberts 1924, p. 52). The earliest map to use hachuring was Vivier's *Carte particulière des environs de Paris* of 1674 (Wallis 1976, p. 27; Harvey 1980, p. 183 disagrees, citing instead a 1718 map of Breisgau by J. B. Homann of Nuremberg).

THE EIGHTEENTH CENTURY

The eighteenth century marks the acceptance of the isoline (both as contour and as isobath), although the exact dates and persons involved are matters for polite scholarly argument. The first appearance of isolines may have been as early as the sixteenth century. Imhof (1982, p. 10) awards the palm to a 1584 map of the ocean off Het Spaarne, near Haarlem, by Pieter Bruinss; Crone, on the other hand, claims that Pierre Ancelin was first with isobaths, in 1697, on a map of Rotterdam and Nieuve Maas (1968, p. 127); while others give N. S. Cruquius's 1728 map of the Merwede the honor (Jervis 1938, pp. 196-97); and still others speak for Philippe Buache (date varying from 1729 to 1737) and his bathymetric map of the English Channel, published in the French Academy of Sciences *Mémoires* for 1752 (Jervis 1938, p. 52; Dainville 1962, p. 161; Larned 1907, p. 18; Kish 1976, p. 129). It is safest simply to say that the system was developed by marine cartographers in about the 1730s.

Spot heights began to be included on maps in the 1740s. Christopher Packe was the first to use spot heights to represent positions of measured altitude above a prescribed datum, in his 1743 map, *Philosophico-Chorographical Chart of East Kent*. In 1749 Milet de Mureau, an officer of the French corps of engineers, expounded on spot heights in his *Mémoire pour faciliter les moyes de projeter dans les pays de montagnes*. Spot heights were generally adopted and used in France in the 1770s and 1780s (Hodgkiss 1981, pp. 43, 159-60).

Milet de Mureau appears again in the history of relief depiction, this time in the matter of the first use of contours to indicate land elevation. Crone (1968, p. 127) believes Milet de Mureau, in the same year (1749), developed practical methods of using contour lines in his fortification plans; Larned (1907, p. 18) plumps for DuCarla's 1768 topographic map of Switzerland.

Dainville (1962, p. 161) and Imhof (1982, p. 12) give DuCarla credit for introducing and establishing the theory of contours, and for making the first contour map of an imaginary land; Dainville mentions Milet de Mureau working on practical applications. But Dainville and many others (Curran 1967, p. 28; Crone 1968, p. 127; Jervis 1938, p. 52) believe that the new method was first used in practice (possibly meaning on a printed and published map) by Jean Louis Dupain-Triel, in 1791, on *La France considerée dans les differentes hauteurs de ses plaines*. With that map the system of contours was "put before the French Academy in 1771 as a way to show relief ... though it was ... only in the second quarter of the nineteenth century that it came to be widely adopted" (Harvey 1980, p. 182; Imhof 1982, p. 12 considers this map to be the first contour map of an existing, as contrasted to an imaginary, land surface). The British Ordnance Survey issued its first contoured map, of Schiehallien in Perthshire, in 1778 (Jervis 1938, p. 52).

Hachures had their strongest and most practised proponent during these years in Johann Georg Lehmann, who in 1799 published a book on their use, *Darstellung einer neuer Theorie der Bezeichnung der schiefen Flächen* (Wallis 1976, p. 29; Curran 1967, p. 28; Thrower 1972, p. 78). He worked with slope hachures (lines drawn in the direction of the slope) and then shadow hachures (lines whose thickness indicates steepness—the thicker the line, the steeper the slope) (Imhof 1982, pp. 9-10). Lehmann was not an exclusionist, however; he used a combination of hachures and contours on some of his maps (Jervis 1938, pp. 196-97).

In spite of all of the progress in methods of relief depiction, most maps of the time, if they showed landforms at all, still used hills and mountains in profile, a style that would persist through the time of d'Anville, who died in 1783 (Jervis 1938, p. 50).

Hachuring was first applied on a large scale in the Cassini *Carte géometrique de France* (1744-60; 182 sheets at a scale of 1:86,400), the results of the first official national survey (Crone 1968, p. 121; Wallis 1976, p. 27; Larned 1907, p. 18). The Cassini map also used the letters D (*douce*) or F (*fort*) to indicate relief (Crone 1968, p. 121). Spot heights, whose marine equivalent had been in use since the sixteenth century—in relief depiction as in planimetry the seamen led the way—was finally put in use by the British Ordnance Survey about 1749 (Dainville 1962, p. 161; Skelton 1952, p. 13). In a list of about 900 state maps dated from the late eighteenth century to 1920, eighty used hachures and about five used contours (Hargett 1971).

THE NINETEENTH CENTURY

During the nineteenth century, over eighty different methods of shading were being used, but none told clearly and accurately enough the four principal facts of relief required on a topographic map: shape, size, slope, and elevation (Greenhood 1964, p. 77; Harris 1960, p. 14).

The use of color, which dates from the early nineteenth century, met with some success; von Hauslab, in 1828, used color intensity to indicate altitude (Lyons 1911, p. 429).

It was in the nineteenth century that contour lines were accepted and began to be frequently used, but progress was slow at first. A commission meeting in Paris in 1802 to work on uniform conventions for maps was in favor of hachures, and felt that contour lines could be restricted to plans of sites (Dainville 1964, p. 171). In 1816, at Laplace's suggestion, the French government survey began using contours, and in 1822 they began to be used in the United States (Jervis 1938, p. 53; Thrower 1972, p. 92). Despite this, by 1833 there were still only about four sheets of contoured maps in existence; in some cases contour lines were drawn as a basis for hachuring and then carefully erased before final sheets were issued (Thrower 1972, p. 80; Wallis 1976, p. 3; Hodgkiss 1981, p. 43).

It was not until the 1840s that contouring displaced hachuring as the most popular method of relief depiction; Denmark was the first to adopt them practically (Van Ornum 1896, p. 358). In the 1850s the British Ordnance Survey began to use them steadily; in 1878, the United States national survey adopted brown contours (Hodgkiss 1981, p. 43).

One of the reasons for the slow acceptance of contours has been that they do not present as aesthetically pleasing an effect as do hachures; it was not until engineering requirements necessitated more exact information that contours finally replaced hachures (Van Ornum 1896, p. 358).

Ironically, it was at this same time (1842-1864) that one of the finest examples of hachured map work, the *Topographische Karte der Schweiz* at a scale of 1:100,000—commonly but reverently called the Dufourkarte, after the person in charge—was issued (Wallis 1976, p. 27).

In 1839 Great Britain introduced contours on its 1:10,560-scale survey of Ireland maps (Hodgkiss 1981, pp. 160-61). Contours were thus first used by the British consistently in 1839 and 1840, during the British survey of Inishowen Peninsula in Donegal (Collier 1972, p. 55), or in 1849 (Thrower 1972, p. 92), or in the 1860s, with final adoption in the 1880s (Yolande Jones 1974, p. 32).

By late in the century, contouring was the preferred method of the great national surveys (Crone 1968, p. 128).

Two other important methods of depicting relief—shaded relief and layer tints—came into being in the early nineteenth century. They were made feasible by the development of lithography by Aloys C. Senefelder in the late eighteenth century, a technical revolution that profoundly influenced map production. First used to produce maps in the early nineteenth century, lithography made it possible not only to print in more than one color, but also to use continuous tonal variation or shading (Thrower 1972, p. 107; Curran 1967, p. 31). Stieler's *Hand Atlas* of 1820 gives excellent examples of printed hypsometric layering (Crone 1968, p. 128).

John Bartholomew, who became head of the firm Bartholomew in 1856, introduced along with his son John George the use of layer tints to the English-speaking world (James 1972, p. 190) and by 1880 their use was widespread (Jervis 1938, p. 55).

THE TWENTIETH CENTURY

In the twentieth century contouring has been the preferred method for showing relief on national survey detailed series sheets and on most detailed maps. Shaded relief has been increasingly used in large part because of the wedding of photography to lithography. Relief may now be drawn on plastic or paper bases with pencil or airbrush, photographed in halftone (replacing the lithographic stone), and then reproduced in a variety of ways (Baldock 1971, p. 75; Thrower 1972, p. 108; Curran 1967, pp. 32-33). This very effective, plastic method of showing relief is frequently used with contouring. Contours satisfy the intellect, as they provide elevation at many points, while shading, with its ability to make the map look like a miniaturized version of reality and not just a symbolization of that reality, appeals to the eye. Imhof (1982) offers a complete study of cartographic relief.

3
TOPOGRAPHIC SURVEYS:
Methodology, Fifteenth Century through Twentieth Century

There is of course hardly a limit to the amount of survey work that can be done in any country.

—West 1959, p. 274

The gathering of information about the Earth's surface is a tough, expensive, difficult job, and really nobody wants to do it if they can get someone else to.

—Hollis Vail
NCIC newsletter, (summer 1977) no. 6:1

Topographic surveys form the basis of all terrain cartography or, for that matter, any cartography at all.

—Imhof 1982, p. 15

And great fun it all is.

—An official of the British national survey
Winterbotham 1936, p. 202

THE GEODETIC BASIS OF TOPOGRAPHIC SURVEYING

Geodesy is fundamental to topographic mapping. It is defined as "a branch of applied mathematics that determines the exact positions of points and the figures and areas of large portions of the earth's surface, the shape and size of the earth, and the variations of terrestrial gravity and magnetism" (*Webster's seventh new collegiate dictionary,* Springfield, MA: Merriam, 1963, p. 349). Only the information needed to understand the linkage between it and topographic mapping will be mentioned here, since it is obviously a substantial topic on its own.

Triangulation, which is at the heart of geodetic surveying, involves selecting two points many miles apart, determining the latitude and longitude of each by astronomical means, measuring the line ("base line") between the two points with great accuracy, and determining the position of a third station by the angle it makes with each end of the base line. This process is continued until the whole area to be surveyed is covered. By 1926, triangulation of all the continents, while not completed, was at the stage where future changes (except in the case of Antarctica) would be relatively minor (Mathieson 1926, p. 347). By 1955, the Amazon basin, central and east Greenland, Arabia, central Asia, northeast Siberia, an area east of the Caspian Sea, and northern Africa were still remarkably short of principal arcs of triangulation (Karo 1955, plate 1; for references on the triangulation of Africa see Chapman 1895, Flotte de Roquevaire 1909, Schierhout 1938, and Bradford 1952; for Australia, Bocksette 1965; for the U.S., Berry 1976 and "Longest triangulation arc" 1943, 1944).

Geodetic networks are expensive and time-consuming to establish, owing to the difficulties of transportation, bulky instruments, and slow, painstaking procedures. Airplane transport, lightweight equipment, and new measuring techniques developed since the 1960s have made triangulation and traverse much quicker, easier, and cheaper (UN 1963a, p. 282).

Advancement has been particularly striking in the area of angular measurement, where accuracy had not increased for 150 years up to the 1960s, when there occurred tremendous miniaturization of equipment (UN 1963a, p. 284). During that decade, electronics (specifically electromagnetics and light waves) came on the scene as well, and allowed very precise traverses (UN 1963a, p. 279).

The innovations of satellite triangulation and electronic distance measurement in the 1970s put geodesists on the threshold of accomplishing their goal of establishing a worldwide geodetic network (A. D. Jones 1978, p. 69; UN 1974b, pp. 109, 203; Huggett 1981; Rueger 1980). Satellites were specifically designed to carry instruments to measure variations in the Earth's gravitational field and to determine the exact geographic position of points on Earth, with the satellite acting as a triangulation point in space and being photographed against a background of stars in order to compare the relative positions of points on the Earth. Three-dimensional, Earth-centered coordinates may be determined from geometric satellite observations when combined with the Doppler effect from other geodetic satellite systems (UN 1974b, p. 120; Aero Service 1982a).

Even with these improvements, by the mid-1970s only one-third of the land area of the world was covered by geodetic networks satisfying the then current requirements (Brandenberger 1976, p. 87). Still, by the early 1980s, satellite geodesy and its earthbound "black boxes" had become an accurate, economical, marvelous commonplace, able to compete with conventional land techniques in both cost and accuracy (Hoar 1982; UN 1979, p. 113).

THE FIFTEENTH AND SIXTEENTH CENTURIES

In the fifteenth and sixteenth centuries regional maps were made by guesswork or with the help of known walking distances, and views from church steeples (Imhof 1964, p. 152). "Triangulation, the fixing of places by intersecting rays, was described by Gemma Frisius in 1533 ..." (Thrower 1972, p. 61) and was relatively commonly practiced from 1550 on (Knox 1955, p. 73). For triangulation, the framework of an accurate map is built up (as one would expect) of triangles, and from the mid-fifteenth century on it was carried out in the following way. The base of the first triangle is a carefully measured base line which, according to Knox, is laid out in some suitable place on the actual terrain to be mapped. Supposing the scale of a map is to be two inches to one mile, and a base-line exactly half-a-mile long is measured on the ground, the surveyor draws the base-line one inch long on his plan. From one end of his half-mile line he takes a bearing—a line of sight—on a prominent landmark and notes its angle. Then he goes to the other end of the base-line and takes a bearing of the same landmark from there. Now, using the two angles obtained, he can draw lines from each end of the base-line on his plan. The point where they intersect is the position, on the map, of the landmark. His first triangle has been plotted, and from each point fixed in this way he can take bearings to other landmarks and plot other triangles until the whole area of his work is triangulated. The long and laborious business of filling in features like roads and rivers and towns comes afterwards ... (Knox 1955, p. 152).

Angle measurement was obtained by using a theodolite. First used in England in the sixteenth century, this surveyor's instrument for measuring angles was perfected for use by the British Ordnance Survey in about 1740 (Jervis 1938, p. 117). In 1571 the plane table, with a sighting rule on the drawing surface enabling the map to be made at the same time that the angles were calculated and laid down, was reported by Leonard Digges (Thrower 1972, p. 61; Taylor 1929). Jervis (1938, p. 117) and Knox (1955, p. 73) say the plane table was invented by Johann Praetorius in 1590, while Finch (1925, p. 323) says that it was first described in 1607.

THE SEVENTEENTH CENTURY

At the beginning of the seventeenth century more accurate measuring instruments, such as the odometer and magnetic compass, were introduced, thus facilitating and improving surveying methods (Imhof 1964, p. 152).

Beginning in the late sixteenth century there was a growing demand for topographical maps by travelers, statesmen, and merchants (Crone 1968, p. 102). Yet even into the seventeenth century relatively few points in central Europe had latitude and longitude fixed by astronomical measurement, although Apian had done some such work in 1561, and Kepler in 1627 (Imhof 1964, p. 152).

The use of the plane table and the practice of plane-tabling—the sighting on a distant object to get its bearing and drawing a line along the edge of a rule to indicate that bearing on the map in hand—were widespread at an early date. In 1625 the plane table was described by Leonhard Zubler in *Fabrica et usus instrumente chorographis,* and in 1657 by William Leybourne in *The Complete Surveyor.* The plane table is a drawing board, usually about two feet square, mounted horizontally on a tripod so that the table may be leveled, twisted, and clamped (Greenhood 1964, p. 219). Because of the lack of instrument sophistication at this early stage, close, minute work was not practicable with either plane table or theodolite in the early years, and would not be until about the eighteenth century (Van Ornum 1896, p. 336).

In 1669 Picard put a telescope on an angle-measuring instrument, and included spider-web hairs to indicate lines of sight.

Late in that century or early in the next, Père Regis, one of the French Jesuits working in China, was the first person to say in print that triangulation was the only adequate and correct basis for topographical work; previously, astronomical controls had been considered sufficient (Van Ornum 1896, p. 336).

THE EIGHTEENTH CENTURY

In 1740 and thereafter the theodolite was improved to the point of being able to measure horizontal and vertical angles simultaneously; it was then called the altazimuth theodolite (Thrower 1972, p. 62). Prior to that date, methods of finding longitude astronomically "were still more or less primitive, surveying instruments were crude, and the art of triangulation was in its infancy" (John Kirtland Wright 1924, p. 21).

By the mid-eighteenth century first in France and then elsewhere in Europe large-scale plans and topographic maps first began to appear (Arthur Robinson 1982, p. 6). As instrumentation improved and as the enormity of the amount of work and time required to properly conduct a survey became evident, private persons gradually ceased making surveys, and national agencies began to take over the work (Satzinger 1973, p. 144).

In 1771 the stadia principle was evolved and used in surveys; this is a surveying method for the determination of distances and differences of elevation by means of a telescopic instrument having two horizontal lines through which the marks on a graduated rod, the stadia, are observed (Styles 1970, p. 9). By 1800, "the quadrant and its variants had been replaced by the theodolite, which is basically a telescope mounted on a frame graduated in degrees.... its invention removed the hit-and-miss element from triangulation" (Styles 1970, p. 9). The superiority of triangulation over astronomical observation as a basis for survey was established when triangulation was used in the Great Trigonometrical Survey of India, undertaken in 1802 (Van Ornum 1896, p. 322).

THE NINETEENTH CENTURY

In the nineteenth century the great national surveys used methods similar to those of the Cassinis in France in the previous century, but with improved instruments. First, mean sea level was determined for at least one point, and all other altitudes referred to that point. Preliminary plane-table reconnaissance to select suitable points for triangulation was undertaken and beacons were erected at triangulation points. Critical latitude, longitude, and azimuthal figures were calculated so that the map was tied to the Earth's surface. Triangulation bases were carefully measured with tape or wire; triangulation calculations were made, and trigonometrically determined points were transferred to the plane table sheets. Finally topographic detail (contour lines, rivers, woods, settlements, etc.) was filled in on the plane-table sheets (Crone 1968, pp. 142-43). All these steps took a considerable amount of time and manpower; the British Ordnance Survey began work on a large-scale map of the British Isles in 1829—the last of the 205 sheets were not completed until 1858 (Tooley 1961, p. 95).

Surveys were assisted by such developments as telegraph lines carrying Greenwich time all over the world. Instrumentation continued to improve; in 1831,

William J. Young invented the engineer's transit, a telescope mounted at right angles to a horizontal east-west axis and used with a chronograph and clock to observe the time of transit of a celestial body over the meridian of a given place (Van Ornum 1896, p. 336; Tooley 1961, p. 95).

By 1885, with the aid of the improved plane table (modified for the better by Survey of India personnel), topographic field notes were laid out on the field table, supplemented with theodolite and stadia work and by direct lineal measurements (Wheeler 1885, p. 79; Jervis 1938, p. 117). The stadia system was adopted and applied in Italy in 1823, in Switzerland in 1836, and in the United States in 1848 (Van Ornum 1896, p. 357). One experienced topographer with two or more soldiers could survey, during the summer survey season in Austria, about one square mile per day at a scale of 1:25,000, in Germany about one-third of a square mile per day, and in Italy (at 1:20,000 scale) one-fifth of a square mile per day. Map reproduction was by hand, or more likely by mechanical engraving on stone or zinc, with photolithography gradually replacing copper hand-engraving (Wheeler 1885, pp. 79-81).

By the end of the nineteenth century, plane-table topographic work had developed into a fine art (Imhof 1982, p. 16). It was ideal for use in the open European countryside, producing accurate contoured maps at scales of 1:63,360 and larger (Sebert 1970b, p. 17).

THE TWENTIETH CENTURY

Modern Mapping Techniques

Surveying methods would stay much as described until the advent of the airplane combined with photography in the early twentieth century. Ground photography had been used in surveys from about 1850 (Quinn 1957, p. 21). Aerial photography first appeared upon the world scene in 1856 with the balloon photography experiements of Gaspard Félix Tournachon—better known as Nadar. In 1904, surveyors began to experiment with aerial photography to obtain ground measurement. In 1909, photography and heavier-than-air craft first came together. Prior to this, aircraft had been employed for photo-mapping, using the photo-theodolite for ground surveys in the United Kingdom, Canada, and Switzerland (Lock 1969, p. 21). "The importance of aerial photography was first recognized during World War I when it became a military necessity" (United States. Dept. of the Army 1970, p. 1-1). The value of photography in mapping was quickly appreciated; it could be used to produce new maps or to revise outdated ones, both in a comparatively short time. The costs of both air and traditional surveying were calculated in 1920, with air weighing in at £5 to £15 per square mile, and traditional at £10 to £1100 per square mile (for 1:25,000-scale mapping) (Newcombe 1920, pp. 202-3).

Between the two World Wars a good deal of progress was made in field methods, although mapping was still rather daunting in those days—survey "parties" are perhaps so called in sarcasm. On the other hand, there were always those several bottles of rum, recommended in case of illness, to be a part of survey party rations (Filchner, Przybyllok, and Hagen 1957, p. 28). Topographers reached an area to be mapped as best they could, and then went to work, using plane table, alidade (a sighting telescope fastened to a flat base with a straightedge for drawing lines on the map manuscript), theodolites and transits (to measure angles), steel tapes and stadia rods (to measure distances), and levels and level rods (to measure elevation). The season's work started with a clean sheet of map manuscript paper on the plane table; on this were plotted projection graticules of latitude and longitude lines and any control stations. The plane table was set up on as large an expanse of ground as could be found, and filling in the blanks began, with distant points plotted by triangulation, intersection and resection, elevations computed, contours sketched in, and drainage located and plotted—after which the planetabler would make a diligent search for such evidence as was needed to plot accurate legal boundaries (Thompson and Speert 1964, p. 34; Leo Roberts 1924, p. 10).

Between 1922 and 1939 the French made extensive use of terrestrial photogrammetry (the science of making reliable measurements by the use of photography) while mapping Alpine regions; ground photogrammetry was widely employed as an adjunct to air photographs or for conditions in which planes could not be flown (John Kirtland Wright 1940, p. 14; "Mapping with the squeeze" 1920).

In early 1931 aerial photography as presently understood was first brought into something like regular use, in France and elsewhere. In 1934, the United States Geological Survey decided to use it for a rush Tennessee Valley Authority job of mapping 40,000 square miles. The benefits of speed and accessibility to difficult terrain were so obvious that photographic surveys were becoming standard by 1939, and by 1941 photogrammetry was a standard method of surveying and mapping. During World War II, the military's need for rapid surveys, frequently of difficult terrain, led to vastly improved techniques, and by the end of the war aerial photography was an even more powerful mapping tool (Worton 1982; Émanaud 1938; Martonne 1947; Crone 1968, pp. 142, 144).

So marked were the advantages of applying aerial photography to mapping that in 1945 Randall stated:

> It is perhaps not too much to say that the airplane and the modern camera have brought about a second age of discovery, comparable in importance and in its implications to the great age of continental discovery typified by Columbus and early navigators.... For whereas Columbus and his contemporaries discovered continents, and traversed their boundaries, the airplane and camera now make it possible to explore and to record in map form not only the fringes but the interior of all lands (p. 2).

By 1949, almost no areas of any extent in the world were being mapped without the use of aerial photography. With the use of the flying camera, detailed mapping of land interiors was finally feasible.

At this point, a systematic topographic survey was composed of the following:

1. Determination of mean sea level at one point, to which all altitudes are referred

2. Preliminary plane table reconnaissance to select suitable points for triangulation, and to erect beacons

3. Determination of initial latitude, longitude, and azimuth (for direction), to tie the map to the Earth's surface

4. Triangulation procedure, with careful measurement of base or bases with tape or wire, theodolite measurement of horizontal angles from base and beaconed points and of altitudes (by readings of vertical angles), with each angle measured thirty-two times

5. Calculation of triangulation data and heights, and transference of trigonometrical points to sheets

6. Use of aerial photography to fill in; field checking

(Crone 1953, p. 152; Conly 1956, p. 345; "Air mapping" 1956; Gerald Fitz-Gerald 1949)

From about 1950 on, map and chart production expanded to undreamed-of proportions. This was largely due to the ongoing improvement in techniques and equipment (many of which meant decreased field work) and to the rude shock received by the military when it discovered during World War II how poorly the Earth's land surface was mapped (UN 1963a, p. 273).

Aerial photography revolutionized cartographic operations. Its only drawbacks are that while it is more economical in the long run (3 percent of the total cost of producing standard topographic maps), it does require a large initial investment amortized over a long period of time, and some land surfaces have too much cloud cover to be photographed more than a few days a year (for example, there are on average only thirty good photography days in England) (Hurault 1963; Carbonnell 1965; Crone 1968, p. 144). Nonetheless, topographic mapping by photogrammetric methods had by 1955 largely replaced the slower and more laborious plane table and traverse methods, although even into the 1960s the older method was still considered "a rational method for the survey of smaller areas" (Imhof 1982, p. 16).

Trimetrogon photography, in which one vertical camera looks down and two other cameras look obliquely left and right from horizon to horizon, was heavily used in the 1940s, and apparently into the 1950s, because so much land could be photographed at one time. Such photographs could not be used to obtain contour information since the necessary stereographic pairs of aerial photographs did not exist (UN 1963a, p. 308; Raisz 1956, p. 89).

At the same time, innovations in reproduction and drafting—photo-lettering, mass production concepts, and negative scribing (supplanting pen and ink drawing)—were speeding up the production of maps (Fuechsel 1953, p. 17). Twelve colors could be printed, allowing an increased amount of information to be presented on any one map.

An innovation in instrumentation during this time was the tellurometer, a radio instrument that allowed for almost instantaneous measurement of distance (Karo 1956, p. 424; Crone 1968, p. 167).

The system for making a standard topographic sheet was to compile original photogrammetry manuscripts at a given scale from aerial photographs. Planimetry, contours, and woodland were penciled on separate coated sheets, and copy was rough-scribed. A field engineer was furnished with a color composite of these sheets, prepared on scribe-coated plastic, upon which would be scribed field additions and corrections. The final color separates, prepared from manuscript, were overprinted with field changes in a contrasting color (United States. Geological Survey 1958, p. 152).

By the early 1960s, it was estimated that a small nation needing 1:250,000-scale coverage of its territory faced only four years of work; a larger scale, say a 1:50,000-scale series of around 200 sheets, would require sixteen years to complete, with a financial investment of $725,000, not counting $475,000 for equipment, and physical plant costs of $12.50 per square foot (Nowicki 1953, pp. 345-48).

The most spectacular instrument innovations of the time had to do with the measurement of distances. The geodimeter measured the length of time required for a beam of modulated light to travel from one point to another; the Shoran system used the speed of electromagnetic waves traveling to each of two ground stations as the airplane carrying the device flies perpendicular to the line connecting the two stations. Electronic digital computers were removing some of the drudgery by processing large amounts of data quickly. The helicopter was proving invaluable for short hops over rough terrain, and the observations of satellites were being used to figure distances (UN 1963b, p. 298; UN 1963a, p. 285). The Airborne Profile Recorder, a precise radar altimeter, was being used to record a continuous profile of the ground under a line of flight (Lock 1969, p. 23; Lawson 1957).

Mapping was going so well that national surveying agencies even had the leisure to worry about revision; prior to that time, just getting an area mapped at all left most such agencies little time to worry about working over maps once completed (Krauss 1965, p. 86).

As a partial answer to some of the problems of revision came orthophotography. An orthophotomap is generated from overlapping conventional photographs; it is an ortho (i.e., rectified) photomosaic prepared in a standard map format, with a limited amount of added cartographic symbols and information, printed in color. Production of such sheets saves time and money because they are prepared with no field checking. The United States Geological Survey issued its first such sheet (of Roanoke, Virginia) in the mid-1960s (UN 1966b, p. 386). The procedure used to make an orthophotomap is called differential rectification; it eliminates the scale variation inherent in aerial photographs, and the image displacements resulting from landform relief and tilt (Lillesand and Kiefer 1979, pp. 323-24).

By the late 1960s the preparation of a topographic map had changed somewhat from the procedure used sixty years earlier. First came planning and prioritizing, field survey, and computations; then vertical photography, horizontal and vertical control establishment, and the construction of glass diapositives from film negatives, for use in stereoplotting instruments such as Kelsh plotters. With this device contours, culture, and drainage are automatically traced by manipulation of a floating dot within the stereo model (generated from a stereo pair, two aerial photographs overlapping each other by about 60 percent) onto the map manuscript; this is called photogrammetric compilation. Then the manuscript was checked for errors by field check, the latter turning up omissions, important details not visible on aerial photographs, and errors. Finally came scribing on a polyester film base, a separate scribe sheet and negative for each category to be printed; then color separation, printing, and publication (Avery 1968, p. 127; Janicot 1969, pp. 68-71; United States. Army Map Service 1966; see Canada. Surveys and Mapping

Branch 1966 for an excellent pictorial presentation of mapping practice in the 1960s).

By the early 1970s, cost per quarter-degree sheet at 1:50,000 scale was calculated to be $2,700, and the cost of supporting mapping at such a scale $50,000 per 100,000 square kilometers (Jerie 1972, p. 19). The big expense was personnel, so virtually every phase of the mapping operation was "engulfed in a tide of automation efforts"—electronics, multispectral sensors, lasers, microwave phenomena, and computer applications (UN 1974b, p. 267). All of this was not, at least at such an early stage, necessarily better or cheaper, but it was quicker, and since a 1976 estimate of the amount of time it would take to complete world coverage at 1:50,000 scale was 300 years, cutting the amount of time was important (UN 1976b, p. 127; Steele 1980). Still, nothing could replace that final field check by human beings.

Measuring elevations was still a problem. Tapes, chains, long-bar bridging and stereotemplet triangulation had all virtually disappeared (UN 1974b, pp. 267, 269). Aerial photography had gone from "elementary uncalibrated cameras mounted insecurely in the open cockpits of planes" to high-speed cameras fitted with special lenses and using improved, chemically treated film, carried by jets (Don Thomson 1975, p. 1).

The 1970s were a time of rapid change in topographic surveying, mapping, and production. Map printing had gone from linotype to phototypesetting, electronic engraving and color scanning, web offset presses, and computerized typesetting (Canada. Dept. of Energy, Mines and Resources 1976; Don Thomson 1975, p. 1).

Remote sensing and automated cartographic data manipulation began to take over, the former represented by orthophotomaps, satellite imagery, and side-looking airborne radar (SLAR). SLAR was especially important when it came to the mapping of regions that could not attract funding for 1:100,000-scale standard mapping procedures (Barrett and Curtis 1977, p. 99).

Photomapping was seen as most promising for a reliable base for planning purposes in that it results in rapidly available and relatively inexpensive (one-quarter the cost of standard sheets) maps. It was still seen as a supplement for existing line maps, to fill in gaps as needed, and as an aid in revising existing maps more rapidly and in greater detail (Weibrecht 1975, p. 45; Lillesand and Kiefer 1979, p. 325). Orthophotomapping, which assumed major importance after about 1972, did so because of its role in speeding up the production of revised maps; map series must now be revised two to four times more often than was necessary perhaps thirty years ago, largely because of an increased rate of cultural change (UN 1974b, p. 186; Petrie 1977, p. 49). In addition, orthophotomaps present an abundance of ground detail and information that cannot be shown on a line map with standard cartographic symbols (McKenzie 1973, p. 327). Orthophotos also offer the possibility of automating the photogrammetric stages of map production, and thus producing bases for maps more quickly and economically. There are drawbacks; while planimetric accuracy is excellent on orthophotomaps, contour lines are only 50 to 60 percent as accurate as contour lines measured directly (Petrie 1977, p. 49). Photomapping techniques continued to develop through the late 1970s, with much achieved in reproduction, cartographic treatment, improved image quality and automation processes (Elizabeth Fleming 1978, p. 141; McKenzie 1973, p. 332; Tennessee Valley Authority 1979; Burnside 1979; Zuylen 1980).

SLAR

Side-looking airborne radar (SLAR)—a radar antenna mounted on the belly of an airplane and aimed to one side—is a recent technique for topographic mapping. SLAR shows terrain in startling relief, and is widely used by oil and mineral exploration companies. Compared with a classic aerial survey, SLAR does give relatively low resolution, shows displacement by local relief and radar shadows, does not give a geometrically true plan, and may "lose" objects when there is a scanning lag (Akovetskiy 1968, p. 276). The United States Army has nonetheless been able to use it to produce 1:250,000-scale sheets, probably due to SLAR's good points. SLAR is usable in all kinds of weather, day or night, because it is an active sensor, penetrating the most dense clouds, and it affords a remarkably plastic overall view of terrain. SLAR acquires data very rapidly; a swath about ten nautical miles wide may be imaged at about 300 knots (ground speed); 3,000 square nautical miles per hour may be covered, at a scale of about 1:200,000 (Gribben 1971, p. 18; Jensen 1977). Some areas, such as Darien province in Panama, are impossible to map using any other method because cloud cover is almost constant; that province was mapped at a scale of 1:250,000 using SLAR (Gribben 1971, p. 28).

Satellite Imagery

Another important innovation of the 1970s was the use of satellite imagery to derive topographic maps:

> Ya se considera, por otra parte, la posibilidad de producir mapas a escala 1:50.000 mediante el uso de la fotografía espacial de extensos territorios continentales, como consecuencia de la alta calidad alcanzada en la técnica fotográfica, en tiempos que superan todo lo imaginable, a juzgar por los resultados obtenidos en el Perú (Turco Greco 1968, p. 58).

> (Now consider, on the other hand, the possibility of producing maps at a scale of 1:50,000, by means of the use of space photography, of extensive continental territories, as a consequence of the high quality reached in photographic technique, at times exceeding all imagination to judge by the results obtained in Peru.)

Even in the early 1960s the possibilities of using satellite imagery for mapping were considered and initial experiments made (UN 1979, p. 197).

Mapping from satellite imagery developed quickly with the launching of, and data generated by, the first United States Earth Resources Technology Satellite, ERTS-1 (later renamed Landsat-1), on July 23, 1972. Landsat-2 was launched in 1975, Landsat-3 in 1978, and Landsat-4 in 1982. The Landsats are designed to orbit the Earth approximately fourteen times per day, with each area being viewed at approximately the same time each day. The sensing devices on the satellites transmit data to United States National Aeronautics and Space Administration receiving stations (and elsewhere—Australia and Brazil, for example, have receiving stations); the data are converted from electronic signals into images and computer compatible tapes. The most important of the Landsat data acquisition systems is the multi-spectral scanner (MSS) (Merideth 1980, p. 1).

By 1970 the tentative conclusion was that topographic maps at scales of 1:25,000 to 1:1,000,000 could be derived from satellite imagery (Petrie 1970, p. 624). But the larger-scale mapping capabilities had not materialized in the early 1970s when a 1:1,000,000-scale mapping program was the largest scale satellite compilation program in existence (Gregory 1971, pp. 7-9; Doyle 1972, p. 32; "Notes" 1973).

One proposal was that satellite imagery be used in concert with conventional aerial photography, with the former serving for aerotriangulation and bridging, and for supplying geometric information, and the latter supplying topographic map information (Kölbl 1973, p. 678). Satellite imagery was not to replace large- and small-scale topographic maps, but was rather to serve as a valuable first look, in part because satellite imagery may often be cheaper and quicker to obtain than that obtained by conventional means, and also because a single Landsat "scene" covers the same area as 1,320 aerial photographs at 1:40,000 scale (William R. MacDonald 1974, p. 1020; Southard and MacDonald 1974 p. 379). One of the first major areas to have satellite imagery applied to its mapping was Antarctica, where Landsat imagery was used for 1:250,000-, 1:500,000-, and 1:1,000,000-scale mapping (Southard and MacDonald 1974, p. 379).

A problem with satellite imagery is that there is marginal overlap between scenes, and therefore stereoscopic work (essential to determine landform relief) is usually not possible. Repetitive imagery may be used for stereoscopic viewing with some degree of success, and computer manipulation of Landsat data can produce stereo pairs (Raju and Parthasarathi 1977, p. 1243). The scale barrier of 1:250,000 was smashed by having lineprinter images of digital Landsat data generated at scales such as 1:24,000, 1:50,000, and 1:62,500 (Ballew and Lyon 1977).

At the end of the 1970s, the more densely populated countries had realized that aircraft systems were the more practical, but that satellite systems, with the "ready adaptability for digital processing" of satellite data, were a "welcome means of developing data-processing techniques" (UN 1979, p. 177). Landsat imagery was then being used in the following ways in the mapping world:

1. as an image base for photomapping at 1:250,000 and smaller scales, in a variety of formats

2. for aeronautical charting (revision of gross features; image base)

3. for mapping of shallow-sea areas

4. "extending and bridging control from mapped into unmapped areas"

5. "providing a means of automated correlation to the figure of the earth"

6. for less detailed thematic mapping, especially that of snow, ice, vegetation, and large cultural features

7. for revising small-scale maps of Antarctica; discovering large geographical and geological features

(UN 1979, p. 62)

Instrumentation for mapping is continually improving. Surveying instruments now come complete with a microprocessor that allows them to combine angle and distance measurements. With the use of a relatively inexpensive receiver that interprets data from satellites, the position of any location on Earth may be instantaneously determined with an accuracy of better than ten meters, in horizontal and vertical coordinates. Space surveying has obvious benefits; it is largely unaffected by climate, it can easily image remote and inaccessible terrain, and repetitive imagery is both inexpensive and frequent. Space imagery is being increasingly used in mapping of all kinds (Zuylen 1978; Zegheru 1980; Baudoin 1980; Hodgkiss 1981, pp. 55-56).

Computers

The last major area of change in map production in the 1970s was computerization used in conjunction with satellite imagery. The idea of putting topographic map data on computer databases in digital form (in order, among other reasons, to enable easy, speedy revision) goes back at least twenty years.

> The topographic map is a marvelous memory device.... In the world of computer technology ... the topographic map stands out as one of the most efficient data devices.... Although it is not reasonable at present to retain a complete topographic map, in binary form, in a computer memory, it does appear reasonable to store sufficient information to describe selected features of maps directly in computer language (James A. Roberts 1962, p. 12).

The topographic map's efficiency as an information device—to the point that a standard United States Geological Survey topographic map has 100 million to 200 million bits of data on it—made computerization a difficult matter; in part, it was a matter of waiting for the computers to reach a point where memories were sufficiently large to store such massive amounts of information. It was thus only in the 1970s that computerization of cartographic data became a reality.

Due to mechanization and automation, the output of relief maps was increasing, but there was a need for even higher output (Lyubkov 1971). Many cartographers' minds turned to the computer. But there was still at least one cautious voice:

> The present passion for converting map information into digital form, often at great expense, only makes sense if we are quite sure that this information is really what it appears to be. and there is some concept of its real informational value (Keates 1972, p. 180).

Nonetheless, several brave—or perhaps desperate—cartographic agencies did indeed work with digitizers, computers, and plotters in the early 1970s (Montagano 1970).

The mid-1970s saw the beginning of a groundswell in topographic map digitizing (UN 1976b, pp. 260-62, 245-49; Margerison 1976, pp. 3-9), even though contour programming was still at a fairly early stage of development. Interest accelerated in the last five years of the decade, not only from federal governments but from commercial businesses, and with the idea of obtaining primary cartographic data in computer form, rather than first putting it in manuscript and then digitizing from the manuscript (Neubauer 1978, p. 5; Teledyne 1978; Margerison 1977; Thompson 1977; Groenningsaeter 1976; National Cartographic Information Center 1980; see entire issue of *Photogrammetric engineering and remote sensing* 44(12), December 1978). The United States was working on a digital cartographic applications program for its national mapping system, directed at that time toward research, pilot projects, and the establishment of a prototype production facility (Beck 1979, p. 300, Southard 1978). Finland was involved in computer-assisted cartography for basic map production, as were Canada, Great Britain, Germany, and Switzerland (Vahala 1978; UN 1979, pp. 115-17, 234-39; "Terrain analysis program" 1979, p. 15). Clearly topographic map production from a computer database is the future, and not very far distant at that. Data digitizing, cost, and the mundane appearance of computer-generated maps are some of the major problems to be attacked. There is a tone of inevitability in the articles on using electronic data processing for topographic map production, a feeling that this is the way it will be.

In the late 1970s such map production followed these basic steps:

1. Aerial photographs are taken

2. Control points are marked on positive transparencies made from negatives

3. The coordinates of each position are measured; the measuring device automatically records the coordinates on computer cards

4. The computer develops three-dimensional coordinates from the cards in a process called analytical aerotriangulation

5. Data from step 4 is combined with other data and fed from magnetic tapes into an automatic plotting machine, which scribes a map on red-coated plastic sheets; these sheets serve as photographic negatives from which the finished map is produced

Alternately, as an operator works on a standard stereoplotting machine, details are automatically drawn on an adjacent plotting machine (Teledyne 1978, pp. 4-5; Masry and McLaren 1979; *Resources* 1982, pp. 75, 79-81, 92-96).

The latest chapter in the story of man mapping the surface of the Earth is one of high-altitude photography, computer applications, advances in satellite geodesy, of rapid but still costly means of collecting and storing vast amounts of information about the Earth's surface, as "the art of mapping is moving into an automated world" (UN 1974b, p. 271).

Part II
TOPOGRAPHIC MAPPING OF AUSTRALIA AND NEW ZEALAND

This is a well-worn subject, and geographers are getting tired of asking whether there is yet a single topographical sheet to be bought in Australia. I believe the answer is still, No.

—Hinks 1925, p. 324

4
AUSTRALIA

Prior to the twentieth century, not only were there no detailed topographic maps of Australia, for many parts of the country there were no maps at all. When Australia became independent in 1901 it was scarcely explored. In 1908 a military survey of Australia, the Survey Section of the Royal Australian Engineers, was formed. This was followed by the establishment of the Australian Army Survey Corps in 1910, which began work on a 1:63,360-scale series for major urban areas, in some cases by adding contours and other details to existing cadastral maps. To establish the former, the Australian General Staff procured the services of a small band of surveyors from the British Ordnance Survey; the latter was to be expanded into the Royal Australian Survey Corps during World War I (Lambert 1969, p. 522; Tyson 1965, p. 1; Ingleton 1958, p. 489).

By 1930, still not a square inch of Australia had been mapped in detail by accurate topographical surveys organized to produce a map series, although the southern and eastern portions had been mapped from less reliable, chiefly nontopographical surveys (Reeves 1917, plate V; Edinburgh Geographical Institute 1922, plate I; Jack 1930, p. 110). Aerial photography as a mapping aid was introduced in 1929 (L. FitzGerald 1951b, p. 244; Montgomery 1928) and there was a general aerial survey conducted in 1930 (Mackay 1934; "Map of the Donald Mackay aerial reconnaissance survey expedition" 1938).

Between the two World Wars, the military survey worked mainly on 1:63,360-scale mapping in New South Wales, Victoria, and Queensland. In 1932, the Survey Section of the Royal Australian Engineers resumed the title of the Australian Survey Corps (Tyson 1965, p. 1). In the mid-1930s mapping activity increased, with air surveys resulting in maps on which several unnamed features were noted; populated eastern Australia had about 59 contoured 1:63,360-scale sheets (about 4 sheets produced per year to 1939) to its name. Mapping of South Australia began in 1934 with work by the Royal Australian Survey Corps; the resulting maps were first produced in 1937 (G. H. C. Kennedy 1976, p. 11). In 1935 the one-inch and half-inch (1:63,360 and 1:126,720) maps, which had been for official use only, finally became available for sale ("Topographic maps of Australia" 1935, p. 575). In that same year a Commonwealth Survey Committee was set up to "effect the much-needed co-ordination"; it "made several unsuccessful representations to Cabinet over the ensuing four years for the initiation of a national geodetic and topographic survey" (Tyson 1965, p. 1). Although aerial photography had been introduced earlier, 1936 marked the issuance of the first sheet to be made by photogrammetric methods and to be compiled completely from aerial photographs—the Sale sheet at 1:63,360 scale (Tyson 1965, p. 2). But even at the end of the 1930s large areas of the interior, especially in the Great Sand and Gibson Deserts, were completely unmapped ("Topographical maps of Australia" 1935, p. 575; Outhwaite 1938, p. 325; Key 1938, p. 128; Jervis 1938, p. 142; Platt 1945, map following p. 180; MacFadden 1941, p. 58; Olson and Whitmarsh 1944, p. 197).

World War II brought about a sudden increase in the demand for maps; an Emergency Mapping Scheme was initiated, aimed at production of maps of strategic areas, particularly those in the north. New series at eight miles to the inch and at four miles to the inch began, as did the production of photomaps. About 170 sheets of the 1:63,360-scale series were published as Emergency Editions, with relief depicted by hachures or, on a few, hill shading; there were also 172 Standard Edition sheets, mostly contoured. Only one-third of the 230 four-mile sheets (many titled *Strategic Series*) were contoured, with most being hachured. During the war years 60 eight-mile, 230 four-mile, and 340 one-mile maps were produced. A military topographic series (*Artillery Map*) at 1:125,000 scale was begun in 1941, with 32 restricted sheets published (Tyson 1965, p. 2; L. FitzGerald 1980).

The postwar years 1945-1956 marked the first stage of a concentrated effort in Australian mapping. In 1945 and 1946 (or 1947), the Australian National Mapping Council or Section (later the National Mapping Office) was established in the Department of the Interior, replacing the Property and Survey Branch, and taking over what had until then been a military responsibility. In the late 1940s, this office began work on a national mapping program, starting with nationwide aerial photographic coverage (Australia. National Mapping Office 1954, p. 21; UN 1968, p. 27; Goodrick 1975, p. 35). The nation was still largely unmapped in any technical sense, with only a 1:8,000,000-scale map covering the entire continent. Only the narrow coastal strip, from Adelaide to Melbourne and from Sydney to Brisbane, had been covered by first class surveys ("Radar's 'magic eye' " 1948, p. 65). The military continued to issue sheets such as those in the four-mile series, and to concentrate on defense mapping.

As a response to the sudden demand for maps came the Survey Co-ordination Act of 1940, which placed responsibility for topographic mapping with the State Surveyors-General, and was initially concerned with the cadastral survey of Crown lands (Frederick Johnston 1949a, p. 69).

Victoria was the first state to embark on a comprehensive scheme of topographic mapping as authorized by the act, in 1944, with the approval of a State Aerial Survey by the Department of Crown Lands and Survey; the initial program was for photomaps at 1:15,840 scale and topographic maps at 1:31,680 scale (Tyson 1965, p. 10). Tasmania formed a mapping branch in its Lands and Survey Department in 1944, to carry on mapping done by the Army from 1941 to 1943 (Frederick Johnston 1949a, p. 69). In New South Wales, a mapping section was authorized in 1945; after a period of research and investigation, the Central Mapping Authority was established, as a part of the Department of Lands, with the mission of working on topographic and cadastral mapping and the production of photomaps. In Western Australia, aerial photography was introduced into the procedures of the Chief Draftsman's Branch in 1949; in 1954 the branch was reconstituted as the Mapping Branch and its work officially recognized as including topographic mapping using photogrammetric methods (Tyson 1965, p. 10). In South Australia, work began late in 1948, with a single cartographer equipped with "a set of drafting instruments, borrowed straightedges and drawing boards, a set of very indifferent K17 photographs, a second-hand stereoscope, and lots of enthusiasm; accomodation being a five by eight feet [sic] office" (G. H. C. Kennedy 1962, p. 108). The following year a Photogrammetric Section was established in the Department of Lands. Until 1951, planimetric maps and mosaics constituted the products of the section; in 1952, the department began its own aerial surveys. In Queensland the Surveyor-General began by recommending the purchase of equipment in 1947, the equipment was actually received in 1950. In 1959 the State Cabinet approved the expansion of the Topographic Branch (Tyson 1965, p. 10). The national agency retained responsibility for topographic mapping of Northern Territory (Lambert 1969, p. 516). Thus state authorities worked on cadastral mapping and on implementation of topographic and thematic mapping programs (Tyson 1965, p. 3; National Mapping Council of Australia 1976; Frederick Johnston 1948 and 1949a and b; L. FitzGerald 1948).

By 1950, between 90 percent and 95 percent of the country was still inadequately mapped; in maps of Western Australia only the prominent features were named (Lambert 1969, p. 515; L. FitzGerald 1951a, p. 127; *Cartography in western Australia* 1946, p. 42). In the early 1950s the Australian government was still fighting the problem of mapping considerable areas in a short time with relatively limited physical resources and finances. There was thus a heavy dependence on aerial photography, noncontoured maps, and photomaps; the latter covered 25 percent of Australia's surface.

Major General R. L1. Brown, Director of the British Ordnance Survey, visited Australia in 1950, and reported, in his book entitled *The Brown Report*, on the work of the Survey Corps and on the integration of civilian and military mapping. In 1954 the report's recommendations were acted upon favorably; "In 1951, the responsibility for national mapping was transferred from the Commonwealth Surveyor-General to a new position of Director of National Mapping," that person becoming the Chairman of the National Mapping Council. In 1954 it was decided to have one authority, the Department of the Interior, responsible for all surveys and mapping, with the Army to carry out some work for that authority (Tyson 1965, p. 8; D. MacDonald 1953; "Preparation of geological and topographical maps" 1953; United States. Army Map Service 1954a; Middleton 1955).

The bulk of map production in the mid-1950s was at a scale of 1:63,360 but there was also a noncontoured 1:253,440-scale series in progress (Australia. National Mapping Office 1954, p. 22 and 1955b, p. 41). By 1955, 5 percent of the 1:63,360-scale photomap series and over 25 percent of the 1:253,440-scale series was completed. In 1956 the first sheet (Mildura West) of the 1:50,000-scale metric series (to replace the old 1:63,360-scale series) was published ("Contemporary cartography: Royal Australian Signal Corps" 1954, p. 151; Australia. National Mapping Office 1955a).

In that same year, the National Mapping Section was transferred to the Department of National Development; the Division of National Mapping—which was responsible for coordination, aerial photography, compilation and publication of topographic maps—was the branch of that department "actively concerned with carrying out those functions" (Tyson 1965, p. 9).

The period from 1956 to 1961 marked the stage of standardization in Australian mapping as new standard map scales were chosen. In 1958 the first truly national mapping program was initiated by the council, with increased output in the four-mile series, and the introduction of the Commonwealth topographic series at 1:253,440 scale. The first sheet of this series was contoured, but it was followed by black-and-white hachured provisional editions. Forty-eight sheets of this series were published to 1960 or 1961, at which time it was superseded by the 1:250,000-scale series.

The outlook for substantial increase in mapping activity in the largely dry and deserted interior of the continent was poor; large inland tracts were still blank on the map, and even some small stretches of coastline were unsurveyed, such as the west coast of Barrow Island (off northwest Australia), which was not surveyed until 1955 (Ingleton 1958, p. 485; UN. Secretariat 1957, p. 6; Karo 1955, p. 64).

Between 1946 and 1959, seventy-eight first, second, or third editions of the one-mile series were published by the Army; in 1959 or 1960 that series was superseded by the 1:50,000-scale series.

In the 1960s matters improved in Australia, formerly "the worst mapped of continents" next to Antarctica (Lock 1969, p. 386). A study made in 1964 and put into action in 1967 by the South Australia Public Service Board recommended acceleration of mapping, centralized small-scale mapping, and the introduction of new large-scale standard series—a general contoured topographic map with a companion cadastral map at 1:50,000 scale, a medium-scale topographic and cadastral series at 1:10,000 scale, and a large-scale contoured 1:2,500-scale series. South Australia was working toward having the first edition of the 1:50,000-scale series completed by about 1980, at which time the 1:10,000-scale series would become the next important standard series (G. H. C. Kennedy 1976, pp. 13-15; "Notes on the application of satellite imagery" 1973).

By the mid-1960s, the two-inch standard topographic series (first proposed in 1944) was a task common to all state lands departments. States were at liberty to adopt other scales as needed; Victoria, for example, had the 1:50,000-scale series as its priority scale (Tyson 1965, pp. 15, 17, 37; Hawkins 1966; Ogrissek 1966; Fletcher 1968). States were partially reimbursed for the cost of topographic mapping. By 1965, coverage at 1:50,000 scale of developed areas stood at about 60 percent but was overall very sparse, being mostly along coasts and in populated areas. The states had published about 300 two-inch series sheets by this time, broken down as follows:

New South Wales	57 +	104 provisional at various scales
Victoria	114 +	7 at 1:63,360
Tasmania	28 +	2 provisional
South Australia	28 +	4 provisional
Western Australia	24 +	19 uncontoured
Queensland	9	

(Tyson 1965, p. 40; "World in the flat" 1965, p. 486; UN 1965a, p. 27; Australia. National Library 1966, p. i).

Priorities for the mid-1960s were the planimetric 1:250,000-scale series, the contoured 1:250,000-scale series, and the contoured 1:100,000-scale series (Tyson 1965, p. 42). The Army and the National Mapping Office were each issuing about 40 1:250,000-scale sheets per year; the Army was also producing priority sheets at 1:100,000 scale and 1:50,000 scale (Tyson 1965, p. 17). In 1966 or 1968 the 1:250,000-scale series (R502) in 541 (or 544) sheets was completed; only a small percentage was contoured (at 250-foot intervals), with the balance of the sheets being planimetric maps with relief shown by hill shading (Lines 1967, p. 133). Work was proceeding on a new contoured 1:100,000-scale series (R652), begun in 1968, to be a joint production of the Division of National Mapping (NATMAP) and the Royal Australian Survey Corps, and designed to cover all of the country except the interior in 3,070 sheets by 1976. A 1:250,000-scale contoured series, to replace the planimetric series, was to be completed in 1978 (UN 1968, p. 73; Goodrick 1975, pp. 35-36; UN 1974b, p. 18).

Strangely enough, there was still no formal dividing line between mapping work to be done by the nation and that to be done by states, although in practice the states concentrated mainly on the 1:31,680-scale series and on more detailed maps, while the Commonwealth worked on the 1:1,000,000-, 1:250,000-, 1:100,000-, and occasionally 1:50,000- (R753) and 1:25,000-scale maps (the last two only for a small number of priority areas) (UN 1968, p. 27; Lambert 1969, p. 517).

By the late 1960s, 2.1 percent of Australia was covered by maps at 1:50,000 scale (190 of about 9,000 sheets total), 0.7 percent by maps at 1:100,000 scale (21 of 3,061), and all of the country by the generally uncontoured 1:250,000-scale maps (UN. Dept. of Economic and Social Affairs 1970, p. 21; Altenhofen 1971, pp. 12-13; National Mapping Council of Australia 1970; Advisory Committee 1969). At this time, the Division was working toward converting 1:80,000-scale super-wide angle photographs into 1:50,000-scale orthophotomaps with map grid, contours, and a limited number of place names, looking toward a future of 1:50,000 supply-on-demand contact printed orthophotomaps, plus computer-produced one-color map overlays on a transparent medium, showing detail that would appear on a normal topographic sheet (Lambert 1969, p. 528; Altenhofen 1971, p. 12; *Australian maps* 1968 lists individual sheets published in the 1:250,000- and 1:100,000-scale series).

In the early 1970s, the various states were involved in their own mapping projects. Queensland was working on 1:25,000 scale; New South Wales was mapping from the coast to the west side of the Great Dividing Range at 1:25,000 scale, mapping in 1:50,000 scale in the central region, and 1:100,000 scale in the west; Tasmania had already completed mapping at 1:100,000 scale; South Australia was working on 1:50,000 scale and West Australia was working on a whole range of scales, from 1:500,000 to the largest scales (UN 1974b, p. 20; Australia. Division of National Mapping 1971; Lambert 1973).

The largest scale to be used for the interior was 1:250,000. By 1975, publication of the contoured 1:250,000-scale series had begun, but there was no definite schedule for completion, priority having been given to the 1:100,000-scale series, which was to be completed in 1977 or 1978 (Goodrick 1976, pp. 231-32 and 1975, pp. 35-36; National Mapping Council of Australia 1976; Urban 1977). By the beginning of 1975, 440 of 2,350 sheets at 1:25,000 scale, 425 of 1,435 at 1:50,000 scale, 624 of 3,061 at 1:100,000 scale, and 3 of 541 contoured 1:250,000-scale sheets had been completed (UN. Dept. of Economic and Social Affairs 1976, p. 23; Fox 1978; Forster 1978).

Australia seized fairly eagerly on the multispectral sensing imagery available from Landsat, since such imagery could contribute substantially toward good 1:250,000-scale sheets (UN 1976b, p. 217); by 1980 Australia had its own Landsat receiving station. While there had been some discussion in the mid-1970s of replacing both the 1:250,000- and 1:100,000-scale series with a 1:200,000-scale series, no precipitate action was taken (UN 1976b, pp. 3, 9).

The various states continued to be active in the late 1970s and early 1980s. New South Wales worked on a 1:10,000-scale series, while Tasmania improved its completed 1:100,000-scale series and formed its own Mapping Division (TASMAP) in 1978.

On the national side, the 1:250,000-scale series was being produced jointly by the Division of National Mapping and the Royal Australian Survey Corps, in the latter case with the series (beginning in 1976) entitled Joint Operations Graphic (JOG). The 1:100,000-scale series was still limited to more densely settled areas and to areas of special interest; by the early 1980s about 1,300 sheets had been published (W. A. Thomson 1980).

5
NEW ZEALAND*

The organized settlement of New Zealand in 1840 provoked its first surveying and mapping, but very little trigonometric surveying was done until about 1854. Between 1854 and 1876 the provincial governments were responsible for surveying and mapping, and trigonometrical surveys became more common, so that by the latter date the provinces of Wellington and Otago had been covered by major triangulation. In that same year, the provincial system of government was abolished, taking with it the nine separate survey agencies that had existed (Barton 1980, pp. 29-30; UN 1968, p. 32). This reorganization was due to a scathing report on the state of the surveys, made to the central government by Major H. E. Palmer in 1875 (*Appendix to the Journals of the House of Representatives*, H.-1, 1975; Barton 1980, p. 35; Feild 1982, p. 25; DeVries 1974; Bradford Patterson 1980).

Relatively little topographic mapping of New Zealand was done until the second half of the twentieth century, although a number of finely executed topographic manuscript maps of limited areas, made in earlier years, are held by the Department of Lands and Survey and the National Archives. This dearth was in part due to difficulties caused by North Island being hilly and South Island mountainous, and neither heavily populated. In the 1870s through the 1890s, because of the Vogel public works policy and the increased importance of export products (e.g., frozen meat and dairy products), there was an increasing demand from the public and politicians for land for settlement, a demand to which the survey department was geared. Following the outbreak of World War I in 1914, topographic maps at scales of 1:15,840; 1:20,000; 1:25,000; 1:31,680; and 1:125,000 were produced, largely to satisfy military requirements. This limited mapping in the main covered the environs of population centers and army training establishments (Barton 1980, p. 35). In about 1920, the first 2 sheets of the contoured 1:125,000-scale series appeared ("Topographical survey of New Zealand" 1920, p. 55).

In 1931, when New Zealand became officially independent, it still had very little topographic map coverage. In 1935, the 1:63,360-scale series for other than military purposes began; the first sheet (N134), of the Napier and Hastings area,

---

*The author is indebted to P. L. Barton, Map Librarian at the National Library of New Zealand, who assisted with the preparation of this section. Barton has written a number of excellent articles offering further information on the New Zealand topographic series. See the Bibliography for full citations.

was published in 1939. In the mid-1930s came the advent of aerial photography and something approaching adequate mapping funding. By 1938, there were a few 1:125,000-scale sheets of such urban areas as Wellington (Jack 1930, p. 110; Hinks 1944, p. 79; Jervis 1938, p. 142; UN 1968, p. 34; Cumberland 1946, p. 135; New Zealand Geographical Society 1964, p. 8; for records and annual reports of the Department of Lands and Survey, see New Zealand. Dept. of Lands and Survey 1925- and various).

The outbreak of World War II revealed the paucity of topographic map coverage of New Zealand. As one writer tactfully commented, "the beautiful topography of New Zealand has not received the attention it deserves from cartographers" (Hinks 1944, p. 79). The war and the accompanying threat of a Japanese invasion provided considerable impetus to the acceleration of mapping. A private company, the New Zealand Aerial Mapping Company, Ltd., was founded in 1936 and was hired that same year by the Department of Lands and Survey to perform aerial photography for the country. With the aid of the army, 1,500 square miles at 1:25,000 scale and 50,000 square miles at 1:63,360 scale (a total of about 200 sheets) were mapped; the sheets were not released to the general public until 1945 (Barton 1980, p. 35; "Maps and mapping" 1968, p. A235; "New Zealand topographic maps and air photographs" 1946, p. 370; Cumberland 1946, p. 135). The 1:25,000-scale topographic map series (NZMS 2) first appeared in 1941 and was completed in 1972; the series covered populated areas, army maneuver areas, and major public works areas.

Full responsibility for the production of maps had rested with the Surveyor-General since 1947. Following World War II, the Survey Division of the Department of Lands and Survey started topographical coverage work at 1:25,000 but soon realized that broad coverage at this level of detail was not realistic and changed back to the 1:63,360-scale series (NZMS 1), mapping only well-populated areas at 1:25,000 scale (UN 1968, p. 349; "Availability of maps" 1949). Within a few years of the close of World War II, more than one-third of the country, mostly the area along the coasts, had been mapped at 1:63,360 scale, using plane-table methods. The 1:250,000-scale topographic map series (NZMS 18) was first issued in 1958, with a projected completion date of 1972. The 1:15,840-scale series (NZMS 86), begun in 1950 and issued only until 1953 with 25 sheets in all, appears to have been of areas considered for the building of hydroelectric projects in the center of North Island (Leikis 1954). In the late 1950s, New Zealand negotiated with the United States for mapping of New Zealand's coastal zone (United States. Treaties 1959).

By 1962 all of North Island had been completely covered by aerial photography, as had two-thirds of South Island. In the mid-1960s, the 1:63,360-scale program was speeded up; by 1964, at least half of the country had been mapped at 1:63,360 scale (Birch 1964, p. 19; Francis 1964 and 1966). In 1968 a new format was instituted for the 1:63,360-scale series, the series to be completed by 1973 (UN 1974b, p. 25 and 1968, p. 34). By late 1969, 180 of about 2,465 sheets (final number not yet determined) at 1:25,000 scale, 234 of 332 at 1:63,360 scale (covering most of North Island except for the East Cape Peninsula, and all of South Island except the southwest coast and part of the southwest interior), and 11 of 26 at 1:250,000 scale had been completed (UN. Dept. of Economic and Social Affairs 1970, p. 62). All of the sheets of that last series, expanded to 31 sheets, were either published or in preparation in 1970 (Lock 1969, p. 391; UN 1968, p. 34; Gurtner 1972). The 1:63,360-scale series was to be completed by 1973 (UN 1968, p. 34). In

January 1973 the Department of Lands and Survey initiated several new map series: NZMS 260, a topographical map of 324 sheets at 1:50,000 scale to replace NZMS 1; a 1:25,000-scale series (NZMS 170, metric); a 1:10,000-scale series (NZMS 269, metric); and a new 1:250,000-scale series (NZMS 262, metric) (New Zealand. Dept. of Lands and Survey 1973, pp. 1-3). By late 1974, 195 of 2,465 sheets at 1:25,000 scale, 307 of 332 at 1:63,360 scale, and 26 of 26 at 1:250,000 scale (respectively NZMS 2, NZMS 1, and NZMS 18, the old series) had been completed; the last sheet of the latter was issued in 1974 (UN. Dept. of Economic and Social Affairs 1976, p. 42; Barton 1978b, p. 219; New Zealand. Dept. of Lands and Survey 1975 and 1976).

By 1975 both North and South Islands had been covered by 1:63,360-scale maps, with many sheets in second or later editions; but in more remote areas there were still some interim sheets with no or only partial contour information. By approximately 1976, 213 sheets of the 1:25,000-scale series had been published; no special attempt was to be made to complete the series (*New Zealand in maps* 1977, p. 135; Stirling 1976). The first metric 1:50,000-scale map was published in 1977; the series is scheduled for completion in about 25 years (Barton 1980, p. 35, 1978a, p. 219, and 1978b; Marshall 1977; New Zealand. Dept. of Lands and Survey 1977). It covered—with the exceptions of the islands of the Great Barrier, Stewart, and Chatham—all of New Zealand (Barton 1978a, p. 219). At this time, New Zealand was working on automated production of 1:50,000-scale sheets (Kihl 1977). The metric 1:250,000-scale series was to supersede the old nonmetric series; while the old series was in 26 sheets, the new was to be in 18, and to be completed in five years (Barton 1978a, p. 220). The old 1:63,360-scale series was to continue to be updated until all of the metric 1:50,000-scale sheets were issued, in about the year 2000 (New Zealand. Dept. of Lands and Survey 1980, p. 5).

**Map of Australia and New Zealand:
Topographic Mapping, 1900-1970
(1:250,000 and more detailed)**

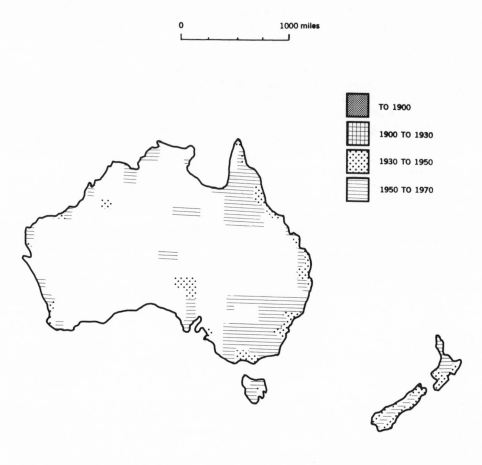

0   1000 miles

TO 1900

1900 TO 1930

1930 TO 1950

1950 TO 1970

Base map: Aitoff's Equal Area Projection.

Sources for Map of Australia and New Zealand:
Topographic Mapping, 1900-1970
(1:250,000 and more detailed)

Australia. National Mapping Office 1955b, pp. 43-44.

Karo 1955, plate II.

Karo 1956, p. 426.

Meine 1972, map facing p. 192.

Platt 1945, map following p. 180.

Raisz 1956, p. 106.

UN 1965a, p. 27.

UN 1966b, annex 3.

UN 1968, pp. 29-30.

UN. Dept. of Social Affairs 1949, map.

UN. Dept. of Economic and Social Affairs 1970, Map XI, p. 95.

Part III
TOPOGRAPHIC MAPPING OF LATIN AMERICA

The hard work in making maps is not done at a drawing board. It is done by geodetic surveyors—specially trained engineers who cross and recross the country through deserts, mountains, and jungle.

—Conly 1956, p. 335

6
INTRODUCTION AND OVERVIEW

The mapping of Hispanic America falls into three categories:

1. Colonial (to early nineteenth century, approximately between 1810 and 1825): broad outline

2. Reconnaissance surveys (date varies from country to country, but 1850 marks the approximate beginning): scales of 1:250,000 and smaller

3. National consciousness and economic development (date varies from country to country; generally 1945 on): detailed topographic mapping

The mapping done by Spain and Portugal before their colonies revolted in the early nineteenth century was usually of the most general kind. Reconnaissance mapping is characterized in its early days in Latin America by the explorations of European surveyors and travelers such as Alexander von Humboldt. By 1851, Europe and North America had some slight interest in Hispanic America as a source of raw materials, but it was not until World War II that this interest was sufficient to provoke programs of systematic topographic survey as a solution to finding out about these resources (Platt 1933, p. 661).

Creation of special bureaus by the countries themselves to carry out surveying began at the end of the nineteenth century, but was not a course followed by all Latin American countries until the middle of the twentieth century (Platt 1933, p. 663; "Cartography in the Americas" 1951, p. 49). Even after the countries established their own cartographic agencies, progress tended to be very slow because of the large scales so optimistically selected—1:25,000 and 1:50,000 in Argentina and Chile and 1:20,000 and 1:50,000 in Uruguay, for example. Peru sensibly chose 1:200,000 as its national scale. The first topographic sheet issued on the entire continent was at one of the larger scales, a 1:100,000-scale sheet of part of the Brazilian state of São Paulo, in 1899, by the State Geographical and Geological Survey. To 1933, only five republics—Argentina, Chile, Uruguay, Peru, and Brazil—had made any substantial progress in the publication of survey sheets (Platt 1933, pp. 661-63; "Bibliografía ..." 1913).

Mid-century saw a much increased demand for large-scale mapping (as large as 1:10,000 scale) due to social reform; the earlier maps had been completed from whatever was available, filled in with guesswork, and were no longer sufficient, if indeed they ever had been (Conly 1956, p. 330; Bennett 1968, p. 7; United States. Army. Inter-American Geodetic Survey 1967, p. 6; Consultation on Geodesy

1950). To 1967, about 2,100 large-scale maps had been prepared, almost all post-1955, and the goal was to have the continent covered by 1:250,000-scale sheets by 1977 (United States. Army. Inter-American Geodetic Survey 1967, pp. 16, 20-21; Freeman, Peacock, and Weil 1963; for general mapping status, see the various editions of the *Handbook of Latin American studies*).

In the early twentieth century, regular field work was not extensive, output was small, quality was not always high, and progress was generally slow. Up to 1920 no general topographic map representing adequately the existing cartographic data for the area covered, of any of the Latin American republics had been produced ("Cartography in the Americas" 1951, p. 58). Matters were at the point where, in 1927, a spokesperson for the American Geographical Society could say:

> The Society is constantly besieged for good maps of one section or another of Central and South America, and similar institutions elsewhere probably have like experience. The answer must of necessity be that there are no good maps: no maps which will at all accurately serve the needs of intensive field work: no maps for the accurate plotting of the distributions in which the geographer, the botanist, and the economist are interested (Platt 1927, p. 302).

In 1928 the Pan American Institute of Geography and History (PAIGH) was founded, with the charge of encouraging geographical and historical studies in Latin America (Randall 1944, p. 3; Calvo 1952). In the American Geographical Society (AGS) landmark publication *Catalogue of maps of Hispanic America*, published from 1930 to 1933, the glaring inadequacy of Latin American cartography was noted. Most significant were the lack of accurate general maps, the difficulty of finding copies of existing maps, and the difficulty of even finding out what had been done, for the unpublished surveys (both commercial and national) were largely confidential (AGS 1930, pp. ix-xi). The situation was such that the society could refer to its heroic effort to compile 1:1,000,000-scale sheets of Hispanic America as work on "so large a scale" (AGS 1930, p. xi). There were still large areas in which no surveys of any sort had ever been made, and virtually the only official topographic survey sheets other than those few issued by Argentina, Brazil, Chile, Mexico, Peru, and Uruguay were 9 sheets at 1:25,000 scale, of about thirty-five square miles of Bogotá and the surrounding area, which had been issued by the Colombian army (AGS 1930, p. ix).

In 1941 the Pan American Institute of Geography and History established a Commission on Cartography, marking a new period (1941-51) in Latin American mapmaking. National agencies developed and intensive inter-American cooperation in various fields of cartography began. In 1946 the United States established the Inter-American Geodetic Survey (IAGS), based at Fort Clayton, Panama Canal Zone. It was a special unit of the Army Corps of Engineers, established to assist Latin American cartographic agencies to become self-sufficient, to secure strong geodetic connections between North and South America, and to obtain aerial photography and geodetic data for map production (PAIGH 1954, p. 1; UN 1963a, p. 333; "Cartography in the Americas" 1951, p. 49; Conly 1956, p. 338; Robertson 1955; "IAGS mapping experts" 1970; Edward B. Brown 1955; Hammer 1963). The agency was established upon request by PAIGH, but not out of sheer benevolence on the part of the United States government; as a U.S. spokesperson put it, "During World War II, we learned the hard way that adequate maps just didn't exist for most parts of the globe" (Conly 1956, p. 338). All of the Latin American countries participated in IAGS except Argentina and Uruguay; they felt their surveying organizations were adequate. There were thus seventeen or eighteen participants in all (Bennett 1968, p. 8).

IAGS had appeared none too soon. Prior to the 1950s, on those relatively rare occasions when topographic mapping was done in and of Latin America, the most frequently used scales were 1:20,000; 1:25,000; 1:31,680; 1:50,000; 1:62,500; and 1:1,000,000 (Pendleton 1944, p. 18). The adverse climatic, vegetational, and physiographic conditions and the unsettled politics of the nations meant that many areas could be mapped only from aerial photography. But extensive clouds in the equatorial regions of Panama and Colombia made such photography almost impossible.

By the 1950s, with many areas in Latin America still unmapped, IAGS and the United States Army Map Service (AMS) concentrated on encouraging regular, systematic surveying with the best available scientific instruments and technical procedures ("Cartography in the Americas" 1951, p. 58). But survey work in Latin American jungles tended to try the participants' good humor.

> To set up just one geodetic control station and complete the necessary observations, survey parties on this mapping project have sometimes had to hack their way through jungle for fourteen days to go twenty miles and then stay on station for weeks, waiting for enough clear weather to make their observations. While they waited, if the weather were wet (as it was in Costa Rica where rainfall is 370 inches a year) fungus formed on the lenses of the surveying instruments.... Wild boars attacked and broke up the campsite, often treed [sic] some of the surveyors for hours.... (Walker 1953, p. 76).

Stoneman (1951, p. 154) concurs in the opinion that fungus growing on the optical elements of the theodolites caused a good deal of trouble. The weather was the worst possible for surveying; airplane crashes, drowning, freezing, and tropical diseases contributed to the surveyors' woes. Triangulation became half trigonometry and half endurance. Surveyors got lost, struck by lightning, and attacked by jaguars (Conly 1956, pp. 338, 345-47).

Such was the setting for the topographic mapping of Latin America. With all the above in mind, the wonder is not that it took so long (as late as 1956, Latin America was still largely uncharted), but that it was ever done at all, and situations in which the existing map showed a large lagoon where in actuality 2,000-foot hills filled the landscape become readily understandable (Walker 1953, p. 76; Castelnuovo-Tedesco 1965). The demand for IAGS collaborative activities, whose chief aim by the 1970s was to assist Latin American countries in the production of first-time mapping coverage, was still growing. By this time the relevant United States agency had changed its name, from the Army Map Service to the Defense Mapping Agency (DMA). DMA's production efforts were designed to supplement rather than to duplicate those of Latin American countries. The program had had an ameliorative effect; during a three-year period in the mid-1970s, 522 sheets at 1:50,000 scale and 35 at 1:250,000-scale were published (UN 1979, p. 57; PAIGH. Commission on Cartography 1965; Kanow 1967; UN 1977a).

In 1979 PAIGH's Commission on Cartography announced the commencement of its 1:250,000 Unified Hemispheric Mapping Series, with the goal of producing complete coverage of the western hemisphere within eight years (1,085 sheets of South America, 53 sheets of Central America, 1,583 sheets of North America, and 8 sheets of the Antilles); the first sheet was to appear in mid-1980. In the early 1980s, distribution, at least to U.S. libraries, was taken over by DMA IAGS* at Fort Sam Houston, Texas, and the program was proceeding well, with all of the Mexico sheets produced and other countries working on theirs (Sebert 1979, p. 3; PAIGH 1978).

---

*Somewhere along the way, IAGS seems to have become a part of DMA.

7
MEXICO

...my country has always lacked good cartography....
−Sanchez Lamego 1952, p. 242

The omens for mapping Mexico were not good from the start. The ship carrying the first *Carta Official de la República* to Europe in 1850 sank (De la Barra 1935, p. 364). Undaunted, the Mexican government started up a Comisión de Cartografía in 1853. In 1857 the Secretaria de Fomento, later to be a key producer of maps, was created (Jáuregui 1968, p. 6). General Riva Palacio, Mínistro de Fomento, created the Sección de Cartografía, sometime in the 1860s (Medina Peralta 1950, p. 2). The Comisión de Cartografía went out of existence in 1876, and in late 1877 (or 1878 or 1886) the Comisión Geográfica-Exploradora was founded (Medina Peralta 1950, p. 3; De la Barra 1935, p. 365). The object of the Comisión was to construct a general map of Mexico (Tamayo 1962, p. 69; Jáuregui 1968, p. 6; Herrera 1945, p. 615). In 1877, 1886, 1891, or 1897 (depending upon the source consulted), the Comisión started work on the *Carta General de la República* at 1:100,000 scale (PAIGH. Centro 1953b, p. 78; Phillips 1900, p. 370; Hoehn 1977, p. 193; MacFadden 1941, p. 75; Anguiano 1914, p. 173). Three sheets were completed by about 1892 ("Maps of North America" 1892, p. 34); sheets were published to 1909, 1911, or 1914 (Medina Peralta 1950, p. 3; Sanchez Lamego 1952, p. 243; "Maps and mapping agencies of Mexico" 1950, p. 2; Mexico. Comisión Geográfica-Exploradora 1893, p. 20). From 1897 to 1911, the Comisión worked on a 1:100,000-scale topographic map of the Gulf of Tehuantepec, on which formlines were more frequent than contours (Thiele 1938, p. 238). What was to become in the mid-twentieth century a central topographic mapping agency, the Dirección General de Geografía y Meteorología, was founded in 1899, as the Comisión Geodésica Mexicana (Lock 1969, p. 321).

At the turn of the century, the Comisión's 1:100,000-scale sheets (128−11 in Sonora, the others toward the Gulf of Mexico and extending from the Rio Grande to the Isthmus of Tehuantepec) had been issued, and 1:20,000-scale topographic and 1:500,000-scale administrative sheets were planned. Yet a person seeking accurate cartographic information about Mexico "or, indeed, accurate information about Mexican maps" met with difficulties (Merrill 1906, p. 281). In 1902 the Comisión Geográfica of the Secretaria de Guerra y Fomento was at work on the *Mapa Topográfico de la República Mexicana* (Alvarado 1900, p. 16; Jáuregui 1968, p. 101). By 1909, the Comisión Geográfica-Exploradora had completed 197 or 198 sheets (21 percent) of a proposed 1,100 in the 1:100,000-scale *Carta de la República Mexicana* (Tamayo 1962, p. 71; MacFadden 1941, p. 75). The last sheet to be published in the series was issued in 1913 or 1914 (Hoehn 1977, p. 193; "Topographic map of Mexico" 1914, p. 433; Mexico. Comisión Geográfica-Exploradora 1974). The approximately 200 sheets published were mainly of Nuevo León, Tamaulipas, San Luis Potosí, Vera Cruz, Puebla, Tlaxcala, part of the Distrito Federal, and, in the north, central Sonora and northern Chihuahua (*Twenty* 1966, p. 100). Had the series been continued—it was terminated when the Comisión was—it would have taken another 144 years to complete coverage of the country at that rate (Tamayo 1962, p. 71).

In 1915 or 1916 the Dirección de Estudios Geográficos y Climatológicos (which would change its name in 1935 to the Dirección de Geografía, Meteorología e Hidrología, until 1950 when it would be replaced by the Dirección General de Cartografía) was established, with the idea of having one agency do all geographic and cartographic work for the nation. Its Sección de Cartografía immediately began work on a topographic map of Mexico. By the late 1920s, the Dirección was working on a 1:100,000-scale series (Tamayo 1962, p. 75; Jáuregui 1968, p. 6; Medina Peralta 1950, p. 3).

By 1930, the Dirección had commenced work on a 1:200,000-scale series (AGS 1930, p. 10; Mexico. Dirección de Estudios Geográficos y Climatológicos 1931). Many unsurveyed areas still existed, including the greater part of the territory between the Tehuantepec railroad and the state of Yucatán, the latter not only unsurveyed but almost completely unexplored. The boundary with British Honduras had never been surveyed (AGS 1930, p. 11; Baker 1967, p. 396). Although Mexico was making some mapping progress, the area covered by sheets was still relatively small; map coverage of northwest and western Mexico was especially patchy (AGS 1930, p. ix, map following p. 142).

In the early 1930s most of the Vera Cruz area was covered by 1:100,000-scale sheets. Aerial surveys had scarcely begun (Cluerg 1933, p. 118). In 1938 or 1939 the Comisión Geográfica Militar was created (in 1954 to become the Departamento Cartográfico Militar) (Tamayo 1962, p. 81; Sanchez Lamego 1952, p. 244; *Twenty* 1966, p. 100). When the United States Air Force decided to obtain aerial mapping photographs of Mexico in 1942, Mexico agreed, stipulating that it was to receive, among other products, contact prints of all photographs taken. The United States made World Aeronautical Charts (WACs; 1:1,000,000 scale) from its prints; Mexico considered its copies of the photographs to be state secrets, and the prints were not available for civilian use. Between 1923 and 1943, Mexico was completely mapped in 51 sheets at 1:500,000 scale by the Dirección de Geografía y Meteorología and its predecessors. In 1945 the Departamento decided to start a map of Mexico at the 1:50,000 scale, working first in northern Chiapas and along the Guatemalan border; fairly soon the scale was changed to 1:100,000, at which point the series became the *Carta General de la República Mexicana*. Also in 1945, the Comité Coordinador del Levantamiento de la Carta de la República was established, to coordinate Mexican map publication; it began work on a 1:500,000-scale series, the new *Carta de la República* ("Maps and mapping agencies of Mexico" 1950, p. 1; Tamayo 1962, p. 81; PAIGH. Centro 1953b, p. 76; Mexico. Dirección de Geografía, Meteorología e Hidrología 1945). The 1940s were marked overall by the indifference of the Mexican government to the need for mapping for civilian uses (Tamayo 1962, p. 88). In 1947, the use of photogrammetry began in

Mexico, and plane-table work went out ("New map of Mexico" 1950, p. 226). The first sheets of the new 1:100,000-scale series were published by the Servicio Geográfico de Ejército (formerly the Comisión Geográfica Militar) in 1949 ("Topographic map series of Mexico" 1950, p. 15; "New map of Mexico" 1950, p. 226; Sanchez Lamego 1949; Mexico. Dirección de Geografía, Meteorología e Hidrología 1950 and 1961).

By 1950 the new map at 1:500,000 scale was completed for the area south of 22°N (Robles Ramos and Ortiz Santos 1950, p. 198). In the same year the Comisión Cartográfica Militar (to be the Departamento Cartográfico Militar) began issuing 1:100,000-scale sheets, and working on a 1:25,000-scale series. Also in 1950 the Dirección General de Cartografía was founded, with as its immediate program to finish 48 sheets at 1:500,000 scale, 21 sheets already issued. Ten of 657 sheets at 1:100,000 scale (between 8°N and 22°N) had been edited to 1950; the first sheet was published in 1951 (Sanchez Lamego 1952, pp. 244-45; Medina Peralta 1950, p. 4; "Maps and mapping agencies of Mexico" 1950, p. 2). Nine of the Dirección's 1:100,000-scale sheets were published by 1953, as compared to 142 sheets of the Comisión's series by 1952 (PAIGH. Centro 1953b, p. 76; Jáuregui 1968, p. 43). In 1953 the United States Army Map Service issued sheets of its 1:250,000-scale series F501, following up on the 1:250,000-scale F541 series (sheets available in about 1948), which was at that time composed of sheets for San Luis Potosí and Vera Cruz, done between 1940 and the early 1950s (Hoehn 1977, pp. 192-93; United States. Army Map Service 1954c, index sheet F541). By the end of 1953, 12 sheets at 1:100,000-scale, 7 more of the 1:25,000 *Carta Táctica del Valle de Mexico*, and 3 of the *Carta Táctica del Istmo de Tehuantepec* (1:25,000) had been issued (Mexico. Comisión Cartográfica Militar 1953).

In 1955, 37 sheets of the Servicio Geográfico's 1:100,000-scale series had been published (Sociedad 1955, p. 7). Public pressure forced the Mexican government to think about doing civilian mapping, since that available was relatively poor (Tamayo 1962, p. 90; Karo 1955, p. 63). Generally accurate military maps extended from the east coast to the Valle de Mexico. By 1958, there were 58 1:250,000-scale sheets issued (Jáuregui 1968, pp. 42-44). In the late 1950s large scale maps became unobtainable even by Mexican citizens (Hagen 1979, p. 109).

The major cartographic problems of the early 1960s were putting all basic cartographic work under one institution's purview, and publishing as soon as possible all of the *Carta Militar* at 1:100,000 scale and the *Carta Táctica del Valle de Mexico* at 1:25,000 scale (Tamayo 1962, p. 96). Only 200 of the approximately 651 total of the first mentioned series had been published (Tamayo 1962, p. 83). The Istmo de Tehuantepec 1:25,000-scale sheets were for confidential circulation only. In 1963 the 1:25,000-scale series was less than 25 percent complete; the 1:100,000-scale series was less than 40 percent complete (Birch 1964, p. 11). By 1966, the last map to be published in the 1:100,000-scale *Carta Militar General de la República* was issued, as was the last sheet in the United States F501 series at 1:250,000-scale (Hoehn 1977, p. 193). There was an "unbelievable array of overlapping series and incomplete projects," (Hagen 1979, p. 108), so that although 300,000 square miles had been mapped it was a problem to figure out at what scale and by what agency (*Twenty* 1966, p. 101; *Geomorfología* 1967).

The Departamento Cartográfico Militar and the Dirección General de Geografía y Meteorología remained the major civilian mapping agencies until October 1, 1969, when the Comisión de Estudios del Territorio Nacional (CETENAL) was founded, and began work on a 1:50,000-scale topographic series of the entire national territory, plus several other thematic series (e.g., geology). When CETENAL took over, the area from 24°N to the United States border was covered with the aforementioned 1:250,000-scale series, a joint effort of the United States Army Map Service and the Departamento (Pan American Union 1965g, p. 4). The formation of CETENAL marked a new era in Mexican topographical cartography, in which large areas of the nation would be quickly and ably mapped. The Departamento Cartográfico Militar continued to work on military mapping while CETENAL took over all civilian map series. By the end of 1974, 480 of the 2,300 sheets at 1:50,000 scale had been completed, covering Coahuila, San Luis Potosí, Zacatecas, Aguascalientes, Guanajuato, and Colima, major parts of Jalisco, Nayarit, México and Morelos, and parts of Sinaloa, Tamaulipas, and Hidalgo, with work ongoing in Nuevo León, Baja, Tabasco, and parts of Campeche and Chiapas (UN. Dept. of Economic and Social Affairs 1976, p. 40). To 1976, 1,010 sheets had been plotted, and CETENAL was looking forward to completion of the series in the early 1980s; by 1977, Baja Norte was covered ("New mapping of western North America" 1977, p. 178; UN 1979, p. 125). In 1978 CETENAL was upgraded to a "dirección," the Dirección General de Estudios del Territorio Nacional (DETENAL). About two-thirds of the country had been mapped at 1:50,000 scale, and DETENAL was producing about 125 new sheets per month. By 1980, all of Mexico was covered with the 1:50,000-scale sheets except for southern Baja, Sinaloa, western Durango, Yucatán, Oaxaca, Chiapas, and Vera Cruz; 1:500,000 scale remained the largest at which the entire country was covered (Hagen 1979, p. 111; Mexico. Dirección General 1980). By early 1983, all the 1:250,000-scale sheets in the PAIGH 1:250,000 Unified Hemispheric Mapping Series had been issued (*1:250,000 Unified Hemispheric Mapping Series, newsletter* no. 6:1, 1/31/83).

8
CENTRAL AMERICA

BELIZE

Belize has been a British possession since 1638, but it was not until 1925 that the British Colonial Survey Committee started a trigonometrical survey of the country. In 1926 and 1927 work was begun on a contoured map series of the colony, various local town plans, general maps at 16 miles to the inch (about 1:1,000,000 scale), and two geological maps (Great Britain. Colonial Survey Committee 1928, pp. 12-14). By the mid-1940s, 6,600 of 8,600 square miles had been topographically mapped (Great Britain. Colonial Office 1946, p. 13).

In spite of this burst of activity, until 1950 Belize was still little surveyed (AGS 1930, p. 112; UN. Dept. of Social Affairs 1949, map following p. 18). There was a formlined 1:50,000-scale British Directorate of Overseas Surveys (DOS) series begun in 1946. In 1952, the Belize Survey Department began issuing a 1:50,000-scale series with formlines and the British Directorate of Military Survey (DMS) began issuing a formlined 1:250,000-scale series in 1954 (Hoehn 1977, p. 190). Publication of 1:50,000-scale sheets by DMS and DOS took place between about 1962 and 1966, with the result that by the early 1960s the series was more than half completed (Birch 1964, p. 11; UN 1979, p. 42). By 1969, all 45 of the 1:50,000-scale maps and all 3 of the 1:250,000-scale sheets were complete (UN. Dept. of Economic and Social Affairs 1970, p. 77). By late 1974, 12 contoured sheets at 1:50,000 scale (DOS 4499; Series E755) had been issued, with completion expected in the late 1970s (UN. Dept. of Economic and Social Affairs 1976, p. 53).

COSTA RICA

Costa Rica does not deviate in any major way from the pattern set by the other countries in this area. It too became independent in 1821; with Honduras, Nicaragua, Guatemala, and El Salvador it formed the Central American Union, which was dissolved in 1839. In 1888 the Instituto Físico Geográfico was founded; it died in 1912.

In 1944, the Instituto Geográfico de Costa Rica was established (Barrantes Ferrero 1954, p. 151 and 1967, p. 40; Lock 1969, p. 327; PAIGH. Centro 1952, p. 290; "Collaborative mapping in Costa Rica" 1956). In 1945, 10 percent of the intermontane area was mapped at 1:25,000 scale (Barrantes Ferrero 1954, p. 158). In 1948 or 1949 the institute began work on a 1:25,000-scale series, using aerial photography (Jáuregui 1968, p. 108; PAIGH. Centro 1952, p. 293). But all in all very little topographic mapping was done in Costa Rica until after 1950.

The actual production of maps began in about 1954, with the 1:25,000-scale sheet of Filadelfia ("Collaborative mapping in Costa Rica" 1956, p. 386; *Twenty* 1966, p. 66; Barrantes Ferrero 1967, p. 40; Palmerlee 1945, p. 25; Hoehn 1977, p. 191; Costa Rica 1954, p. 1, map facing p. 2). The 1:50,000-scale series was begun in about 1955, and made Costa Rica virtually the only country in Central America at that time with an active, ongoing mapping program (Hoehn 1977, p. 191; Karo 1955, p. 63).

The 1:25,000-scale series was suspended in 1962 after 99 sheets had been published. Forty-one sheets at 1:50,000 scale had been issued to 1964, covering less than 25 percent of the country (Pan American Union 1965c, p. 4; Birch 1964, p. 11; Barrantes Ferrero 1967, p. 41). In 1968, the institute, renamed the Instituto Geográfico Nacional, began work on a 1:200,000-scale series (Hoehn 1977, p. 191). By late 1968, only 1 of 9 sheets at 1:200,000 scale, 120 of 138 at 1:50,000 scale (to be completed in 1969), and 100 of 552 at 1:25,000 scale (now revived, but slated to cover only densely settled areas) were complete (UN. Dept. of Economic and Social Affairs 1970, p. 41). By late 1974, all of 138 sheets at 1:50,000 scale (E762), 100 of 490 at 1:25,000 scale (E862), and all of 9 at 1:200,000 scale (E561) had been completed (UN. Dept. of Economic and Social Affairs 1976, p. 28).

EL SALVADOR

To 1930, the only detailed accurate surveying done in El Salvador—a country that became independent in 1821—was the surveying done for the Intercontinental Railroad Commission and a few surveys related to possible road routes (AGS 1930, pp. 112, 114). The Dirección General de Cartografía was founded in 1946; the Oficina de Cartografía y Geografía was founded in the same year, to work at scales of 1:200,000; 1:50,000; 1:20,000; and 1:10,000. The Dirección was renamed the Dirección de Cartografía in 1950 (PAIGH. Centro 1953a, p. 102).

In 1954 or 1955, the 1:50,000-scale series sheets were first published (Hoehn 1977, p. 191). By 1956, a 1:200,000-scale contoured series was completed. To 1960, at least 35 sheets at 1:50,000 scale had been published (Paris 1967, p. 21; El Salvador. Sección 1961). By 1964, 46 of 58 sheets of the 1:50,000-scale series, covering 90 percent of the national territory, had been published and maps covering the remainder, extending to the northern frontier, were in preparation (Pan American Union 1965d, p. 5; El Salvador. Dirección 1963; *Twenty* 1966, p. 83). In the same year, a 1:100,000-scale series was begun with an estimated completion date of 1970. By spring of 1969 the 1:200,000-, 1:100,000-, and 1:50,000-scale series were all complete, and 155 of 188 sheets at 1:20,000 scale had been published (Bennett 1968, p. 8; UN. Dept. of Economic and Social Affairs 1970, p. 44). By late 1974, the Instituto Geográfico Nacional "Ing. Pablo Arnoldo Guzmán" had issued all of the now 196 sheets at 1:20,000 scale (UN. Dept. of Economic and Social Affairs 1976, pp. 29-30; Bergquist et al. 1978, p. 28; El Salvador. Instituto 1977, pp. 14-19).

GUATEMALA

As part of the relatively densely settled portion of Central America, Guatemala was mapped in outline by 1600 (Bettex 1960, front endpapers). This fine old tradition of outline mapping continued into the twentieth century; by 1930 planimetric maps, mostly sketch maps, were still virtually the only maps available. In fact, outside of Sapper's surveys in Alta Vera Paz and Lake Petén, Guatemala was practically unknown cartographically, especially in the north and central areas (AGS 1930, pp. 112, 114). There were no national survey series in progress. In 1934, the Geographic Branch of the United States Army did issue a 1:250,000-scale map of Guatemala (PAIGH. Centro 1952, p. 6).

In 1945, Guatemala set up the Departamento de Mapas y Cartografía under the Ministerio de Communicaciones y Obras Públicas ("Collaborative mapping in Guatemala" 1957, p. 126; Lock 1969, p. 325; Santiso 1944). By 1949, the only mapping on scales more detailed than 1:250,000 were some sheets of inferior quality, between scales of 1:25,000 and 1:75,000, of areas in western Guatemala just west of Guatemala City; some 1:200,000-scale preliminary maps were compiled in 1949 (McBryde 1969, p. 291; UN. Dept. of Social Affairs 1949, map following p. 18; Guatemala. Instituto 1978, p. 32).

In 1954, the Departamento became the Dirección General de Cartografía, and began an intensive program to complete the basic map at 1:250,000 scale by 1958 ("Collaborative mapping in Guatemala" 1957, p. 126; Lock 1969, p. 325). In 1958, the Dirección, IAGS, and the United States Army Map Service began work on a 1:250,000-scale series (E503). In about 1959 the Dirección began the 1:25,000-scale series, and in 1959 or 1960 a 1:50,000-scale series; in the latter series 53 sheets were completed to 1963 (Paris 1967, p. 21; Hoehn 1977, p. 191; Guatemala. Dirección 1958).

In 1964, the Dirección changed its name to the Instituto Geográfico Nacional de Guatemala (*Twenty* 1966, p. 89; Lock 1969, p. 325). By this time, traditional methods of triangulation had been replaced by modern methods. The 1:250,000-scale series covered all of Guatemala south of 15°N, while 1:50,000-scale sheets covered the southwest and southeast portions of the country plus a band extending across the center of the nation and a portion of the central Petén region (Pan American Union 1965e, p. 4). The base map of the country was the 1:250,000-scale series, with the 1:50,000-scale series as the next most important (Guzmán 1967, p. 52). By late 1969, some 171 of the 332 sheets at 1:50,000 scale, and all 13 (in some cases reported as 16, since 1 sheet combined 4 partial sheets) sheets of the 1:250,000-scale series were complete (McBryde 1969, p. 291; UN. Dept. of Economic and Social Affairs 1970, pp. 49-50). All of the 1:50,000-scale series (now in 330 sheets) was complete by 1977, except for the upper right hand corner of the country, west of Belize (Guatemala. Instituto 1978, pp. 30-35).

HONDURAS

Honduras, which became independent in 1821, remained mostly unmapped topographically until after 1950 (AGS 1930, pp. 112-14; UN. Dept. of Social Affairs 1949, map following p. 18). In November of 1946, the Comisión Geográfica Especial was constituted in a provisional form as a part of the Secretaria de Guerra, Marina, y Aviación (PAIGH. Centro 1952, p. 174). Its tasks were to complete the aeronautical chart program, work on geodetic measurements, and construct basic maps at scales of 1:50,000; 1:100,000; and 1:250,000 (*Twenty* 1966, p. 96).

In 1954, the Honduran Comisión, IAGS, and the United States Army Map Service were working in concert on a 1:50,000-scale series (E752), to total 285 sheets (Hoehn 1977, p. 192). In 1956 the Comisión was transferred to the ministry of development; in 1957 its name was changed to the Dirección General de Cartografía, and in 1958 to the Instituto Geográfico Nacional (*Twenty* 1966, p. 96). Apparently the name was soon changed back to Dirección General de Cartografía.

By 1967, 77 sheets of the 1:50,000-scale series had been published, as had 2 sheets of the 1:250,000-scale series (E503) compiled from the former (Caceres 1967, p. 61). By mid-1968, 104 of the 275 sheets at 1:50,000-scale (*Mapa del Territorio Nacional*) had been published (UN. Dept. of Economic and Social Affairs 1970, p. 50; Saubers 1969, p. 210; Honduras. Instituto 1967, 1969-71; *Honduras cartográfica*).

In 1970, with 50 percent of the national territory covered by 1:50,000-scale sheets (42 percent actually published), field operations began in the Mosquito area. The area measured 16,360 square kilometers, about the size of New Jersey, and had been a blank area on the map (Hughes 1971, p. 307; Saubers 1969, p. 210; Honduras. Instituto 1969b, p. 45). By late 1974, 224 of 275 sheets at 1:50,000 scale were complete, and 7 of about 14 at 1:250,000 scale (UN. Dept. of Economic and Social Affairs 1976, p. 35). Sometime in the 1970s, the civilian mapping agency was again named the Instituto Geográfico Nacional (Bergquist 1981, p. 38). By 1977, only about 24 sheet areas were not mapped either at 1:50,000 or 1:25,000 scale; between 5 and 7 of the 1:250,000-scale series were left to do, and those sheets published were issued by the Instituto or by the United States Defense Mapping Agency (Granados Garay 1977, lamina VII).

NICARAGUA

Nicaragua, independent since 1821, is noted for its paucity of surveying and mapping for many years into the twentieth century (AGS 1930, pp. 112, 114-15; "Bibliografía..." 1914). The United States Marines issued an uncontoured map in 1934 (Thiele 1938, p. 235; Monteiro 1967a, p. 150). In 1946 the Oficina de Geodesía was organized as a part of the Ministerio de Guerra, Marina, y Aviación, and an agreement was made between Nicaragua and the United States to establish basic geodetic control in Nicaragua (Núñez 1967, p. 74).

In 1954, the first sheet of the 1:100,000-scale series was issued by the Oficina de Geodesía. In 1955 (or 1960) the Oficina became the Dirección General de Cartografía. The Dirección placed emphasis on working on the planimetric 1:100,000-scale series and on the topographic 1:250,000-scale series of Nicaragua west of 85°30'W ("Collaborative mapping in Nicaragua" 1957, p. 4; *Twenty* 1966, p. 105). Conventional methods of mapping were impossible in the undeveloped eastern two-thirds of the country, with its constant cloud cover, vast areas, lack of roads, flat terrain combined with heavy jungle, and extensive coastal swamps, all making plane-table techniques unworkable ("Collaborative mapping in Nicaragua" 1957, p. 5). In 1956 the first sheet of the 1:50,000-scale series appeared, completed with the assistance of IAGS (Hoehn 1977, p. 195; Núñez 1967, p. 74; Monteiro 1967a, pp. 147-49).

In 1960, at least 123 sheets at 1:50,000 scale had been issued (Núñez 1967, p. 74; Paris 1967, p. 22). In 1962 the Dirección began issuing 1:250,000-scale maps, and by 1964, the western one-third of the nation was covered by the 1:50,000-scale series (Hoehn 1977, p. 195). By late 1968, 11 of 13 sheets at 1:250,000 scale, 214 of 300 at 1:50,000 scale, and 4 of 1,200 at 1:25,000 scale (the latter intended to cover only densely populated or special areas) were complete (UN. Dept. of Economic and Social Affairs 1970, p. 62). By late 1974, the number of sheets in the 1:250,000-scale series (E503) had been revised to 12, and all were complete, as were 27 of 100 at 1:100,000 scale (E651; planimetric with hachures), 288 of 300 at 1:50,000 scale (E751), 4 of 1,200 at 1:25,000 scale (E851), and 1,032 of 4,130 at 1:10,000 scale (E951; orthophotomap) (UN. Dept. of Economic and Social Affairs 1976, p. 42). The issuing agency was the Instituto Geográfico Nacional (Bergquist 1978, p. 51; Nicaragua 1977).

PANAMA

Panama's political history is considerably more complicated than that of its northern neighbors. It was a segment of the Spanish Viceroyalty of Peru in 1542; in 1717 it became part of New Granada, which, as Colombia, became independent in 1819. Panama remained part of Colombia until 1903, at which time the United States Army Corps of Engineers began work on the Panama Canal.

The corps worked on maps of the area from about 1904 to about 1935 (Thiele 1938, p. 235; United States. Library of Congress. Map Division 1918, p. 154). The rest of the country, except for the north and south coasts, was cartographically ignored (AGS 1930, p. 112). In 1946 aerial photography began to be used for Panamanian mapping; a 1:20,000-scale map of the Canal Zone was made by the corps (PAIGH. Centro 1952, p. 419; UN 1979, p. 193).

The Sección de Cartografía was established in the same year; it would eventually be renamed the Instituto Geográfico Nacional "Tommy Guardia" (UN 1979, p. 21; *Twenty* 1966, p. 108). As late as 1949 there were features that did not appear on then current maps, such as a range of mountains 120 miles long and over 5,200 feet high only sixty miles from the Canal Zone (Conly 1956, p. 338; "Cartography in the Americas" 1951, p. 53).

In 1954, the Sección became the Oficina de Cartografía, and in 1955, the Dirección de Cartografía (*Twenty* 1966, p. 108). Between 1958 and 1960 the United States Army Map Service began a 1:25,000-scale map series (Hoehn 1977, p. 195), which was less than 25 percent complete in 1963 (Birch 1964, p. 11). By 1964, the AMS series at 1:50,000 scale covered the south coast, the peninsula west of Panama City, and islands in the Gulf of Panama. In 1962, the Dirección began work on a 1:10,000-scale map series (Pan American Union 1965i, p. 4).

One of the major reasons for such sparse and patchy cartographic coverage in such a relatively small country was the almost continuous cloud cover, which for twenty years precluded obtaining satisfactory aerial photography. At the same time the vegetation, fauna, and physiography militated against the use of plane-table mapping. To 1965, about 47 1:50,000-scale sheets had been issued (Paris 1967, p. 22). In 1967, side-looking airborne radar (SLAR) cut through the clouds and provided imagery that could be used in the compilation of 1:250,000-scale sheets (UN 1976b, pp. 204, 215; Viksne, Lister, and Sapp 1969, p. 54). By late 1968, all 12 of the 1:250,000-scale sheets, 109 of the 199 1:50,000-scale sheets (covering

55 percent of the country), and 47 of the 700 1:25,000-scale sheets (covering the Canal Zone) had been completed (Saenz 1969; UN. Dept. of Economic and Social Affairs 1976, p. 44). By 1976, the 1:50,000-scale series covered 70 percent of the national territory (UN 1979, p. 21; Cardoze and Tempone 1978, pp. 15-18).

9
SOUTH AMERICA

ARGENTINA

The Oficina Topográfico Militar was established in Argentina in 1879 to carry out basic geodetic surveying and frontier and boundary surveying, and to compile military maps. In 1884 it became the Instituto Geográfico Militar (IGM) (AGS 1932b, p. 5; Luxardo de Castro 1952, p. 84; Benjamín García 1913, p. 63).

Early in the twentieth century, in 1904, IGM began work on a geodetic framework for the country ("Cartography in Argentina 1953, p. 43; Luxardo de Castro 1952, p. 87). In 1905 the first map sheets made by the institute were completed; they were, as might be expected, of the area around Buenos Aires. Mapping of the various provinces started in some cases prior to 1910. All of this early survey work was exclusively plane-table compilation, mainly by the División Central Nacional Cartográfica. The scales chosen were 1:25,000 for cities, 1:50,000 for other urbanized areas, and 1:100,000 for rural areas, the latter being the majority of the nation (Ruiz Moreno 1917, pp. 27, 33). In 1914, Argentina's first topographic sheets were published (Platt 1933, p. 662; Mori 1914).

The first stereo-photogrammetry field team, using ground photography, was organized in 1920; it completed a survey of the province of Mendoza at 1:25,000 scale (Gast 1922). In 1920 some sheets of Santa Fe province at 1:25,000 scale appeared, and soon after, a few 1:50,000-scale sheets were published. From 1922 to 1925, about 14 of the 1:25,000-scale sheets of Mendoza were published; in 1924 or 1925 some 1:50,000-scale sheets of the same province were issued. In 1929 experimental aerial surveying began, and some 1:100,000-scale sheets of Corrientes province were published ("Cartography in Argentina" 1953, p. 54; Argentine Republic 1927).

By 1930, IGM's basic program was composed of triangulation and precise leveling carried out by its geodetic section; topographic surveys for the general map of the republic at 1:100,000 scale; topographic surveys at scales of 1:25,000 and 1:50,000 for areas of special administrative or military importance; 1:250,000-scale sheets for geographical surveys, and the compilation of the Argentinian sheets of the *International map of the world* at 1:1,000,000 scale (AGS 1932b, p. 5).

Argentina has taken its mapping program seriously since the end of the nineteenth century, and documentation of its publication program, unlike that for other countries in Latin America (with the exceptions of Brazil and Mexico), is plentiful. The status of topographic maps published in Argentina from 1900 to 1940 is given in the accompanying figure (see page 64).

IGM worked mainly on 1:25,000-scale sheets prior to 1925, on 1:50,000-scale sheets in the 1930s and 1940s, and on 1:100,000-scale sheets thereafter (Olson and Whitmarsh 1944, p. 196; Monteiro 1967b, pp. 3-30; Conferencia 1937).

Province	Series Scale	Comment
Buenos Aires province	1:25,000	about 40 done, 1900-1939
	1:50,000	about 40 done, 1913-1939
	1:100,000	10 completed by 1939
Catamarca province	1:100,000	9 done by 1936
Córdoba province	1:25,000	4 sheets, 1912-1915
	1:50,000	31 done by 1935
	1:100,000	29 done by 1939
Corrientes	1:50,000	begun 1909; no sheet production given
Entre Ríos	1:25,000	21 done, 1910-1933
	1:50,000	about 70 by 1939
	1:100,000	21 done by 1939
Jujuy	1:50,000	10 done 1935-1937
Mendoza	1:25,000	about 14 by 1935
	1:50,000	about 30 by 1935
	1:100,000	about 15, 1900-1937
Salta	1:25,000	8 in 1912; 5 in 1935
	1:100,000	2 done 1934-1935
San Juan	1:50,000	19 done 1934-1935
	1:100,000	1 done in 1936
San Luis	1:50,000	1 done in 1936
Santa Fe	1:25,000	10 done to 1935
	1:50,000	27 done to early 1930s
	1:100,000	6 done 1933-1934
Tucumán	1:50,000	3–1928, 1932, 1935
Chubut	1:50,000	1 in 1936
	1:100,000	2 in 1934
Misiones	1:100,000	4, 1934-1935
Neuquén	1:50,000	24, 1934-1939
Río Negro	1:100,000	9, 1935-1937
Santa Cruz	1:100,000	4, 1934-1935

(Argentina 1940)

Argentinian Topographic Map Sheet Issuance, 1900-1940

Until 1932, most work was concentrated in the provinces and gobernaciones (sparsely populated territories) of Buenos Aires, Córdoba, Corrientes, Entre Ríos, Mendoza, Santa Fe, Tucumán, Jujuy, and Neuquén. In 1941 came the Ley de la Carta, in which 1:100,000 and 1:50,000 were made the official national topographic scales. Before the law, about 32.6 percent of the national territory had been surveyed (Arredondo 1957, pp. 91, 93). In the same year as the law's appearance, IGM published its first colored 1:250,000-scale sheet.

From 1933 to 1943, as aerial survey gradually became a standard technique, IGM extended its work to San Luis, Río Negro, Chubut, Santa Cruz, Tierra del Fuego, and Formosa ("Cartography in Argentina" 1953, pp. 43, 57; Argentine Republic 1943 and 1947). By 1949, a combined procedure of classic plane-table and modern photogrammetric methods was being employed ("Cartography in Argentina" 1953, p. 57).

By about 1950, there were 434 (or 306) sheets at 1:50,000 scale, 515 (or 229) sheets at 1:100,000 scale, and 122 at 1:25,000 scale available (Luxardo de Castro 1952, p. 88; Wilhelm Schulz 1951, p. 183; Congreso 1951; Calvo 1956; Ronchetti 1954, p. 37). A new format for 1:50,000-scale sheets was introduced in 1955; the new format for the 1:100,000-scale sheets began in 1945 (Paris 1967, pp. 1-2; Argentine Republic 1955, p. 109). By 1955, accurate detailed contour sheets were concentrated along the Paraná and the Plata, with the northern half of the country generally better mapped than the southern half (Raisz 1956, p. 106; Argentine Republic 1956; PAIGH. Sección Naciónal Argentina 1955). Sheets at 1:50,000 scale existed for northeast Buenos Aires province, central and eastern Entre Ríos, eastern Corrientes, western Mendoza, southeast Córdoba, and southwest Neuquén; 1:100,000-scale coverage existed for about a third of the country—parts of Buenos Aires province, Corrientes, Entre Ríos and Córdoba, and parts of the territories of Neuquén, Chubut, Santa Cruz, and Tierra del Fuego (UN. Secretariat 1957, p. 6).

In 1964, IGM's 1:25,000-scale series (which had obviously been in existence for some time since about half the country was covered with it) finally was mentioned in the literature (Pan American Union 1965a, p. 4; Wilhelm Schulz 1962 and 1963). A 1:100,000-scale series covered most of the northeast, four large regions in the Cordillera, and Patagonia; a 1:50,000-scale series covered large regions of the north central and eastern provinces. The 1:50,000-scale series was less than 25 percent complete, and the 1:100,000-scale series less than 50 percent complete (Pan American Union 1965a, p. 4; Birch 1964, p. 11). By late 1968, 76 of 246 sheets at 1:250,000 scale, 642 of 1,860 at 1:100,000 scale, and 1,467 of 7,065 at 1:50,000 scale were complete (UN. Dept. of Economic and Social Affairs 1970, p. 34).

BOLIVIA

The Instituto Geográfico Militar "General Juan Mariano Mujía" was founded in 1936, based on the Mesa Topográfica del Sudeste and the Gabinete Topográfico del Estado Mayor General. It was reorganized in 1939 at Cochabamba, and in 1942 transferred to La Paz. But in spite of the existence of the institute, Bolivia was cartographically impoverished until after 1950 (Edinburgh Geographical Institute 1922, plate I; Platt 1945, map following p. 18; Karo 1955, plate II; "Cartografía extranjera" 1913; Twenty 1966, p. 40). There was some work done in the 1940s, mostly at 1:100,000 scale in the Cordillera and Altiplano. Some work was also done at 1:25,000 scale in the Cordillera and at 1:20,000 scale in the Altiplano, but none of it was published. In 1948, the institute became responsible for production of the national maps (Consultation on Geodesy 1945, p. 144; Pan American Consultation on Cartography 1950, p. 208; *Twenty* 1966, p. 40; Medina Ruiz 1954).

A Comisión Nacional de Cartografía was apparently in existence in the 1950s. In the 1960s some detailed topographic work was done by the institute and by Yacimientos Petrolíferos Fiscales Bolivianos, both of which, in 1964, were working on a 1:50,000-scale series based on aerial photography. Apparently there was an "old" series at 1:250,000 scale dating from the 1950s that was between 25 and 50 percent complete (Birch 1964, p. 11; Lock 1969, p. 337; Pan American Union 1964a, p. 4). Nonetheless, "Cartography has come into being [in Bolivia], we might say, somewhat belatedly, in the past twenty years" (A. García 1967, p. 1). At the time of that quote, aerial photogrammetric plates were being assembled and work being done by United States companies as Gulf and Shell (A. García 1967, p. 2). By the late 1960s, 250 of 2,357 sheets at 1:50,000 scale and 3 of 84 at 1:250,000 scale had been completed (UN. Dept of Economic and Social Affairs 1970, p. 37). By the mid 1970s, the relevant cartographic agency was the Instituto Geográfico Militar y Catastro Nacional (Bergquist 1978, p. 17).

BRAZIL

In 1825, three years after Brazilian independence, Brazil's—and South America's—first official mapping agency, the Comissão do Imperio do Brasil, was formed. Two state agencies appeared before the end of the century, the Comissão Geológica do Estado do São Paulo in 1866, and the Comissão Geográfica e Geológica, the official mapping agency for the state of Minas Gerais, in 1892 (Brazil. Conselho 1951, p. 61). In the late nineteenth century, the Instituto Geográfico e Geológico do Estado do São Paulo produced the first 1:100,000-scale map of the nation René de Mattos 1967, p. 6).

In 1909, the Diretoria do Serviço Geográfico do Exército produced some 1:10,000-scale sheets (René de Mattos 1967, p. 6). In 1913 or 1914, photogrammetry (probably with ground photography) was first used in Brazil (Lock 1969, p. 333). In 1917 the Serviço Geográfico Militar was founded (Oliveira 1952, p. 220). By 1919 the Club de Engenharia of Rio de Janeiro had reached the dismaying conclusion that it would take 690 years just to survey Brazil at 1:100,000 scale at what was the present rate of progress, let alone actually issue the maps ("Proposed map of Brazil" 1919, p. 260). In 1922, the first map compiled using photogrammetric procedures was published; it was of the Distrito Federal (René de Mattos 1967, p. 5).

In spite of all this cartographic preparation, in 1930 the status of cartographic knowledge of the country was generally speaking far below that of similarly populated sections in other South American republics. Vast stretches of the Brazilian interior were only mapped, if at all, by reconnaissance surveys (AGS 1933, p. 85). The state mapping programs were by definition limited to areas within a given state's boundary, and there seemed not to be a national mapping program, or at least not an active one.

The Comissão da Carta Geral was created in 1930 to carry out a plan of mapping Rio Grande do Sul, initiated by the Army General Staff. Later, the Servico

Geográfico Militar (a similar unit) was established in Rio de Janeiro under the direction of Austrian technicians from the Geographic Military Institute of Vienna. In 1932 the army reorganized its mapping units, and formed the Serviço Geográfico do Exército. The Conselho Nacional de Geografía, a civilian agency, was established in 1937 or 1939 (Brazil. Conselho 1951, p. 61; Allyrio H. de Mattos 1944, p. 23; Castro 1940; *Twenty* 1966, p. 50).

In spite of all these organizational efforts, Brazil remained without a national mapping program throughout the 1930s. Only 32 sheets at 1:100,000 scale (covering one-third of the state of São Paulo) and 40 sheets at 1:100,000 scale of the southeast corner of Minas Gerais had been issued to 1935, and those by the states' own mapping units (Thiele 1938, p. 234).

In 1943, two-thirds of the country was covered by trimetrogon photographs (René de Mattos 1967, p. 5). By 1944, a 1:200,000-scale *Carta das Excursionistas*, with contours, was being developed by the Instituto Astronómico e Geográfico do São Paulo, and the Serviço Geográfico do Exército was working on 1:250,000- and 1:50,000-scale sheets (Olson and Whitmarsh 1944, p. 198; Castro 1945, p. 11; Allyrio H. de Mattos 1944, pp. 21-23; United States. Dept. of State 1946). By the end of the 1940s, the Serviço Geográfico do Exército, which had responsibility for topographic maps (at scales of 1:25,000; 1:50,000 (the prime series); 1:100,000 and 1:250,000), was working in the southern part of the Rio Grande do Sul on 1:50,000-scale sheets, in the Distrito Federal at 1:100,000 scale, and in northeast Brazil at an undefined scale (Brazil. Conselho 1951, p. 62 and 1950; Rio de Janeiro 1951). The Instituto Geológico e Geográfico do São Paulo had completed half of a 1:100,000-scale series of that state; the Departamento Geográfico do Estado do Minas Gerais was working on its 1:100,000-scale series, with one-third of the southern part completed; and the Conselho had completed eight maps at 1:250,000 scale, based on trimetrogon data and field traverse, mostly in the São Francisco River basin (Minas Gerais, Bahia, Pernambuco, Piauí, Alagoas, Sergipe, and Goiás provinces), and the coastal area of Bahia (Brazil. Conselho 1951, pp. 62, 65-67). Reconnaissance topographic mapping of east and central Brazil at 1:250,000 scale was reported to be the Conselho's next task (Brazil. Conselho 1951, p. 62).

In 1952, Brazil entered into a treaty agreement with the United States in which the latter agreed to take trimetrogon and vertical aerial photography of Brazil and to give sets of the resulting prints, negatives, sheets at 1:50,000 scale and 1:100,000 scale compiled from the photographs, and much more, to Brazil, while Brazil agreed to complete the necessary ground control (United States. Treaties 1955).

By the mid-1950s, several dozen sheets at 1:25,000 scale had been issued by the Conselho, and 1:50,000 *Carta Normal* sheets covered the regions of the states of Rio Grande do Sul, Ceará, and Rio Grande do Norte. Maps at 1:100,000 scale covered northwest Paraná; 1:25,000-scale sheets (mostly planimetric) of 75 percent of Santa Catarina and Rio Grande do Sul, 65 percent of Paraná, and 10 percent of Mato Grosso had been made. The Conselho had also issued 40 sheets at 1:250,000 scale of east and central Brazil. Some 60 sheets at 1:100,000 scale of São Paulo and 55 sheets of Minas Gerais had been issued by the state mapping agencies (UN. Secretariat 1957, p. 8; Brazil. Diretoria 1954; Brazil. Conselho 1957). Photogrammetry was very much in use throughout the 1950s and afterward (Corrêa Filho

1957, p. 719). By 1958, one-eighth of the country was covered with 1:250,000-scale sheets, and the remainder with 24 1:1,000,000-scale sheets ("Mapping progress in Brazil" 1958, p. 290; Serviços 1962).

The major mapping agencies in the 1960s were the Conselho, the Diretoria do Serviço Geográfico (DSG) do Exército (which worked on all series at 1:250,000 and more detailed scales, with major effort on 1:25,000-, 1:50,000-, and 1:100,000-scale series in potentially important industrial and agricultural areas), and the Instituto Geográfico e Geológico for the state of São Paulo. Although detailed mapping coverage was very limited, reconnaissance mapping did cover most of the populated regions of eastern Brazil. The Conselho had 1:250,000- and 1:50,000-scale mapping in progress in that area, with a 1:250,000-scale project covering parts of Bahia, Goiás, Piauí, and Pernambuco, and all of Alagoas and Sergipe. The 1:50,000-scale series was slated to cover only the states of Rio de Janeiro and Guanabara ("Mapping progress in Brazil" 1958, p. 291; Pan American Union 1965b, p. 4). The Diretoria was concentrating on areas in the south and on the northeast coast, in some of the same regions. All agencies had the major problems of the immense size of the country and the difficult terrain and weather conditions. In 1962, the Divisão de Cartografía started an accelerated production program at scales of 1:100,000 and 1:50,000, while continuing to work at 1:250,000 scale ("O programa" 1963, p. 100).

The São Paulo Instituto had been working on a 1:100,000-scale series based on aerial photography since 1952, the earlier series based on field mapping having been discontinued. The Departamento Geográfico de Minas Gerais discontinued its 1:100,000-scale series in 1952 (Pan American Union 1965b, p. 4).

In the Amazon basin and the Mato Grosso there was very little topographic mapping of any kind, even in the 1960s, and none of the series in progress were more than 25 percent complete for the country as a whole (Birch 1964, p. 11). In 1964, the Conselho began sheet production on a new 1:100,000-scale series (René de Mattos 1967, p. 6). In late 1968, 19 of 805 of the contoured 1:250,000-scale series, 39 of 2,982 at 1:100,000 scale, and 376 of 11,928 at 1:50,000 scale were complete (UN. Dept. of Economic and Social Affairs 1970, p. 38).

In 1971, Brazil was 12 percent mapped. The Instituto Brasileiro de Geografía e Estatística (IBGE) became responsible for the 1:100,000- and 1:50,000-scale series; in some way the Diretoria de Servico Geográfico retained responsibility for systematic mapping at 1:100,000 scale. IBGE also published the topographic map of the northeast Brazil at 1:100,000 scale, by agreement with the Superintendência do Desenvolvimento do Nordeste (SUDENE). SUDENE had its own Divisão de Cartografía that performed the 1:100,000-scale work (Gardini 1979, pp. 42-46; Brazil. Superintendência 1965). In the early 1970s, about 345,000 square kilometers were being systematically mapped at 1:100,000 scale, as a result of an agreement signed between IBGE and the Superintendência do Desenvolvimento da Amazônia (SUDAM) ("Mapeamento topográfico na Amazônia" 1973 p. 142). Four areas to be concentrated on in this program were:

1. 55°30' to 57°30'W, 13°-16°S

2. 48°-49°, 6°-17°S
   49°-51°W, 7°-9°S
   50°-51°31'W, 9°-10°S

3.   50°30'-52°W, 10°-15°S
     51°-52°W, 15°-15°30'S
     51°30'-52°30'W, 15°30'-16°S

4.   47°-48°W, 3°30'-5°S
     47°-49°W, 3°30'-5°S
     47°-47°30'W, 3°-3°30'S

The job of mapping Brazil seemed hopeless until Projeto RADAM, which took remote sensing imagery, specifically SLAR, of all of Brazil; by 1975, radar mapping of all of Brazil, the data in the form of computerized information, was done. In the process, some persons died in helicopter crashes, fell victim to disease and Indian arrows, or "just disappeared into the wilds" (Hammond 1977, p. 514). The results of this work were embodied in precise topographic maps that included such discoveries as finding a previously unmapped river 400 miles long. The information gathered by RADAM took the form of a series of maps accompanied with a thick book of supporting data for each section—18 volumes, for example, for the Amazon basin. Brazil also began to use Landsat imagery heavily in the late 1970s (Simon 1978; *Resources* 1982, pp. 317-35; A. J. Lewis 1976, p. 393).

CHILE

In 1849, the Comisión Topográfica was established; by 1870, 13 sheets at 1:250,000 scale were ready for engraving. In 1873, the *Plano Topográfico y Geológico de la República de Chile*, by Pissis, at 1:250,000 scale, was issued (United States. Library of Congress 1904, p. 55; Ruge 1883, p. 530; Wheeler 1885, p. 460). In 1891, the Instituto Geográfico Militar (IGM) was formed, as the Oficina Geográfica; at various times over the years, it would be called the Sección Cartográfico, the Sección (or Departamento) de Levantamiento, the Oficina de la Carta de la República/Estado Mayor, the Servicio Geográfico, and the Departamento de Levantamiento (Arce 1967, p. 14; "Cartografía chilena" 1955, p. 28; Chile 1950, p. 97; "Collaborative mapping in Chile" 1956, p. 139; "Labor ejectuada" 1953, p. 5). In 1894, work on 1:25,000-scale topographic sheets was initiated (*Twenty* 1966, p. 55).

Triangulation for the *Carta de la República* at 1:50,000 and 1:100,000 scales was begun in 1903 (Bertrand 1915, p. 664; Fraguela 1909). The first Chilean topographic sheets appeared in 1914 or 1915; five 1:25,000-scale sheets appeared in about 1918 (Platt 1933, p. 662; Paris 1967, p. 9). In 1922, the Servicio Geográfico was renamed the Instituto Geográfico Militar (IGM) ("Collaborative mapping in Chile" 1956, p. 139). By 1930, IGM and the Inspección General de Geografía were working on 1:25,000-scale sheets; IGM was also working on 1:50,000- and 1:100,000-scale series (AGS 1932b, p. 145; Platt 1930, p. 142). Large areas of the interior south of Puerto Montt remained unexplored, and the interiors of most of the islands were unmapped (AGS 1932b, p. 147). By 1935, there were a few 1:25,000-scale sheets available for the area around Iquique, from the central valley to the coast south of Santiago (Thiele 1938, p. 235). Between 1933 and 1937, at least 12 1:100,000-scale sheets were issued; aerial photography was being used to compile maps (Paris 1967, p. 9; Saavedra Rojas 1939; Brunner 1939).

In the early 1940s, the 1:250,000-scale *Carta Preliminar*, using aerial photography for compilation, was begun (Monteiro 1967b, pp. 171-72; UN. Secretariat 1957, pp. 9-10). In 1947, IGM had begun to work with the Inter-American Geodetic Survey on 1:100,000-scale sheets; IGM edited a preliminary map at 1:250,000 scale covering the metropolitan area from Arica to Cabo de Hornos, based on trimetrogon photography ("Cartografía chilena" 1955, p. 29).

By 1950, the northern half of the nation was covered with accurate maps; by 1961, 105 contoured preliminary sheets at 1:250,000 scale were published (Pan American Union 1964c, p. 4; Lock 1969, p. 338). In the 1950s, the main objectives of IGM were the 1:250,000- and 1:100,000-scale sheet completion. By 1953, the *Carta Preliminar* at 1:250,000 scale was completed ("Labor ejectuada" 1953, pp. 7-8; Chile. 1955; "Cartas geográficas" 1958). In 1959, the first 1:100,000-scale modern topographic sheet of the country was published (*Twenty* 1966, p. 55).

Earthquakes in 1960 and 1964 made retriangulation and releveling necessary for some areas of Chile (Lock 1969, p. 338). Official mapping activities were concentrated on the 1:50,000- and 1:100,000-scale series in the late 1960s, since continental Chile, the coastal islands, and the Chilean Antarctic Territory had been mapped (Arce 1967, p. 15). Up to 1964, the 1:50,000-scale map had not been a major concern; 12 sheets had been published between 1935 and 1939, 6 between 1955 and 1964. The 1:25,000-scale series, begun in 1897, had been the preferred scale, with 440 sheets published by 1964, most based on aerial photography of 1947 or later vintage. Between 1960 and 1967, new-format 1:100,000-scale sheets appeared (Paris 1967, p. 9). By late 1968, all of the 1:250,000-scale sheets and 60 of 445 sheets at 1:100,000 scale were complete. In the 1:100,000-scale new-format series (begun in 1963, and intended initially to cover the northern part of the country, from 17°S to 28°S), 60 of the 116 sheets for the north and 140 of the 1,700 sheets needed to cover the central and southern part of the country from 28°S to 53°S (which were begun in 1965) were completed. In all, 440 of 6,800 sheets at 1:25,000 scale were completed (UN. Dept. of Economic and Social Affairs 1970, p. 40; "El primer symposium" 1972).

By 1976, 10 percent of the regular 1:250,000-scale series (covering the northern one-third of the country), 20 percent of the 1:100,000-scale series (covering the same area), 70 percent of the 1:50,000-scale series (covering the north except around Antofogasta, and all the rest except the border with Argentina), and 8 percent of the 1:25,000-scale series were completed (UN 1979, p. 3; Chile 1975). In 1978, Chile was in the process of reevaluating its topographic mapping program; all northern area sheets were classed as restricted (Mrowka 1978). In the late 1970s, Chile was working especially hard on the 1:50,000-scale series, and on the new regular series at 1:250,000 scale (Santiago de Chile 1978, p. 12; Chile 1978, pp. 14-26).

COLOMBIA

The cartographic section of the general staff of the Colombian army began work on the *Carta Militar* at a scale of 1:25,000 in 1903; some eight sheets were published by 1920. The Servicio Geográfico del Ejército was formed at about this time (Thiele 1938, p. 236; Rozo M. 1952, p. 186; Bogotá 1923). The Oficina de Longitudes was suspended in 1905 and then recreated in 1909 as the Oficina de Longitudes y Fronteras; it was first assigned to the Ministerio de Guerra y de

Instrucción Pública, but was returned eventually to the Ministerio de Relaciones Exteriores, where it had been located under its first name (Rozo M. 1952, p. 186; PAIGH. Centro 1954, p. 12). From about 1915 on, United States and European petroleum companies mapped thousands of square miles of Colombia and Venezuela with high-grade topographic surveys; for business reasons, such mapping was considered confidential, and will not be discussed here (Martin 1929, p. 621).

By 1930, the only detailed official topographic sheets available to the public were nine sheets at 1:25,000 scale, which covered about thirty-five square miles in and around Bogotá (AGS 1930, p. ix). Very little progress had been made on the *Carta Militar*, and by the middle of the 1930s it seemed to have been abandoned (Thiele 1938, p. 236). The Dirección de Minas, Geología e Hidrología began a 1:200,000-scale topographic series in the early 1930s (AGS 1932a, pp. 57-58; Posada 1938-39, 1942). The dense jungles inhibited topographic mapping of the nation; aerial photography finally came to the rescue (Lasche 1937, pp. 35-36).

In 1940 the name of the mapping agency was Instituto Geográfico Militar y Catastral; it had begun as the Instituto Geográfico Militar in about 1936. In 1944 or 1946 it started work on a contoured 1:25,000-scale series as a *Carta Preliminar*; in 1948 it started with a 1:100,000-scale series covering the north and northeast (Rozo M. 1952, p. 187; PAIGH. Centro 1954, p. 13; Pan American Consultation on Cartography 1950, p. 212; Lock 1969, p. 336; Monteiro 1967b, p. 203; *Twenty* 1966, p. 60).

In 1950 the institute was renamed the Instituto Geográfico Augustín Codazzi (Rozo M. 1952, p. 187). In 1952, it planned to finish basic topographic mapping in ten years, but an informed guess was that it would take more like 21 years (Arjona Esponda 1952, pp. 9-10; Colombia. Instituto 1955).

In 1967 SLAR imagery was obtained of areas of northwest Colombia, where almost continuous cloud cover had made obtaining aerial photography very difficult (UN 1976b, p. 204; Smit 1975). By the fall of 1969, one of 30 sheets at 1:250,000 scale, 111 of 569 sheets at 1:100,000 scale, 2,523 of 7,927 at 1:25,000 scale, and 206 of 25,710 at 1:10,000 scale had been completed; the province of Antioquía was covered by provisional 1:100,000-scale sheets (Antioquía 1969, p. 25; UN. Dept. of Economic and Social Affairs 1970, p. 40). As of late 1970, the country was 30.9 percent covered at 1:100,000 and 1:200,000 scales (Escoria Marín 1972, p. 375). By late 1974, 11 of 31 at 1:250,000, 2 of 66 at 1:200,000, 202 of 569 at 1:100,000, 149 of 2,996 at 1:50,000 (basic compilation scale for the 1:200,000-scale series), and 3,233 of 7,937 at 1:25,000 scale (basic compilation scale for 1:100,000-scale series) were completed (UN. Dept. of Economic and Social Affairs 1976, pp. 27-28).

ECUADOR

The Servicio Geográfico Militar (SGM) was established in 1928 (Lock 1969, p. 336). Between 1928 and 1930, SGM produced nine sheets at 1:20,000 scale of the area around Riobamba (Pan American Union 1964c, p. 4; *Twenty* 1966, p. 79). In 1930 the following sad commentary on Ecuadorian cartography appeared: "it is a record of a succession of crests and depressions with little or no actual progressive development" (AGS 1932a, p. 101).

The service began work on a series of 1:25,000-scale sheets in the 1930s and 1940s. The main program in the 1940s was the 1:250,000-scale series; beginning in

1935, 6 percent of the sheets had been done in 15 years ("Mapping in Ecuador" 1949, p. 295). Some 85 sheets (or 93 to 1951), from Sierra north to Tulcán and south to San Isidro, had been published by 1952. A 1:50,000-scale series, less than one-fourth complete in the early 1960s, with about 39 sheets issued, was to cover the coast and Sierras regions; a 1:100,000-scale series was planned to cover the area east of the Sierras. As of about 1962, 25 sheets of the 1:50,000-scale series had been produced (Pan American Union 1964c, p. 4; Paris 1967, p. 12; *Twenty* 1966, p. 79). To about 1965 or 1966, 39 sheets had been issued, as the new standard sheets. By late 1968, 27 of 245 at 1:100,000 scale, 112 of 1,036 at 1:50,000 scale, and 62 of 4,144 at 1:25,000 scale (the published sheets in the latter series covering part of Loja Province) had been completed (UN. Dept. of Economic and Social Affairs 1970, p. 43; *Twenty* 1966, p. 79).

GUYANAS*

The Guyanas are to be noted, if not commended, for their lack of detailed official topographical maps. The coastlines have long been acceptably mapped, first appearing on maps about A.D. 1500. To 1930, the coastlines and major river courses remained all that was mapped. Considering that Guyana became British Guiana in 1796 (and had been in Britain's sphere of interest since 1621), Surinam became Dutch Guiana in 1667, and French Guiana was annexed in 1674—making the Guyanas among the oldest of these nation's colonies—such a cartographic non-record is truly remarkable, at least until distance from Europe and the climate and vegetation of the colonies are considered; all constitute adverse mapping conditions. Indeed, the boundaries of French Guiana were not finally fixed until 1900 (France. Armeé 1931, p. 197).

Although maps had been made, prior to the 1930s, of the colonies, such maps were on scales less detailed than 1:250,000 (AGS 1933, p. 47). In 1934, a small topographic military bureau, the Service géographique de l'Inini, was formed at Cayenne in French Guiana, charged with working on local mapping (UN 1979, p. 14). In the late 1930s, the colonies' owners were engaged in their own diplomatic problems, and this factor plus distance and the relative smallness of their South American holdings precluded any topographical survey work in any of the colonies during that decade. Surinam had no contoured maps except for the extreme south, although it had at some point been surveyed by the Netherlands government (Thiele 1938, p. 237). The first aerial photographs of the Guyanas were made in 1939 by the KLM airplane, *Snip*, marking the beginning of a new and far more fruitful period in mapping (Bubberman 1973, p. 92).

In 1944, the United States Army Map Service issued map series E691 at 1:250,000 scale, of parts of northern British Guiana; after World War II, the French Institut géographique national began to do aerial photography of French Guiana, and the Dutch did some work in Surinam (Brasseur 1974, p. 56; Hurault 1949, p. 157). By 1949, Surinam had been mapped at scales more detailed than 1:250,000 (UN. Dept. of Social Affairs 1949, map following p. 18; UN 1977, p. 10). The

---

*Either Guyana or Guiana is correct.

French did reconnaissance mapping of their portion of the Guyanas in 1949 and 1950 (UN 1979, p. 14).

The French Institut issued 11 sheets at 1:200,000 scale between 1954 (or 1956) and 1958; these were based on aerial photography and not field surveying, so they remained as manuscripts and were not published. The British Directorate of Overseas Surveys (DOS) completed some 1:50,000-scale sheets for British Guiana; the Netherlands Central Bureau Lucktkartering issued some 1:100,000-scale sheets of Surinam in 1953, just in time for the latter's independence in 1954 (Brasseur 1974, p. 57; Monteiro 1967b, pp. 245-57; United States. Army Map Service 1954c, index map E691). In 1955, Surinam was still the only one of the Guyanas to have any extensive coverage at 1:250,000 or more detailed scales; its first complete topographic map was issued in that year (Koeman 1973, p. 8; Karo 1955, plate II). In 1956 the bureau issued some 1:20,000-scale sheets for a small area in Surinam; in 1958, it began work on a 1:200,000-scale series in 29 sheets. Between 1953 and 1964, the bureau also worked on a planimetric 1:100,000-scale series (Koeman 1973, pp. 59, 61). Between 1955 and 1962, 25 sheets at 1:50,000 scale were made of French Guiana's littoral (Brasseur 1974, p. 57).

By 1964, British Guiana's 1:50,000- and 1:250,000-scale coverage was less than 25 percent complete, as were French Guiana's 1:50,000-scale series and Surinam's 1:50,000-scale series; the 1:100,000- and 1:200,000-scale series of French Guiana and Surinam were more than half done (Birch 1964, p. 11; Lock 1969, p. 332). British Guiana became independent Guyana in 1966; in the same year, Surinam's 1:200,000-scale series was completed (Koeman 1973, p. 59). By this time, both Guyana and Surinam had their own mapping agencies. By late 1968, Guyana had completed 82 of 294 sheets at 1:50,000 scale (some sheets with hachures or formlines); these sheets covered the coastal belt and the developed portions of the country. French Guiana's 1:200,000-scale (complete) and 1:100,000-scale sheets (10 of 35 completed) were formlined only; 16 of the 37 sheets of a contoured 1:50,000-scale series were complete. Surinam's ongoing series were at scales of 1:200,000, 1:100,000 (to total 103 sheets), 1:40,000 (later to be abandoned), and 1:20,000; the first two were almost complete, and the last three about one-third to one-half complete, in 1970 (UN. Dept. of Economic and Social Affairs 1970, pp. 46, 50; Bubberman 1973, p. 112; Zarzycki 1972). By late 1974, 16 of 37 sheets at 1:50,000 scale of French Guiana were completed; for Guyana, all 11 at 1:200,000 scale, 10 of 35 at 1:100,000 scale, and 193 of 294 at 1:50,000 scale were done; and for Surinam, all 29 at 1:200,000 scale, 97 of 104 at 1:100,000 scale, 188 of 374 at 1:40,000 scale, 425 of 1,394 at 1:20,000 scale, and all 140 at 1:10,000 scale (*Landbouwarealen;* of agricultural areas only) had been completed. Yet even in the early 1970s, relatively little ground survey work had been done in western Guyana (UN. Dept. of Economic and Social Affairs 1976, pp. 31, 35, 47).

PARAGUAY

Since the Paraná River bisects national territory, and since the country is relatively flat, the general layout of Paraguay was tentatively known by A.D. 1600, and fairly definitely by the time of Paraguayan independence in 1811 (Debenham 1960, p. 238). By 1900, little of Paraguay was unexplored except for an area in the middle west, just north of the Confuso River (Cyrus Adams 1907, p. 307). Yet to 1930:

Cartographically Paraguay ranks lowest of all of the countries of South America. In fact the number of copies or reproductions of original surveys in Paraguayan territory found in the libraries and map collections covered by this extremely comprehensive catalogue is so small as to be almost negligible (AGS 1933, p. 191).

When it is realized that the American Geographical Society was including all surveys of whatever kind and had spent 15 years searching, the problem is clearly staggering. Virtually all that had been done in Paraguayan mapping were boundary surveys (AGS 1933, pp. 192-93).

In 1941, the Instituto Geográfico Militar was created; but the government apparently had no program of topographic mapping until about the 1950s. In 1958, the institute issued four 1:50,000-scale sheets of the area of Asunción (Monteiro 1967b, p. 261; *Twenty* 1966, p. 113). Some 1:50,000-scale maps of the Colonia Iguazú were produced prior to 1964 (Pan American Union 1964d, p. 5). The major cartographic program was a 1:100,000-scale series; its first sheets were published in 1967 (Monteiro 1967b, p. 261). By 1970, perhaps one-sixth of the 1:50,000-scale series and one-fourth of the 1:100,000-scale series were available; those sheets published covered parts of eastern Paraguay. To late 1974, 60 of approximately 270 sheets at 1:50,000 scale (of the eastern region) and 29 of approximately 68 at 1:100,000 scale (apparently also intended to cover the eastern region only) had been published (UN. Dept. of Economic and Social Affairs 1976, p. 44).

PERU

In 1904, the Sección Topográfica of the Escuela Militar was formed; in 1907, it became part of the Estado Mayor General del Ejército, and was renamed the Servicio Topográfico. In 1911 or 1912 its name was changed again, to the Servicio Geográfico del Ejército (Peru. Instituto 1969, p. 100; Dianderas 1936, p. 42; Barriga 1972, p. 49). The service produced two sheets at 1:40,000 scale and three at 1:100,000 scale to about 1915. In 1915 it was reorganized into a Servicio (or Sección) Topográfico and a Sección Cartográfica; it issued nine sheets of Arequipa at 1:20,000 scale (Barriga 1972, p. 49; *Twenty* 1966, p. 117). In 1920 or 1921 it again became the Servicio Geográfico, and began work—with the assistance of Colonel George Thomas (a member of the French military mission in Peru)— on the *Carta Nacional* at 1:200,000 scale ("Collaborative mapping in Peru" 1957, p. 290; Peru. Instituto 1969, p. 100; *Twenty* 1966, p. 117). The first sheet of the series was issued in 1923 or 1925 (Perrier 1924; Platt 1933, p. 667; Monteiro 1967b, p. 267; MacFadden 1941, p. 81). By 1930, 23 sheets, covering the coastal plain and the eastern border of the Andes, from the boundary with Ecuador to Chimbote Bay, had been issued (AGS 1932a, p. 134). By 1935, 45 or 48 sheets were available, the newer sheets covering the area from the Chilean boundary to Lake Titicaca (Platt 1943, p. 63; MacFadden 1941, p. 81). In 1939 the Servicio Geográfico changed its name to the Instituto Geográfico Militar (IGM) (Peru. Instituto 1969, p. 100). In succeeding years Peruvian mapping continued in the areas just mentioned, with the unmapped area in the center of the country slowly becoming smaller. In the 1940s, IGM adopted the 1:200,000 scale for a major series, first mapping the western part of the country, and next the forest regions, using aerial photography (Consultation on Geodesy 1945, p. 154). Between 1929 and 1955, at least 76 1:200,000-scale sheets were issued (Paris 1967, p. 11). To about 1957, IGM had published about 281 sheets, of which 95 were 1:200,000-scale sheets ("Collaborative mapping in Peru" 1957, p. 290). IGM worked to 1958 on 1:200,000-scale sheets; the series was then discontinued at a total number of 98 (or 96) sheets issued out of a total of 280 sheets; it covered 35 percent of the country—the coast, western sierra, and south (Temple 1964, p. 47; Pan American Union 1964e, p. 4; Peru. National Office 1979, p. 34).

In the early 1960s IGM concentrated on the 1:100,000-scale series, based on recent United States Air Force aerial photography. Between 1959 and 1963, 21 sheets at 1:100,000 scale were published (Temple 1964, p. 52). There was little mapping of any kind at any scale for the eastern Andes and the Amazonian part of the country (Pan American Union 1964e, p. 4). In 1968 there were 92 of 504 sheets at 1:100,000 scale published; the series was primarily intended to cover the coastal and mountain areas (UN. Dept. of Economic and Social Affairs 1970, p. 64). To late 1974, 172 of 1,860 at 1:50,000 scale (J731), 188 of 504 at 1:100,000 scale (J631), and 21 of 97 at 1:250,000 scale (1501) had been issued (UN. Dept. of Economic and Social Affairs 1976, p. 44). By the mid-1970s, aerophotogrammetric maps at 1:250,000 scale, 1:100,000 scale, 1:50,000 scale and 1:25,000 scale (rural cadaster; monochrome) had been issued (Peru. National Office 1979, pp. 34-44).

URUGUAY

Another country that has kept a low profile in the mapping world is Uruguay. Although its coast was mapped by A.D. 1600 and all of its interior explored in less than 25 years after its independence in 1828, detailed mapping made a leisurely appearance (Debenham 1960, p. 238).

The first cartographic agency was the Comisión Geográfica, which was replaced by the Servicio Geográfico Militar in 1913; the first detailed topographic sheet was issued in 1920 (Mato 1917, p. 10; Platt 1933, p. 662; AGS 1932b, p. 262; "Uruguay" 1912). The service adopted a 1:100,000 scale for a series to cover the entire country, and the 1:25,000 scale for maps of more populated sections in the south and southwest (AGS 1932b, p. 262). Nine sheets, at 1:20,000 scale, for Montevideo and vicinity and 4 sheets, at 1:50,000 scale (published in 1926 or 1929), covering part of the same region appeared prior to 1930 (Lock 1969, p. 392; Carlberg 1935, p. 190). Publication of sheets in the 1:50,000-scale series stretched from the 1920s to the 1940s (Monteiro 1967b, p. 291). By about 1944, the 1:50,000-scale sheets covered about 10 percent of the country, mostly along the coast (Consultation on Geodesy 1945, p. 157).

In the early 1960s, the 1:50,000-scale series was less than 25 percent complete (Birch 1964, p. 11). By the mid-1960s, 10 percent (40 of 292 sheets) was still the only coverage reported in the 1:50,000-scale series (Viglietti 1967, p. 104). By the end of 1968, only 40 sheets—the same number—were reported to be complete, and the total number of potential sheets had increased to 303 (UN. Dept. of Economic and Social Affairs 1970, p. 82). The civilian mapping agency in the mid-1970s was the Dirección de Topografía, Ministerio de Obras Públicas (Bergquist 1978, p. 70).

VENEZUELA

Venezuela is another country whose coastline was mapped fairly early on—about A.D. 1600—and whose interior stayed a mystery for several centuries thereafter; the southeast remained unknown nearly to 1900, more than 50 years after the nation's independence in 1830 (Cyrus Adams 1907, p. 307; Debenham 1960, p. 238).

In 1905, the Venezuelan government made its first move toward a systematic topographic survey when it initiated a program for the production of a *Plano Militar*; in 1908 the name of the series was changed to *Mapa Física y Política de Venezuela*, and triangulation was begun. Some sheets, without contours, had been drafted but not published when work was halted by World War I (AGS 1933, p. 7). After 1914, topographical surveys by petroleum companies were the most important work done until the interwar period and even later; such sheets are usually unavailable to the general public and will not be considered here (AGS 1933, pp. 7-8).

In 1935 or 1936, the Dirección de Cartografía Nacional was created; the same year saw the founding of the national aerial photographic service. In 1937, the 1:25,000 scale was adopted for the base map. In 1939, the Dirección was reorganized, and the name of the Servicio Aerofotográfico was changed to the Servicio Cartográfico Nacional (Lock 1969, p. 331; Quijada 1967, p. 106; Mohn 1968, p. 43; Romero 1964, pp. 66-71; Venezuela.Ministerio... 1938). The Dirección established some topographic series at scales of 1:25,000, 1:50,000 or 1:100,000, and 1:250,000; the latter was begun in 1948, with work in the north (Lock 1969, p. 331; Mohn 1968, p. 424). The Dirección issued some 1:25,000- and 1:100,000-scale sheets in the 1940s (Monteiro 1967b, pp. 303-4). By 1955, about 280 sheets of the old 1:100,000-scale series and 42 sheets of the 1:250,000-scale series had been issued (UN. Secretariat 1957, p. 24; Paris 1967, p. 19; Pan American Consultation on Cartography. Delegación de Venezuela 1955). By 1957, the United States and Venezuela had negotiated an aerial mapping treaty (United States. Treaties 1957).

By the early 1960s, the 1:25,000-scale series was less than 25 percent done, the 1:100,000-scale series was 25 percent to 50 percent complete (37 new series sheets, in color, beginning in 1962), and the 1:250,000-scale series was more than 50 percent done (Birch 1964, p. 11; Mohn 1968 and 1969, p. 424; *Twenty* 1966, p. 125). By about 1963, the country was 26.6 percent covered with 1:250,000-scale sheets and 38.9 percent covered at 1:100,000 scale; the 1:25,000-scale coverage stood at 10.1 percent (Romero 1964, pp. 69-71). A preliminary 1:100,000-scale map series had been discontinued in 1964, after 81 of 287 sheets were issued. The 1:50,000-scale sheets were classified (Pan American Union 1964g, p. 4). The 1:100,000-scale sheets in existence were largely of the coastal region and near the Colombian border, just east of 70°W (Quijada 1967, p. 108; Paris 1967, p. 19). By late 1968, 16 of 42 sheets at 1:250,000 scale (of the area north to 8°N; a new contoured edition begun in 1962), and 117 of 526 maps of the new series at 1:100,000 scale had been completed (UN. Dept. of Economic and Social Affairs 1970, p. 82). More than one-third of the country was covered with preliminary 1:25,000-scale sheets, and 10 percent in contoured 1:25,000-scale sheets (Mohn 1969, p. 425). To late 1974, series coverage was as follows:

1:250,000	17 of about 42; no longer published
1:250,000	new series since 1970; 8 of 82
1:100,000	120 sheets, since 1966, preliminary information on areas loacted south of 6°N
1:100,000	233 of 542
1:50,000	23 sheets issued; regular publication not yet firmly decided upon
1:25,000	162 sheets; suspended in 1958
1:25:000	574 sheets; suspended in 1958
1:25,000	3,911 of 7,277; published since 1958; adopted in final form from original survey for basic map of the country at at 1:25,000 scale

(UN. Dept. of Economic and Social Affairs 1976, p. 62.)

**Map of South America:
Topographic Mapping, 1900-1970
(1:250,000 and more detailed)**

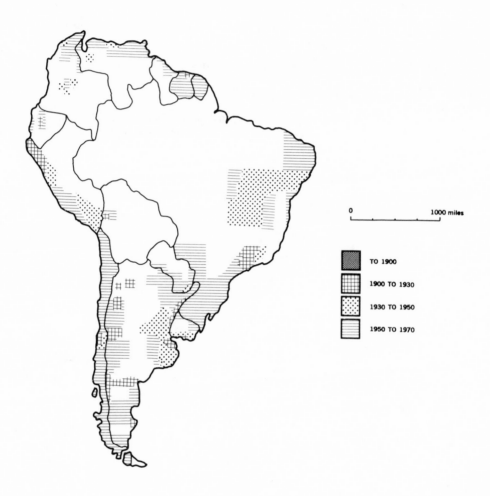

0   1000 miles

TO 1900

1900 TO 1930

1930 TO 1950

1950 TO 1970

Base map: Aitoff's Equal Area Projection.

**Sources for Map of South America:
Topographic Mapping, 1900-1970
(1:250,000 and more detailed)**

AGS 1930-1933.

Argentine Republic 1947.

Brazil. Conselho 1951, p. 65.

René de Mattos 1967, p. 12.

Pan American Union—all.

Platt 1945, map following p. 180.

Turco Greco 1967, maps.

UN. Dept. of Social Affairs 1949.

UN. Dept. of Economic and Social Affairs 1970.

(NOTE: Mexico and Central America are depicted on the map showing topograhic mapping of North America)

Part IV
TOPOGRAPHIC MAPPING OF NORTH AMERICA

10
GREENLAND

From 1917 to 1923, the Danish polar explorer, Dr. Lauge Koch, compiled a map of the northern and northwestern parts of Greenland, from Melville Bay to Peary Land. The map was produced in 18 sheets at a scale of 1:300,000, with hill shading and some spot elevations ("Danish topographical maps of Greenland" 1956; Koch 1940; Gertsen 1970, p. 121; United States. Dept. of the Army 1956, p. 44). Except for this effort the vast majority of Greenland was unmapped, an icy expanse crisscrossed with route sketches. As for topographic maps, there were almost none (Edinburgh Geographical Institute 1922, plate I).

In 1927 the Danes, who gained control of Greenland in 1729 and retain it to the present, began topographic mapping of Greenland at 1:250,000 scale (with contours and spot heights), even though there were still some unknown regions in interior Greenland and areas in the north central, central, and south central regions that were poorly known (Outhwaite 1938, p. 325; Gertsen 1970, p. 114; Nørlund 1939, p. 38; Baker 1967, p. 471).

Based on ground and aerial surveys performed from 1932 to 1937, maps at 1:250,000 scale of the south, east, and west coasts (from 67°30'N to 73°N) were issued between 1937 and 1946; thirty-four maps were issued to 1939 (Nørlund 1939, p. 38; Loewe 1933, p. 218; Gertsen 1970, p. 114; B. Schulz 1938, pp. 201-2; Buhler 1948). In the late 1930s, the Danes were doing cartographic work on the coast to 77°N on the east coast and 73°N on the west coast (Nørlund 1939, p. 38).

To 1956, the above-mentioned 1:250,000-scale sheets and the Koch maps were the major official maps of Greenland. The rest of the island was either roughly mapped or not mapped at all (United States. Dept. of the Army 1956, p. 44; Raisz 1956, p. 106). By 1961, almost all of the coastline of Greenland was mapped at a scale of 1:250,000. To late 1968, 69 sheets at 1:250,000 scale had been issued. In 1970 the series as a whole was a long way from completion, and the Danish Geodetic Institute had no plans to complete it; the series was not to cover the icecap areas in any case (UN. Dept. of Economic and Social Affairs 1970, p. 43; Gertsen 1970, p. 114; Lillestrand and Johnson 1971; Toniolo 1972; Helk 1961a, 1961b, and 1966). By the end of 1974, 71 sheets, covering approximately three-quarters of the coastal area, had been published (UN. Dept. of Economic and Social Affairs 1976, p. 29).

11
CANADA

We are pleased with our contractors, our product and the excellent cooperation between the various sub-disciplines of surveying and mapping. Our specifications appear to work—no one has yet threatened to sue us—and even our somewhat unorthodox procurement procedures have withstood the usual onslaughts of furious purchasing officers.

—Haddon 1979, p. 33

The Technical Branch of the Department of the Interior began mapping Canada in 1873, establishing a map series at six miles to an inch (1:380,160 scale) in the west (Sebert 1967, p. 112). Photomapping (ground phototopography, where photographs replace the topographer's view of terrain through the alidade—an extension of the plane-table method) was used in the mountainous regions beginning in the 1880s and well into the 1930s, at scales of 1:253,440 and 1:63,360 (Gamble 1964, p. 573). This was necessary because:

when the surveys of the Dominion Lands were extended to the Rocky Mountains region it was found that the methods hitherto employed were inadequate. The operations in the prairies consisted merely in defining the boundaries of the townships and sections; these lines form a network over the land by means of which the topographical features, always scarce in the prairies, are sufficiently well determined for general purposes. In passing to the mountains the conditions are entirely different; the topographical features are well marked and numerous, and the survey of section lines is always difficult, often impossible, and in some cases useless ... The ordinary methods of topographical surveying were too slow and expensive for the purpose; rapid surveys based on triangulation and on sketches were tried and proved ineffectual, then photography was resorted to and the results are all that could be desired.

(Surveyor General E. G. D. Deville's introduction to *Photographic Surveying* Don Thomson 1975, p. 11).

The first photographic survey party set out in 1886, to the Rocky Mountains. While the Yukon was being explored, the Topographical Survey Branch (having changed its name from the Technical Branch in 1890) was issuing a few 1:40,000-scale sheets of mountains further south during the time period 1888 to 1892 (United States. Library of Congress 1904, p. 45; Don Thomson 1967b, p. 120; Frances Woodward 1981). This "charming but relatively unimportant little series of 21 sheets" was the first Canadian attempt at a "truly topographic series" (Nicholson and Sebert 1981, p. 15).

In 1891, the survey's standard scale changed from 1:380,160 to 1:190,080, and the first of the sectional map series sheets appeared. These sheets never covered more than the three provinces of the interior plus British Columbia and Dawson in the Yukon; the maps themselves did not cover areas of uniform size, and there was no progressive system of numbering to allow for complete coverage (Don Thomson 1967b, p. 121; Sebert 1967, p. 112). Topographic surveys at scales of 1:62,500 and more detailed were limited to the far east, New Brunswick, and the Gaspé Peninsula (Bartholomew 1891, map following p. 610). Surveys were mostly confined to the Crown lands ("Maps of North America" 1892, p. 34). In the west, especially in British Columbia, reliable topographic data continued to be sketchy, but by 1893, phototopographic triangulation had begun; map scales were 1:633,360; 1:1,000,000; and 1:1,900,800 (Pearson 1974, pp. 121-22).

Remaining completely unmapped in 1900 were Labrador's interior and northern portions, and stretches of the Yukon and Canadian Rockies in British Columbia (Debenham 1960, p. 238; Baker 1967, p. 374).

In 1901 the Surveyor-General's office issued maps at a scale of 1:190,080 of lands "surveyed, sold, settled, etc." of Alberta, Saskatchewan, Assiniboia, and Manitoba. These maps were uncontoured, and topographical information given on them was sparse; this three-mile series was the first extensive map series, and had been started as a result of the movement of settlers into the interior (United States. Library of Congress 1904, p. 46; Sebert 1976, p. 123; Nicholson and Sebert 1981, p. 19). Very few, if any, of the maps issued by official sources in the early 1900s in Canada were true topographic maps (Sebert 1976, p. 123).

In 1903, the Canadian Department of Militia and Defence, Intelligence Section (to become the Survey Division in 1906), with the assistance of the British War Office, set up the nucleus of a mapping unit. At that time, only 1,600 square miles of 3.5 million square miles had been topographically mapped, so the British visit and the evaluation carried out by Major E. H. Hills, were timely (Hay and Davidson 1951, p. 28; Canada. Surveys and Mapping Branch 1951, p. 74; Nicholson and Sebert 1981, p. 36). This was in effect the revival of the British military topographic mapping of Canada that had begun in the late nineteenth century and then been restricted to areas adjacent to garrisons.

In 1904 the Survey Branch of the Army's Intelligence Department was formed, and the 1:63,360-scale series was begun, the latter occurring in large part because Great Britain had loaned a unit of Royal Engineers to Canada (Sebert 1976, p. 123). In 1903 or 1906, the Topographical Survey Branch was formed (UN 1974a, p. 73). In 1909 the Geodetic Survey of Canada was formally launched (Don Thomson 1967a, p. 72), and the Topographical Survey Division of the Geological Survey was formed (from Branch) (Nicholson and Sebert 1981, p. 36).

In 1912, the Geological Survey produced some excellent contoured maps of Ontario (Don Thomson 1967b, pp. 125-26; Canada. Archives 1912; Zaslow 1975). Some topographic sheets were issued as part of the Survey's A series (e.g., 686A, Chalk River). The Survey Division was firmly established by 1913, and was preparing contoured maps at a scale of 1:63,360 as well as other detailed maps, for troop maneuvers (Don Thomson 1967b, p. 252). In 1916, the 1:20,000-scale series, to be published by the military's Survey Division, was started; in future years it would be followed by 1:21,120-, 1:31,680-, and 1:25,000-scale sheets (the latter aimed toward satisfying military needs) until the series was standardized at 1:25,000 scale (Sebert 1975, p. 68). From 1916 to 1917, about 128 sectional sheets, covering 500,000 square miles, were issued, and sheets of the Topographical Series, a product of early contour mapping work, on several scales, were spotted around British Columbia (Pearson 1974, p. 123). By 1920, there were some 1:63,360-scale contoured maps of small areas in Canada, primarily around Montreal and north of Lake Erie (Great Britain. War Office 1920, index map XIII). From 1920 to 1955, 132 cadastral sheets of the Sectional Map Series at 1:190,080 scale, covering the Great Plains west to the Pacific, east into Ontario and north to Dawson, were converted to topographic maps; after 1955, these sheets were superseded by the 1:250,000-scale sheets of the National Topographic System (Sebert 1967, p. 112).

Canada was one of the first nations to use photogrammetry, initially—as has been mentioned—with photography taken from ground stations. The first periods of such activity were 1886 to 1906 and 1911 to 1923 (Canada. Topographical Survey 1925; Don Thomson 1967b, p. 144; Canada. Surveys and Mapping Branch 1951, p. 74). The introduction of aerial photography revolutionized Canadian mapping; by 1930, aerial surveys had covered vast areas (Sebert 1970a, p. 18; Pearson 1974, p. 123; Baker 1967, p. 374). Ontario, for example, was mapped accurately for the first time by 1920s aerial surveying; some 3,000 lakes in the north that had never been previously mapped finally showed up on the sheets (Montagnes 1929, p. 215; Don Thomson 1969, p. 8). An oblique aerial photograph of Pelican Narrows, Saskatchewan, taken in 1922, is generally accepted as the first aerial photograph used for mapping purposes (Don Thomson 1975, p. 36).

By 1922, the welter of bureaus doing mapping—the Topographical Survey of the Department of the Interior, the Geographical Section of the Department of Militia and Defence, and the Bureau of Geology and Topography of the Department of Mines—had become so confusing that it was very obviously time for reorganization (Don Thomson 1975, pp. 15, 298; Canada. Geographic Board 1918). In that year, the Topographical Survey Branch was renamed the Topographical Survey of Canada (Nicholson and Sebert 1981, p. 37). The Canadian National Topographic System (NTS) had an experimental start in 1923, with the 1:253,440-scale series; its official formal beginning was in 1927, with a full panoply of scales, 1:63,360; 1:126,720; 1:253,440, and 1:1,013,760 (Sebert 1970b, p. 15; Don Thomson 1967a, p. 72; Greene 1971, p. 269). In 1924, the Survey Division of the army was renamed Geographical Section, General Staff; in 1925 the Board of Topographical Surveys and Maps changed its name to the Board of Topographical and Aerial Surveys and Maps (doubtless the result at least in part of the block of aerial mapping photographs taken in 1924) (Hay and Davidson 1951, p. 28; Canada. Surveys Branch 1917 and 1930). To finish off the decade, the area from Wood Buffalo Park (boundary of Alberta and Northwest Territories—the sixtieth parallel) down through northern Alberta, Saskatchewan, Manitoba, and Ontario, to the St. Lawrence River, had had aerial photographs for mapping taken (Montagnes 1929, p. 214).

In the early 1930s, the 1:190,080-scale planimetric maps were, as was earlier indicated, in some cases being converted to contoured 1:253,440-scale sheets, and mapping was in general proceeding more quickly than in another former British colony—Australia. This was of some consolation to the Canadians (Sebert 1970b, p. 17; Curnow 1930, p. 92). Several uncontoured 1:253,440-scale sheets of the Canadian Arctic were mapped from oblique photography during the decade (Waugh 1953, p. 405). In 1932 the British Army decided that 1:25,000 was the best scale for artillery operations, and Canada conformed by standardizing its varying 1:20,000- to 1:31,680-scale series at 1:25,000 (Sebert 1975, p. 71).

By the mid-1930s, 17 percent of the country was accurately mapped while large areas in the north were still largely unsurveyed and unmapped. In 1934, due to lack of funds, the 1:253,440-scale series was at a standstill; in 1939, with 84 sheets issued, it was shelved, and mapping agencies concentrated their efforts on aeronautical charts at 1:506,880 scale (Sebert 1970b, p. 19; Peters 1936, p. 16; Canada. Surveys and Engineering Branch 1939). In 1936, the Department of the Interior went out of existence, and was replaced by the Department of Mines and Resources (which was to become, in 1949, the Department of Mines and Technical Surveys) (Hay and Davidson 1951, p. 26; Chipman and Hanson 1944). The Topographical Survey Division of the Surveyor General's office was attached to the Topographical Survey, now a part of the newly formed Bureau of Geology and Topography, which in addition to a topographical branch had Geological Survey with no topographical division of its own; this marked a formal end to warfare between the two civilian surveys, although informal animosities would continue into the 1950s (Don Thomson 1969, p. 255; Nicholson and Sebert 1981, p. 40).

Although Canada had made great progress in topographic mapping in the early twentieth century, areas of the Yukon and British Columbia remained unmapped, and some of the northern island interiors were still unexplored. In spite of 250,000 square miles of vertical aerial photography (used to make maps at scales of 1:63,360 and 1:126,720), less than 5 percent of the country was covered by aerial photography. By 1939, about 600,000 square miles had been flown and oblique aerial photography taken, and mapped at a scale of 1:253,440 (Carroll 1947, p. 8; Outhwaite 1938, p. 325; MacFadden 1941, p. 73).

The mapping picture remained complex through the early 1940s. At scales more detailed than 1:300,000, there were sheets issued in the 1:63,360-scale series (British GSGS), the 1:126,720-scale NTS series, the 1:190,080-scale sectional sheets (Topographical Survey), the 1:250,000-scale Standard Topographical Map (Natural Resources Intelligence Service), and the 1:253,440-scale NTS series (Olson and Whitmarsh 1944, p. 201; Peters 1943). Whereas some of the populated areas in the southeast had almost an embarrassment of maps, Canada in toto had large areas where no mapping work at all had been done—especially north of 60°N. Even in the east, there were large unmapped areas of Labrador and Newfoundland; mapping of the latter only began in 1939 (Peters 1945, p. 27). In 1944 Canada began its Arctic mapping program, starting with 1:1,000,000-scale aeronautical charts and working toward 1:250,000-scale sheets (Waugh 1953, p. 404; Canada. Bureau 1945; "Maps of the Northwest Territories" 1952; "Mapping the northland" 1947).

Up to the end of World War II, the only maps of some parts of the Arctic coastline of North America had been made from charts of sailing ships 100 years before (John Lewis Robinson 1954b, p. 291). This situation more than justified the reactivation of the national mapping program in 1946, now including work in earnest on mapping the Arctic—the latter at least in part to strengthen the claim of ownership (Greene 1971, p. 270). In 1947, Canada's first serious long-range mapping program was approved by the Cabinet Defence Committee, extending geodetic control and aerial photography so that 1:50,000-scale sheets could be produced quickly in case of emergency. The completion date for the 1:250,000-scale coverage was set for 1977 (Sebert 1970b, p. 20; Collins 1951; Boyer 1953; John Lewis Robinson 1954a). Following the war, the first task was to produce detailed 1:50,000-scale sheets for resource investigations; provisional 1:50,000-scale sheets issued after the war had no contours. Some 1:63,360-scale sheets were still being made; 9 planimetric sheets and 1 contoured sheet of Newfoundland were compiled following the war, with field operations in 1949 and map compilation in October of that year (Gamble 1957, pp. 333-35).

Except for field checking, plane-table surveying was almost completely abandoned in favor of aerial photography after World War II. Trimetrogon photography (a system of aerial photography for which three high-speed, wide-angle cameras are so placed in an airplane as to take photographs of the Earth from horizon to horizon) was developed by the United States Air Force during the war; this method was useful for mapping large areas planimetrically. By 1948, all of Canada not previously photographed vertically was photographed from 20,000 feet with the trimetrogon camera, on flight lines sixteen miles apart. Since little reliable contour information could be produced from trimetrogon photographs, the system was soon dropped (Carroll 1945, p. 10; Sebert 1970a, p. 19; Alcock 1950; W. H. Miller 1951).

In spite of all former efforts at consolidation, two agencies were still producing topographic maps. The two therefore decided to split the territory, with the army compiling the west and Arctic sheets, and the Surveys and Mapping Branch of the Department of Mines and Technical Surveys working in the east. In November of 1948, standard scales were set at 1:50,000; 1:250,000; and 1:500,000 (Pearson 1974, p. 123). Fewer than 150 of the 1:125,000-scale sheets, and those mostly of Quebec and Ontario, had been made previous to standardization (Knowles and Stowe 1976, p. 12). In 1949 the Surveys and Mapping Branch (hereafter, the branch) completed 8,800 square miles of 1:50,000-scale mapping and 38,000 square miles of 1:250,000-scale mapping, totaling ten times the 1939 output (Sebert 1976, p. 123; Canada. Surveys and Mapping Branch 1951, p. 75). Several provinces, such as Ontario, Alberta, and British Columbia, had their own mapping units as well, and were involved in such projects as 1:63,360/1:50,000-scale mapping (Canada. Surveys and Mapping Branch 1951, p. 75).

By 1950, the 1:250,000-scale project was moving along well; the 1:50,000-scale mapping program had been reduced in order to accelerate the mapping at the former scale ("Mapping" 1964, p. 314). The plan was to complete the 1:250,000-scale project as speedily as possible and then to shift to the 1:50,000-scale series, which would probably take about 100 years to complete for well-populated areas, even if all efforts were devoted to it (Canada. Surveys and Mapping Branch 1951, pp. 74-77; Sebert 1976, p. 130; Palmer 1957). Considering that Canada was attempting to map about the same area as the United States, but with one-tenth the population and more adverse climatologic and physiographic conditions, this was a sensible order of priorities (C. H. Smith 1951, p. 368). The 1:250,000-scale series (25 percent complete in 1953) demonstrated quickly the need for its existence;

in the remapping of the northeast coast, some 5,000 square miles of islands were discovered where maps had shown only empty sea (Wyener 1953, p. 17; Walker 1953, p. 72).

In the 1950s the emphasis was not only on mapping at 1:250,000 scale but also on expanding work into remote areas. One-third of the mapping was at 1:250,000 scale, the rest at 1:50,000 scale. The mapping of Nova Scotia, New Brunswick, Prince Edward Island, and Newfoundland was "well in hand" by about 1955 ("Summary of surveying" 1956, p. 216; Klawe 1955). Existing 1:63:360-scale sheets were being converted by photographic enlargement to 1:50,000-scale sheets. Between 1949 and 1955, 159 of 167 1:50,000-scale maps of Newfoundland were compiled (Gamble 1957, p. 336; Nicholson and Sebert 1981, p. 34). By 1955, 20 percent of Canada was covered by 1:50,000-scale sheets (either published or in hand) and about 52 percent covered at scales of 1:250,000 and 1:253,440; the latter percentage dropped to about 37 percent when the Arctic Archipelago was included ("Summary of surveying" 1955, p. 592). The only series completely covering Canada by the mid-1950s was an uncontoured 1:506,880-scale series compiled from trimetrogon photographs (UN. Secretariat 1957, p. 9). The northern coast and islands, and the area immediately west, south, and east of Hudson Bay remained mostly unmapped (Karo 1955, plate II; Douglas Woodward 1955). As for other scales, the 1:25,000-scale series got a new lease on life in about 1953 when the Department of National Defence required larger training areas, and needed large-scale map coverage of them (Sebert 1975, p. 75). The highlight of the 1956 mapping season was the completion of Yukon mapping at 1:250,000 scale. In 1957, the last two-mile (1:126,720) federal sheet was published. In 1959, 237 sheets at 1:50,000 scale and 20 sheets at 1:250,000 scale were issued, but many large areas in the north were still unmapped (Tuttle 1961, p. 45; Nicholson and Sebert 1981, p. 77; Canada. Surveys and Mapping Branch 1957; "Surveying and mapping" 1957).

With 230 of 940 sheets at 1:250,000 scale completed, the primary goal for the branch remained completion of mapping at that scale. Some of the most difficult areas, such as Baffin and Ellesmere Islands, remained to be mapped (Tuttle 1961, p. 46). In 1963, the Canadian petroleum industry became interested in northern Canada, thus giving additional impetus to the branch to complete the 1:250,000-scale survey. In 1964 the branch decided to extend the 1:25,000-scale series beyond the coverage required for military purposes and to begin mapping heavily populated areas in Ontario and Quebec and some regional cities, with the series reaching a theoretical total of about 30,000 sheets. By about 1965, 60 percent of Canada's developed areas was covered with 1:63,360/1:50,000-scale sheets ("World in the flat" 1965, p. 486; Klawe 1965; Flötner 1963). The 926 maps of the 1:250,000-scale series were to be completed by the end of 1967 or 1968; remaining to be done in 1966 were 200 sheets of interior Quebec and 50 sheets in Ontario, all to be derived from more detailed scale mapping (UN 1966b, p. 32; "Mapping" 1964, p. 314; "Activities" 1969, p. 83). By 1967, all sheets were compiled except those covering three islands in the far north of Hudson Bay—Coats Island, Mansel Island, and Nottingham Island (Sebert 1970b, p. 25). By 1970, all were completed, and the older 1:253,440-scale maps were being replaced by 1:250,000-scale sheets (UN 1974b, p. 65). Much of the country still remained to be mapped at detailed scales; in early 1969, 530 of the 1:25,000-scale series, 3,450 of

13,200 total at 1:50,000 scale, and 915 of 918 at 1:250,000 scale (no 1:253,440-scale sheets included) were completed (UN. Dept. of Economic and Social Affairs 1970, pp. 38-39).

By 1971, approximately 30-40 percent of Canada was covered by 1:50,000-scale sheets, with 400 sheets per year being issued, working toward a goal of 500 per year by 1976 (Greene 1971, p. 270; Knowles and Stowe 1976, p. 12; Klawe 1971; Olsen 1971; Harris 1972b). By this time, the 1:50,000-scale sheet had been through many style changes: 1950 Standard; 1953 Standard; Preliminary; Arctic Provisional; 1959 Provisional; 1966 Provisional; 1967 Standard; and 1972 monochrome (Nicholson and Sebert 1981, pp. 50-56).

In the early 1970s, the computer began to be applied to the 1:50,000-scale series production, with the aim of immediate processing and plotting of digitized data, digitizing of additive data for revision and editing, speedy drafting from a minimal number of input coordinate points by data reduction and data intrepretation, creation of one type of data tape only, and flexibility in handling input (Harris 1971, 1972a, and 1973, p. 17).

By 1972, 1:50,000-scale sheets covered everything south of 55°N except for a large blank about 300 miles south of Hudson Bay (from York east to the mouth of the Harricanaw River), an area just south of the line in Labrador, and two small areas (about 2,000 square miles) in south central Quebec (Sebert 1976, p. 236). There were also two large empty blocks in British Columbia north of 55°N, along the Mackenzie River to its mouth, and north of 60°N in the Yukon (UN 1976b, p. 236). In 1972, the branch decided to expedite production of northern topographic maps by publishing a monochrome version of the standard 1:50,000-scale series; it was necessary to redesign certain symbols and there was some loss of both readability and information. The line separating the areas to be mapped in color from that to be mapped in monochrome was called the Wilderness Line. Only 138 sheets south of the line remained to be published in 1974 (Sebert 1974, pp. 167-68).

By late 1974, all 918 at 1:250,000 scale, 6,100 of 13,200 at 1:50,000 and 723 at 1:25,000 scale (for cities over 35,000 population and for highly industrialized areas) were completed (UN. Dept. of Economic and Social Affairs 1976, p. 27; "Panel discussion" 1975; Ebner 1975; E. A. Fleming 1975; *Canadian map makers* 1975). Between 1973 and 1976 the branch was barraged with heavy demands for production of new maps, especially in the more northerly areas, in support of the development of natural resources. At the same time, it continued a modest program of map revision and of remapping of more densely populated areas (UN 1979, p. 22; Sebert 1973; UN 1974b, pp. 64-66; Young 1973). The 1:25,000-scale series seemed to have met its demise in 1976; the branch's work on the series was reduced to completion of editions already being worked on and revision of published sheets. The urgent demand for 1:50,000-scale sheets in the Arctic continued (Nora Williams 1976, p. 13; Nicholson and Sebert 1981, p. 119). At 1:125,000 scale, 95 sheets had been completed and 46 more were in production (UN 1976b, p. 22).

By about 1976, half of the 1:50,000-scale sheets had been compiled, and the major thrust of the branch was toward completing that series and revising existing maps. Automation was being very seriously looked at and worked with. The base concept was to store terrain data in digital form by digitizing existing map sheets or edited map manuscripts, and to develop in the future a system that would permit terrain information, "digitized directly on the photogrammetric plotting instruments, to be used as input into the data base" (UN 1979, p. 215). This would eliminate the necessity for digitization of compilation graphics, resulting in higher resolution and a saving of time. The ultimate objective would be to create a terrain information database into which new information could be fed and from which revised maps could be generated quickly via an attached drafting machine (UN 1979, p. 215; Canada. Surveys and Mapping Branch 1982a and 1982b; *Resources* 1982, pp. 92-96).

In 1977 the Ontario government entered into mapping in a fairly big way; the north was to be covered at 1:20,000 scale and the south at 1:10,000; the Hudson Bay and James Bay Lowlands coverage would be provided by orthophotographs with spot heights and the remainder by line maps with contour intervals; all urban areas were to be covered by 1:2,000-scale sheets. The program was to be completed by 1992, with the lower one-third of Ontario mapped to specifications by 1982 (Haddon 1979, pp. 30-32).

The provinces had for many years played an important role in mapping data collection. British Columbia had worked with the federal government on the production of 1:25,000- and 1:50,000-scale sheets, and other provinces had shown interest in mapping at 1:25,000 scale (Sebert 1975, p. 79). By the early 1980s, all of the provinces were involved in their own mapping programs, with many of them working on very large scale cadastral mapping (1:1,000; 1:2,000; 1:5,000) and on 1:20,000-scale resource mapping (Edward Kennedy 1981; Nicholson and Sebert 1981, pp. 152-63).

Nicholson and Sebert (1981) provide an excellent and detailed survey of the mapping of Canada.

12
UNITED STATES

In imagination the mind climbed rapidly through cool dark forests, up ragged rock precipices, across shining snowfields and glistening glaciers, occupying peak after peak and gazing afar on the silent grand array ... with a shock the mind returns to the realities and wonders how in creation survey instruments, cameras and necessities of existence are ever to be taken up to these outposts of the earth.

—A. O. Wheeler, 1905
Don Thomson 1975, p. 11

Topographic mapping of the United States began in 1775 with the appointment of Robert Erskine by General Washington as topographer for the Continental Army. In 1777 the Continental Congress authorized the appointment of a geographical surveyor, "to take sketches of the country and seat of war," at which time the Geographer's Department was created ("Cartography in the United States of America" 1951, p. 85; Andregg 1976, p. 385). The Geographer's Department was dissolved in 1783 (Friis 1976, p. 358).

In 1813 Congress authorized the appointment of eight topographic engineers and eight associate topographic engineers to a Topographical Bureau, under the War Department's General Staff. The first crude contour map of the United States was made in 1835 (Pendleton and Hall 1928, p. 339). Between 1838 and 1863 (when the sixteen engineer positions were absorbed by the Corps of Topographical Engineers), the Topographical Bureau played a considerable role in exploring and mapping the trans-Mississippi West, and all with a staff never larger than thirty-six (Goetzmann 1959). There was a general lack of topographic maps of the United States to the mid-nineteenth century, although most of the country had at least been explored—the exceptions being some areas in the Rockies, the Cascades, and the Sierra Nevada (Debenham 1960, p. 238).

In the years following 1865, interest in the west increased, and several surveys from 1867 to 1879 produced the first maps of large areas of the west, mapping some 600,000 square miles in all (Don Thomson 1967b, p. 116). These surveys and their resultant maps have the Superintendent of Documents classification numbers of I 17; I 18; W 7.10: vol. 18; W 8; and the Serial Set (for an index to part of the Serial Set see: Claussen, Martin Paul, and Friis, Herman R. 1941. *Descriptive catalog of maps published by Congress, 1817-1843*. Washington: privately printed).

The four surveys are as follows:

1. Geographical Surveys West of the 100th Meridian (1868-1879): led by Captain George M. Wheeler; surveyed 360,000 square miles (two-thirds mapped at 1:500,000 scale, hachured); some sources feel that Wheeler in 1874 was "deliberately surveying areas already covered by previous parties in an obvious attempt at empire building" and that the maps were inaccurate and useless for geologic purposes (Goetzmann 1966, p. 480); 95 sheets at eight miles to the inch (later changed to four miles to the inch) were proposed; 29 had been completed by 1879 when the survey was terminated (Moffat 1981, p. 16); W 8

2. Geological and Geographical Survey of the Territories (1867-1879); led by Ferdinand Vandiveer Hayden; mapped 167,000 square miles in the Rocky Mountains at 1:253,550 scale (four miles to the inch), using contours in some cases; best known for work in Colorado and in Yellowstone area; I 18

3. Geographical and Geological Survey of the Rocky Mountain Region (1869-1879); led by Major John Wesley Powell; mapped 67,000 square miles of Utah and Arizona, using plane-table work and triangulation; for a report concerning Powell's work, see: United States. Congress. House 1878 (in bibliography); I 17

4. U.S. Geological Exploration of the 40th Parallel (1871-1879/1867-72): led by Clarence King; 86,500 square miles surveyed; W 7.10: vol. 18/1-9

(Stephenson 1949, p. 7; UN 1979, p. 146; Gannett 1892a, p. 151; Winslow 1894, p. 29; Goetzmann 1966, p. 582; Henry Nash Smith 1947).

The surveys were evenly divided between the War Department and the Department of the Interior; the Hayden survey was primarily concerned with exploration and reconnaissance mapping, the Wheeler survey with transportation routes, and the Powell survey with systematic surveying and mapping in detail (Lyddan 1976, p. 344). It was the latter that set the tone for the Department of the Interior, which decided that the "one great object" of its survey work was "the construction of suitable maps of the country surveyed for the use of the Government and the nation" and that a uniform mapping plan should be followed (Rabbitt 1979, p. 224). In July of 1874 Interior Secretary Columbus Delano sent forth instructions for constructing an atlas of the United States west of 99°30'W, at a scale of 1:253,440; this was perhaps the beginning of the idea of a topographic "atlas" covering the entire territory of the United States (Rabbitt 1979, p. 224).

In 1878, the Special Committee on Scientific Surveys of the Territories of the United States—a committee of the National Academy of Sciences—issued a report recommending that the various geological and geographical surveys be abolished, and that a central mapping organization be created. It further stated that the United States Coast and Geodetic Survey (established in 1878 to replace the Coast Survey, established in 1807) should be that organization, and that, in pursuance of its goal, it should be transferred from the Treasury Department to the Department of the Interior. It should then be charged with undertaking a geodetic survey, a topographical survey (both detailed and reconnaissance work), and public land, or landparceling, surveys (National Academy of Science 1878; Rabbit 1979, p. 272; "Federal mapping" 1938, p. 244). The proposed United States Geological Survey would be charged with geological structure and economic resource studies only, although it might make topographic surveys for special purposes (Rabbitt 1979, pp. 273-74). The full program recommended was not adopted; the Coast and Geodetic Survey did eventually take on the geodetic work for the nation (as of the early 1980s, renamed the National Geodetic Survey, a unit of the National Ocean Service).

On March 3, 1879 the United States Geological Survey (USGS) was created, with a $6,000 appropriation. The first actual director was Clarence King; the first regular director was John Wesley Powell, who held the office from 1880 to 1894.

Ostensibly the survey was to concern itself only with geological mapping, and between 1879 and 1881 it did work on mineral surveys, but Powell soon realized it was impossible to do geological mapping without topographic mapping, since all reliable geological mapping is based upon topographic sheets. Powell made the national topographic map a personal quest; nonetheless, there is some argument that the topographic mapping program should be credited not to Powell but to Henry Gannett—who returned to the survey in 1882 after serving as Geographer for the 1880 Census—or to Powell's successor, Charles D. Walcott, who established "regular and substantial funding" from Congress for the program (Lynn 1979, p. 338; Gannett 1892b).

Be that as it may, immediately after congressional consent for the survey to move east—in 1882—a topographical division and a plan for topographic mapping of the nation were established (Manning 1967, p. 93). The original plan was to complete the topographic mapping by quadrangle areas, that is, areas bounded by lines of latitude and longitude; the complete set of sheets was to be known as the Topographic Atlas of the United States. The scales were to be 1:250,000 for undeveloped areas in the west, 1:125,000 for the east, and 1:62,500 (for areas of heavy cultural development in the east). All of the work was to be done in twenty-four years' time (Altenhofen 1971, p. 5). The topographic quadrangle that started out and has remained the basic unit of the U.S. topographic (and, for that matter, geologic) survey is defined as "a topographic map of a rectangular area, usually bounded by given meridians of longitude and parallels of latitude, or by other given guidelines"; frequently referred to as "quad" (Ehrenberg 1982, p. 56).

One of the most innovative aspects of USGS's program was the decision to depict relief by the use of contour lines. The birth of the program came in 1882, with the surveying of the Wingate, New Mexico, 30-minute x 30-minute sheet, though the 1:125,000-scale sheet resulting from the survey was not published until 1886. Interestingly enough, that same four-year time lag between survey and publication continued into the 1970s (Ehrenberg 1977, p. 141; Joseph Roberts and Robert Bloomer 1939, p. xiii; Gerald FitzGerald 1956, p. 447; Knowles and Stowe 1976, p. 12). In the same year, USGS began its extensive topographic mapping program (for preparation of the geologic map of the United States), the Coast Survey received congressional authorization to make a map of the eastern United States, and, in 1884, to make a map of the entire country (Rabbitt 1980, p. 90). In the 1880s topographic mapping was being done in eastern Kentucky, the mining areas of California and Colorado, the mountain/valley/plateau regions of Tennessee, large upland portions of North Carolina, Georgia, and Alabama, as well as in many other places (Snyder 1973, p. 130; Manning 1967, p. 101).

The initiation of cooperative state surveys in the 1880s inaugurated a new age in topographic mapping (Walling 1884 and 1886, p. 334; Bechert 1956, p. 467; Gannett 1892a, p. 152). In 1883 a campaign to map West Virginia began, and in 1884, Missouri, Kansas, Texas, southeastern Utah (between 1884 and 1896, 17 of 23 1:250,000-scale sheets were issued), southern Nevada, New Jersey, and Massachusetts followed suit. On July 6 of the latter year, USGS took over the topographic work of New Jersey from that state, while Massachusetts chose the cooperative route, with a four-year project to map the state by 1888 at 1:62,500 scale. Agreements were made to map Rhode Island, Connecticut, and New York (Manning 1967, pp. 97-98, 101; Lyddan 1976, p. 347; Rabbit 1980, pp. 90-91).

By 1885, 1:125,000-scale mapping was being done more than was 1:250,000-scale mapping, although the latter was still used extensively in the west, in areas such as the Grand Canyon, where the first standard series of topographic sheets was the 1:250,000-scale sheets, two in the 1° x 1° reconnaissance map series—Kaibab (1886) and Echo Cliffs (1891); they would be reprinted as late as 1937 (Seavey 1980a, p. 10). Arguments as to what agency was to do the nation's topographic mapping continued (United States. Congress. Joint Commission 1886).

Rhode Island mapping took place between 1888 and 1889, Connecticut mapping between 1889 and 1890. There was some feeling that the Massachusettes mapping was "hasty, inaccurate" work, and that the California 1:250,000-scale maps published during the 1880s were also mostly inaccurate (Manning 1967, p. 101; Wing 1949, pp. 204-5).

The survey's budget in 1889 was $199,000; the first appropriation specifically for topographic surveys made by USGS was in the sundry civil act of October 2, 1888, for fiscal 1889 (United States. Geological Survey 1926, p. 1; Sargent 1912, p. 483; United States 1888, pp. 505-26). In the same year, one of the first topographic sheets of the eastern United States issued by USGS came out, the Asheville, North Carolina-Tennessee sheet (Rabbitt 1980, p. 94). By the end of the decade the publication of 1:250,000-scale sheets had virtually ceased (Altenhofen 1971, p. 5).

The earliest topographic mapping of Indiana was largely that of quadrangle maps done for other states in which the quad boundaries extended into Indiana, especially in the southwest (due to interest in coal-bearing lands). The first Indiana sheet was a 1:62,500-scale sheet issued in 1889 (Bechert 1956, p. 467). Between 1888 and 1890, USGS mapped 46,807 miles in twenty states (Rabbitt 1980, p. 162).

By the 1890s, New Hampshire, New York, Pennsylvania, New Jersey, Kentucky, Wisconsin, Minnesota, Missouri, Arkansas, Texas and California had portions of their territory mapped but by 1893 still only about 8 percent of the conterminous United States was surveyed. USGS sallied next into central Alabama, the piedmont of North Carolina, and the Virginia coastal plain. Mapping of California mountainous areas at 1:125,000 scale started in the 1890s and continued—with many errors—into the early 1930s (Wing 1949, p. 205).

In 1892 a Topographical Conference was held in Washington by the Coast and Geodetic Survey, and the decision was made to map the mountains at 1:40,000 scale and the rest of the interior at 1:30,000 scale, a decision that was obviously completely ignored (Van Ornum 1896, pp. 347-51). By that same date USGS had completed 703 sheets, 291 at 1:62,500 scale, 352 at 1:125,000 scale and 60 at 1:250,000 scale. The survey had accurately surveyed approximately 60,000 square miles, and the total area surveyed was 650,000 square miles (Gannett 1982a, p. 152). In fiscal 1891 the survey's topographic survey budget was $325,000; between

1890 and 1892, the Topographical Branch was under Henry Gannett, and had mapping underway in nineteen states east of 97°W. About 40 percent of the area under survey was to be mapped at 1:63,360 scale (Rabbitt 1980, p. 189).

Between 1892 and 1894 Powell pointed out that the preparation of the geological map of the United States was taking a long time because of the necessity of preparing a topographic map first, and because of the time required for research in systems of mapping and cartography. Powell was also ready to argue against USGS's topographic work being transferred to the Coast and Geodetic Survey if such arguments were still needed, as they very much had been in the 1880s (Rabbitt 1980, p. 215).

The eastern division of the Survey (under Gannett) had mapped 26,060 square miles in fourteen states in two years, mostly at 1:62,500 scale. The cooperative survey of New York had been greatly enlarged and mapping was continuing in New Hampshire, Vermont, and the southern Appalachians. In the central division, 16,000 square miles had been mapped in North Dakota, South Dakota, Nebraska, Kansas, and Oklahoma, while in the western division 11,630 square miles in California (mainly in the Los Angeles and San Francisco regions), Colorado, and South Dakota had been mapped (Rabbitt 1980, pp. 215, 233). In 1893 the survey's topographic budget was $240,000 (United States. Geological Survey 1926, p. 2). By 1894, the Topographic Division had worked in every state and territory, and had mapped 600,000 square miles—20 percent of the national territory (Manning 1967, p. 93). By the time that Powell resigned, in that year, "topographic mapping had become by far the largest single activity of the Survey. The mapping had progressed, and continued to progress, beyond the needs of the Survey itself for strictly geologic purposes. The maps were becoming basic and standard for all purposes" (Rabbitt and Rabbitt 1954, pp. 751-52).

Between 1894 and 1897 USGS received the statutory right to have as one of its functions the making of a topographic and geologic map of the United States. The survey mapped in twenty-one states, more than one-third of which were in the central division. In 1897 USGS received the authority to sell topographic sheets to the public (Rabbitt and Rabbitt 1954, p. 752; Rabbitt 1980, p. 242). The topographic survey budget for 1897 was $175,000 (United States. Geological Survey 1926, p. 2).

The survey began topographic mapping of Alaska in 1895, with small field parties. These field parties combined geologic and topographic mapping in four-month survey parties of six men each. They worked in areas of potential mineral value; this was principally due to the gold rush of 1898 which had resulted in increased congressional appropriations for work in Alaska. Monies for this work ranged from $5,000 in 1895 to a peak $100,000 each year from 1913 to 1917. Work was begun in the main river valleys, such as Kuskokwim, Susitna, Copper, Tanana, and White (Gerald FitzGerald 1951a, pp. 2, 3, 8, 9; and 1953, p. 406).

Between 1897 and 1900, the Topographic Branch worked in thirty-one states and territories, with the bulk of the mapping for publication at 1:125,000 scale, although more than 20 percent was at a scale of 1:62,500. New York and Missouri contributed increased funds, and West Virginia began to participate in the cooperative program (Rabbitt 1980, pp. 272-88). The first 1:62,500-scale sheets of California, specifically of the San Francisco and Los Angeles areas, appeared in the late 1890s. In 1899 the Topographic and Geologic Commission of

Pennsylvania was established because of the demand for topographic maps of the state; in 1900 Pennsylvania began working on a 50/50 cooperative basis with USGS (Stephenson 1949, p. 11). In 1898 the survey's topographic surveys budget was $150,000, and in 1900 it was $240,000 (United States. Geological Survey 1926, p. 2).

Between 1900 and 1902 the survey continued onward; its goal was to become "the best geological survey in Christendom" (Rabbitt 1980, p. 299). Twenty-seven percent of the United States had been surveyed as of 1900, but more than 200,000 square miles, mapped in the early years at a scale of 1:250,000, needed to be resurveyed—so in actuality only 19 percent was adequately mapped. The director of the survey stated at that time that it would take 100 years to complete coverage of all of the states, 110 years if the necessary resurveying for old 1:250,000-scale sheets was figured in. In that year detailed topographic mapping was done in thirty-two states and territories, amounting to 35,123 square miles (one-third at 1:62,500 scale). The eight states working on cooperative mapping were contributing $101,000; this dollar-for-dollar cooperation with the survey was not law, but simply the survey's way for those states desiring speedy survey to obtain it (Rabbitt 1980, pp. 299-326; Friis 1952).

By 1902 the topographic mapping program was almost independent of the rest of the survey. In the east areas were chosen to be mapped according to the availability of cooperative funds; in the west much of the work was in the forest reserves. Between 1902 and 1904, 16,278 square miles east of the Mississippi were mapped, of which 84 percent was in the eleven states having cooperative mapping agreements with USGS. Approximately half of that mapping was done in New York, Pennsylvania, Ohio, and Virginia. In the west, 18,913 square miles were mapped, nearly 60 percent of that in California, Arizona, Washington, and Montana. By 1904, 929,850 square miles had been topographically mapped, in 1,327 atlas sheets. This represented 26 percent of the country including Alaska, 31 percent excluding it (Rabbitt 1980, pp. 338-55).

California began state participation in 1903, the same year that mapping in the Central Valley commenced (at 1:31,680 scale) (Wing 1949, p. 206). In 1904, the survey celebrated its twenty-fifth anniversary; it now had a permanent workforce numbering 678 (Rabbitt and Rabbitt 1954, p. 752). In Alaska, from 1902 to 1910 the survey would go from 1:500,000-scale exploratory mapping to 1:250,000-scale reconnaissance mapping (Gerald FitzGerald 1951a, pp. 10-12). Members of the survey developed a panoramic camera in 1905, which was successfully used for many years for topographic mapping of Alaska (Gerald FitzGerald 1951a, p. 1). In New Jersey, the last new sheet in the state's 1:25,000-scale series appeared in 1905 (Snyder 1973, p. 132).

During the early part of the century, there was a brief flurry of 1:31,680-scale sheets; the 1:24,000 scale, which was also implemented early in the century, would eventually become the established scale. By 1906, USGS had completed topographic sheets for about one-third (1,025,000 square miles) of the United States. Connecticut, Massachusetts, New Jersey, and Rhode Island were covered, West Virginia was to be completed by 1907, and work was proceeding mainly in Ohio, Pennsylvania, Illinois, West Virginia, Kentucky, and New York. USGS was spending about $350,000 per year on topographic mapping, and the cost per square mile was up from the $4 it had been in the early 1890s to $10 (Wilson 1907, pp. 13-14). In 1909 Virginia and Texas (the latter in the official body of the

State Levee and Drainage Board) joined the ranks of states having cooperative programs with USGS (Webb 1978, p. 38; Baskin 1980, p. 2).

The only completely unknown areas in the United States by 1910 were in Alaska, particularly in the northern half. Surveying in Alaska had its difficulties; the season was short—June 15 to September 15 as a maximum—and in the southeast the dense forest, fallen timber, and continual rains meant that surveying costs shot up to $42 per square mile (Sargent 1912, pp. 486, 489). By 1910 USGS had done an exploratory survey of 47,680 square miles (8.16 percent of the total area), as well as 114,045 square miles of reconnaissance surveys (19.45 percent) and 3,022 square miles of detailed survey work (0.52 percent). The goal was to map Alaska on 1:250,000-scale contoured sheets (Sargent 1912, p. 491; Gerald Fitz-Gerald 1957, p. 484). By 1911, about 2,000 quadrangle sheets had been issued, and three-eighths of the United States had been surveyed (United States. Geological Survey 1911, p. 3). Relatively few of those sheets had been made of Arizona, which entered the Union as a state in 1912 with only 1 percent adequate topographic coverage (UN 1959, p. 35).

By 1913 about 37 percent of the nation was mapped topographically, albeit in a scattered pattern (Joerg 1912, p. 842; Baker 1967, p. 393). Pennsylvania suffered a two-year lapse in its cooperative funding, from 1916 to 1918, and then resumed it; to the 1940s it would be exceeded only by the state of New York in duration of cooperative efforts (Stephenson 1949, p. 11). From 1916 up to about 1934 Texas maintained a cooperative program to map lowland areas and state prison system properties (Baskin 1980, p. 2). In 1917 USGS's topographic mapping budget was $350,000 (United States. Geological Survey 1926, p. 2).

Between 1898 and 1920 USGS did 152,000 square miles of reconnaissance mapping and 3,700 square miles of detailed mapping, the latter at a scale of 1:24,000 or 1:62,500) (Gerald FitzGerald 1951a, p. 13). Between 1911 and 1920, R. H. Sargent supervised topographic mapping operations in Alaska. These were primarily at 1:250,000 scale in the Copper River valley, the Kenai peninsula, the south flanks of the Alaska Range near Broad Pass, and along the Richardson Highway (Valdez to Thompson Pass) (Gerald FitzGerald 1951a, p. 12).

Indiana, via the office of the State Geologist, began participating in cooperative mapping in about 1919 or 1920; prior to this only 25 15-minute (1:62,500 scale) quads had been produced for the state (Bechert 1956, p. 467).

By 1920, about 43 percent of the conterminous United States was mapped topographically; Delaware, Maryland, West Virginia, and Ohio joined the roster of states completed, and New York was more than 90 percent mapped ("Progress in the work of mapping the United States" 1921, p. 165). At least half of the topographic work done was so old that it had little worth; large areas of the west had not been surveyed in forty years. In addition, although the standard scale was 1:62,500, in practice scales varied a good deal, and sheets did not always fit together well ("Unmapped United States" 1922, p. 24; Davis 1922, p. 557). Cooperative programs continued; in 1923, the Texas Board of Water Engineers signed a two-year agreement with USGS (Baskin 1980, p. 2). By the mid-1920s, USGS had about nine million topographic sheets on hand, and sold a half million per year (Bechert 1956, p. 167; Glenn Smith 1924; United States. Geological Survey. Alaska Branch 1926).

The Temple Act, which provided for mapping the United States in twenty years (with the states matching the federal government dollar for dollar), was passed February 27, 1925 (Pendleton and Hall 1928, p. 343). More than half of the states were already participating in the cooperative program. Although the act was passed, no federal funds were appropriated to carry it out; possibly the total amount–$50 million–stuck in the congressmen's gullets. Over $15 million had already been spent on the topographic atlas of the United States. About 45 percent of the total national area was covered with sheets, but perhaps 15 percent of that amount was small-scale and reconnaissance mapping. At that rate of progress, it would take another 100 years to finish the task (Mitchell 1925, p. 221). Instead of full funding for the total program, USGS received $325,000 for topographic mapping in fiscal 1920, $500,000 in 1924, $485,000 in 1926, and $451,700 in 1927 (United States. Geological Survey 1926, p. 3). In fiscal 1927, the states allotted $378,791.88 to the cooperative program (United States. Geological Survey 1926, pp. 3, 7). To 1928, about 57 percent of the continental United States had never been mapped "even in the roughest manner" (Pendleton and Hall 1928, p. 340). In 1929 the survey celebrated its fiftieth birthday; its total federal funding now amounted to more than $2 million; its total expenditure for fifty years was about $75 million, of which about $10 million was state funding. It had 998 employees, and the expenditure for fiscal 1929 was $3,875,000 (United States. Geological Survey 1930; Curnow 1929).

The first 1:24,000-scale sheets of California were of the Los Angeles area, and were issued between 1923 and 1930 (Wing 1949, p. 204). Between 1926 and 1929 USGS was making its first attempt to use aerial photography as an aid to mapping Alaska (Gerald FitzGerald 1951a, p. 35).

By 1930 Connecticut, Delaware, Maryland, New Jersey, New York, Ohio, Rhode Island, West Virginia, the District of Columbia, and the Hawaiian Islands were covered by maps "considered adequate at the time" (Wrather 1949, p. 2). At last the survey began working on mapping north of the Arctic Circle, although with reconnaissance mapping methods that had been used in the west since the 1880s; triangulation was nonexistent in that area except for the 141st meridian and a few areas spotted along the Arctic Coast. The rising young surveyor in those days traveled in Alaska via pack train, poling boat, canoe, dog team or snowshoes, as the season required (Gerald FitzGerald 1951a, p. 406).

One reason for the slowness of mapping progress was that although USGS and the Army Corps of Engineers had first tried aerial photography in about 1920 in connection with planimetric mapping and flood control, previous to 1935 almost all topographic work was done by plane table ("Cartography in the United States of America" 1951, pp. 81, 87). The impetus for the changeover to aerial photography in 1935 was apparently due to a large portion of the U.S. oil-producing territory being flown (and presumably mapped) by commercial firms in 1934. Within a few years of 1935 USGS began making standard topographic quadrangles from aerial photographs, and was devoting considerable effort to the improvement of equipment such as cameras and stereoplotters ("Cartography in the United States of America" 1951, pp. 81, 87; Frederick McDonald 1935; Wilby 1935; Carlberg 1931).

In 1934 the topographic mapping of the alluvial floodplain of the Mississippi River at 1:62,500 scale (177 sheets in six years, 1929-1932 for surveying and 1930-1933 for publication) was complete ("Completion" 1934, pp. 651-52). In that year the portion of the conterminous United States mapped rose to 45 percent, but with only 60 percent of that percentage–that is, 26 percent of the total area–*adequately* mapped (Joerg 1935, facing p. 204; United States. National Resources Board 1934, p. 177; Bowie 1936).

In that same year the National Resources Board proposed that topographic mapping series become exclusively the responsibility of the federal government, instead of being a shared financial responsibility of state and federal governments, and that the United States be mapped in ten years at a cost of $117,531,000 (United States. National Resources Board 1934, pp. 77, 451-53). The aim was not only to save money by being able to plan properly for such matters as highway construction and mineral resource development, but to bolster United States prestige on the international front.

> All first class foreign powers have accurate maps of their territory, usually several series of them on scales appropriate to different uses. The United States still has more than half its territory unmapped, and for 75 percent of it no modern maps exist (United States. Science Advisory Board 1935, p. 152).

Not only was U.S. mapping generally inadequate, it was also confusing. Federal mapping activities were "enormous in volume," of "confusing variety," and had developed independently and without correlation in many different executive agencies, leading to duplication of effort and wasted funds. The Science Advisory Board recommended the consolidation of the USGS Topographic Branch, the Coast and Geodetic Survey, the Lakes Survey, and the International Boundary Commission (United States. Science Advisory Board 1935, p. 46). As was the fate of the fourteen other commissions that had investigated federal mapping activities between 1842 and 1938, their advice was ignored and no observable changes were made.

By 1937 some 48 percent of the conterminous United States, including Connecticut, Delaware, the District of Columbia, Maryland, Massachusetts, New Jersey, New York, Ohio, Rhode Island, and West Virginia had been mapped. The standard scale in the 1930s was 1:62,500. By 1939, the largest unmapped areas in the United States were in the northern half of Alaska, the southeast central area, west Texas, the north central Great Plains, and the northeast and southeast Pacific Northwest (Platt 1945, map following p. 180; Thiele 1938, p. 123; Bowie 1938, p. 88; John Kirtland Wright 1950; Raisz 1937). Two-thirds of the 1939 output was at 1:62,500 scale; 45.4 percent of the conterminous United States was covered with topographic sheets (Joerg 1940, p. 275).

In 1937, after a mapping bill had been in almost every Indiana state session since 1923, a disastrous flood pushed through a mapping program bill. As a result of this Indiana entered into a cooperative agreement with USGS for 1:24,000-scale sheets (Bechert 1956, pp. 467-68). Also in the late 1930s, a 1:24,000-scale series was initiated in Virginia and a resurvey program was begun in New Jersey that would lead to sheets at that scale in 1944 (Webb 1978, p. 38; Snyder 1973, p. 130).

In 1939 a joint letter from Harry H. Woodring, the Secretary of War; J. M. Johnson, the Acting Secretary of Commerce; and Harold L. Ickes, the Secretary of the Interior protested the lack of topographic mapping, and recommended the expanded program detailed in Senate Resolution 87 (Woodring, Johnson and Ickes 1939, p. 276).

Between 1920 and 1940, most mapping had been done by field methods, and published at 1:62,500 scale in 15-minute quadrangles; in succeeding years, most of the publishing would be of 1:24,000-scale maps in 7½ minute quads (Lyddan 1976, p. 347; Kenneth T. Adams 1941). In 1940, the Bureau of the Budget heeded the

National Resources Board's call (and probably that of the President) and began to work on coordination of some of the various cartographic activities and programs.

To 1940, USGS had done 1:250,000-scale mapping of 185,586 square miles and 4,552 square miles at 1:62,500 scale of Alaska. Nearly one-half of Alaska was mapped in some manner, although it was largely at scales of 1:250,000 and 1:500,000 (Gerald FitzGerald 1951a, p. 8).

In 1942, the director of the Bureau of the Budget was specifically directed to coordinate and promote improvement of federal surveying and mapping activities ("Cartography in the United States of America" 1951, p. 83). The Federal Board of Surveys and Maps, established in 1919, was abolished and the director took over the work of that board (United States. President 1942; Randall 1948, p. 8). The United States continued to compare unfavorably in the mapping world not only with most European countries, but, as far as the *International map of the world* at 1:1,000,000-scale coverage was concerned, with Paraguay (Marschner 1943, p. 215).

During World War II the mapping of areas considered strategic because of location or resources proceeded fairly quickly. By the early 1940s Alaska was 50 percent covered with topographic maps—15 percent at 1:500,000 scale, 29 percent at 1:250,000 scale, and the remainder at 1:62,500 scale. Much of Arctic Alaska was covered by trimetrogon photography during the war years (Gerald FitzGerald 1953, p. 407, and 1957, p. 484; Olson and Whitmarsh 1944, p. 7; Hinks 1944, p. 115; Gill 1945; Fuechsel 1944). The trimetrogon mapping had been developed largely by USGS personnel engaged in Alaska mapping and by members of the Army Air Force (Gerald FitzGerald 1951a, p. 1). By about 1944, 1:62,500- and 1:31,680-scale sheets covered half of the United States; the emphasis on mapping in the early 1940s had been in the coastal belt and extending inland 100 to 200 miles (Lobeck 1945, p. 417).

By 1944 topographic mapping had been going on for sixty-five years in California. Seventeen percent of the state was still unmapped. Forty-four percent of the mapping was obsolete and 39 percent acceptable, but two-thirds of the latter was so old that it needed revision, so actually only 13 percent of the state was acceptably mapped. In 1945 Olaf P. Jenkins recommended that topographic mapping of California be completed in ten years, at a cost of $6 million (Wing 1949, p. 206). In that same year, California began to match USGS dollar for dollar in mapping funds for the state (Troxel 1960, p. 8).

The influx of War Department funds had stepped up the snail's pace of pre-war mapping considerably, and in 1945 the hope was that United States mapping would be completed in twenty-five years (Gerald FitzGerald 1945, p. 26; Randall 1946). In 1946 the percentage mapped was given as 47 percent ("Topographic maps of the USGS" 1946, p. 161). A return to normal USGS operations began in 1947, with 27 percent of the country having adequate coverage. That year also marked the beginning of the National Topographic Program at 1:24,000 scale, and the first major expansion of the topographic mapping program since 1920 (Lyddan 1974, p. 347). The nation was just less than half mapped, including over half of Pennsylvania, 12 percent of Colorado, and 38 percent of California (Colbert 1947, p. 8; Federal Map Users Conference 1964, p. 10). In late 1947 the Army Map Service began working on a 1:250,000-scale series of the United States, an "economical solution to our mapping dilemma," detailed enough in scale to provide useful information and compact enough to be rapidly accomplished (Zelinsky 1951, p. 662). This project was to include 153 sheets for Alaska, 42 of those north of the

Arctic Circle (Gerald FitzGerald 1953, p. 407; Skop 1947). In 1949 New York, Ohio, West Virginia and Maryland were completely mapped, and Pennsylvania nearly so except for eight 15-minute quads in the north central area (Stephenson 1949, p. 11; Fuechsel 1949; Carlton 1949). At this point, about 2,000 quads were in process and about 500 were completed each year; at that rate it would take until A.D. 2000 to complete coverage (Wrather 1949, p. 7). On a happier note, more progress had been made in the surveying and mapping of Alaska between 1940 and 1950 than in any previous period, largely due to Alaska's having been a strategically important area during the global war (Gerald FitzGerald 1951a, p. 19; United States. Map Information Office 1950).

In 1950 came yet another drive to accelerate the topographic mapping of the United States, with what would have been the National Surveying and Mapping Act of 1950; it was not passed. In 1950 about 50 percent of the country was covered by topographic maps of some sort, but only 10-20 percent was mapped adequately, that is, covered with relatively recent maps at a scale more detailed than 1:100,000. Only Massachusetts and Rhode Island were completely and adequately mapped; in the eight other states where mapping was technically complete, the sheets needed revision (as in Hawaii, where the topographic work had been done forty or fifty years before). There were cooperative programs in twenty-six states, including two fairly new recruits, Utah and Kentucky (Kilmartin 1951, pp. 222, 227-28; Gerald FitzGerald 1951b; King 1951; Ralph Leroy Miller 1951). For 40 percent of the national territory, there were no topographic maps whatsoever (Crone 1968, p. 153; James Patterson 1951, p. 345; "Cartography in the United States of America" 1951, p. 87). To map the remaining 75 percent in 20 years, instead of the 40 to 100 years required at the then rate of mapping, would cost $480 million, or $24 million per year, in comparison to the $9 million per year then being spent. It was anticipated that this mapping program would save $5 billion just in the areas of highway, railroad, and industrial location planning (Mahoney 1950, pp. 5-11, 19). The plan was that half of the unmapped area of the conterminous United States would be covered at 1:24,000 scale, the other half plus one-third of Alaska at 1:62,500 scale, and the rest of Alaska "where maps of any scale are sadly lacking," at 1:250,000 scale (Mahoney 1950, p. 21). There was once again an appeal made to national pride.

> Despite the fact that the United States is one of the most advanced nations of the world in respect to its position in science, engineering, transport, business, and industry, it has lagged far behind other forward-looking nations in completing topographic and geological maps of its area. In fact most of these other nations have long ago completed their entire series of detailed maps and maintain adequate mapping forces to keep maps revised and up to date (United States. Congress. House 1950, p. 2).

Once again, it failed, in spite of enactment being unanimously recommended by the House Committee (United States. Congress. House 1950, p. 14). USGS continued to plod along, doing about 80 percent of all the topographic mapping of the country, mostly at scales of 1:24,000; 1:31,680; 1:62,500; and 1:250,000 ("Cartography in the United States of America" 1951, pp. 81, 85; Joerg 1951).

The Army Map Service had by 1951 completed about 84 sheets out of 469 in the 1:250,000-scale series, most derived from recompilation of more detailed existing maps (Zelinsky 1951, pp. 662-63). As for USGS work, the 1:31,680-scale series was being replaced by 1:24,000-scale sheets; about 3,000 quads were in the course of preparation, and emphasis was placed on the 1:62,500-scale series, with over 4,000 sheets published (UN. Secretariat 1957, p. 23). The scales for the conterminous United States and Hawaii were 1:250,000; 1:125,000; 1:62,500; 1:31,680; 1:48,000; and 1:24,000. The scales for Alaska were 1:63,360 and 1:250,000 (United States. Geological Survey 1952; Alaskan Science Conference 1953; Arthur Robinson 1956; Gerald FitzGerald 1952). Some of the western states had thousands of square miles completely unmapped; the lack of detailed maps for large areas of the United States was considered by one observer to be "a national disgrace" (Karo 1955, p. 4).

USGS's budget had gone from $5 million in 1946 to $17.5 million in 1952, the latter sum including $4 million from Defense Department funds. Over 10,000 titles had been published in the topographic atlas over the previous seventy years, and between 900 and 1,000 new titles were coming out each year (Lloyd Arthur Brown 1953; Stiefel 1953, p. 162). In 1953 the last sheets of the *Alaska Reconnaissance Topographic Map Series* at 1:250,000 scale were completed. It was followed almost immediately by the Brooks Range Project at 1:63,360 scale, to be completed in 1958. Mark Hurd was doing aerial photography for this, on a large fixed price contract in 1955 on the north slope of the range; the fliers waited six weeks for clear weather, finally got three days of it, and completed over 90 percent of the project in that time (Bock 1979, p. 6; Gerald FitzGerald 1956; United States. Army Map Service 1954a).

The last Vermont quad, Burke (1:62,500 scale), was compiled in 1951 and printed in 1954. In the same year the Indiana state government, faced with only 245 of 691 1:24,000-scale sheets done, realized that it would take almost forty years to finish the state at that rate, and state industry did not see much use in such mapping if it were not completed in ten years—at which point the Department of Conservation received an extra $400,000 for mapping (Bechert 1956, p. 469).

In 1954, the survey had more than 6,000 permanent employees and was funded at about $48 million per year; in 75 years, the total expenditure had been $475 million (Rabbitt and Rabbitt 1954, p. 757).

By the mid-1950s, New Jersey was covered with 1:24,000-scale quads (Snyder 1973, p. 130), considerably better off than the rest of the United States, which in 1956 stood at 37 percent covered with adequate topographic maps (Conly 1956, p. 338).

Prior to 1957, most of the USGS sheets were 15-minute quads at 1:62,500 scale; in that year the survey began compilation of all except Alaska maps at 1:24,000 scale, on 7½-minute sheets (United States. General Accounting Office 1968, p. 2). By the same year, the United States was covered with 1:250,000-scale sheets (Griffith 1957, p. 51; American Society of Civil Engineers 1958; Randall 1958; "Tendances" 1959; Meine 1959; Gerald FitzGerald 1960).

A long, searing drought between 1950 and 1956 in Texas finally made the need for topographic mapping of the state obvious; the Texas Water Planning Act of 1957 included funds for topographic mapping. In addition, a strong state and federal cooperative mapping program became active in 1958, following more than three decades of state inactivity; funding went from $180,000 to $520,000 per year and was administered by the Texas Water Development Board. In about the same year, Florida began a cooperative program ("Topographic mapping completed for Florida" 1979; Baskin 1970).

In about 1960, while USGS was about to complete the Brooks Range Project in Alaska (with 18 of 21 sheets done), California was contributing about $3 million per year to topographic mapping; about 100 or more new sheets (at scales of 1:24,000 and 1:62,500) of the state were being produced each year, and the estimated date of completion was 1962. At this rate, the first sheet of a print run was costing several thousand dollars (Troxel 1960, p. 9). USGS issued a few sample shaded relief maps at 1:24,000 scale; the first, in 1961, was of Santa Fe. By 1962, the 1:62,500-scale series was about 40 percent complete, and the 1:24,000-scale series about 20 percent complete (Griffith 1962, p. 392; Baughman 1961). In 1963, survey director Thomas B. Nolan announced a plan to complete the topographic atlas of the United States by 1981 (Manning 1967, p. 227).

By 1964, about 70 to 75 percent of the conterminous United States was covered with 1:62,500 or more detailed scale maps (Thompson and Speert 1964, p. 34; "World in the flat" 1965, p. 486; Witkege 1965). The standard topographic quadrangle series was 60 percent complete, with another 9 percent in manuscript form, and the estimated date of completion of the 1:24,000- and 1:62,500-scale series was 1976 (UN 1966b, p. 90; UN 1976 b, p. 105).

In 1966 Minnesota began an accelerated program, in cooperation with USGS, to provide standard map coverage of the entire state; the unmapped area was mainly remote regions consisting of vast swamps, peat bogs, and muskegs (Hudson and Johnson 1972, p. 337).

By 1967 about 47 percent of the 48 contiguous states were mapped (United States. General Accounting Office 1968, p. 2; Fuechsel 1967; Borgerding 1966). In the same year, the Office of Management and Budget (OMB) issued *Circular 16* specifying responsibilities for coordination of mapping, charting, and geodesy, calling upon the Department of the Interior to exercise government-wide leadership in assuring coordinated planning and execution of topographic mapping (Radlinski 1978, p. 1).

By 1968, the 1:24,000-scale series stood at 40 percent complete, with completion date set for 1981; the United States had 16,000 map personnel and spent $300 million on mapping activities between 1966 and 1968 (Brandenberger 1970, p. 356; Harris 1970, p. 103). In that same year 1:24,000-scale coverage stood at 48.2 percent published and 18.5 percent in progress; revision was on 5- to 20-year cycles (Altenhofen 1971, p. 13). By 1968, 21,760 of 53,700 sheets (excluding Alaska) at 1:24,000 scale, 6,100 of 13,650 sheets (excluding Alaska) at 1:62,500 scale, and 2,117 of an estimated 2,920 sheets of Alaska at 1:63,360 scale had been published (UN. Dept. of Economic and Social Affairs 1970, p. 81; Southard 1969).

Almost all of the United States except for scattered areas in the west and a substantial block in northern Alaska was covered by some form of topographic mapping at scales more detailed than 1:250,000 by 1970. Puerto Rico was comfortably covered at 1:20,000 scale (UN 1970, p. 82). The 1:24,000-scale mapping in Vermont was concentrated in the western part of the state, with the exception of the central portion from Rutland east to Hanover, New Hampshire (Cobb 1971). The discovery of oil on the North Slope of Alaska "caused the Geological Survey to reappraise its Alaska mapping program," and to initiate a program providing for detailed 1:63,360-scale topographic mapping in the central part of the Brooks Range; field operations in 1970 started on a 26,700-square-mile area that encompassed the proposed Trans-Alaska Pipeline route north of the Yukon River (Stubbe 1970, p. 428).

So deeply involved in topographic mapping was USGS that in the early 1970s, geologic maps—which one would think would be a Geological Survey's major concern—composed less than 7 percent of all titles issued. Geologic maps were, and are, a major concern to the survey, but good geologic maps must be based on good topographic maps, and therefore the topographic mapping has to be done first.

By early 1972, 79 percent of the United States was covered by 1:24,000- and 1:62,500-scale sheets; after a ten-year cooperative effort, Virginia was covered by 1:24,000-scale sheets (UN 1976b, p. 105; Calver 1974, p. 46). A steady map revision program of 900 sheets per year was also in progress (UN 1976b, p. 105). The 1:24,000-scale series was over 60 percent complete and the 1:62,500/1:63,360-scale series was 84 percent complete. The 1:24,000-scale series had a completion date of 1983 (Sibert 1972, p. 239; Webb 1978, p. 39). Another study of the nation's problems was made by the U.S. Federal Mapping Task Force on Mapping, Charting, Geodesy and Surveying, again with little result (United States. Federal Mapping Task Force 1973).

In 1974, USGS began work on digitizing projects; the data for the 1:250,000-scale Army Map Service (as of 1972, the Defense Mapping Agency, but the sheets were still usually called "the old AMS sheets") sheets were all on magnetic tape. USGS was issuing about 4,000 orthophotoquads per year as an interim or companion project (UN 1979, p. 60).

In the late 1960s USGS began going to orthophotomapping, since such maps could be generated quickly, economically, and accurately. An orthophotoquad is either an orthophotograph or a mosaic of such photographs in standard quadrangle format (in this case, 1:24,000 scale) with little or no cartographic treatment. In orthophotographs displacements of images caused by camera tilt and ground relief are corrected, and the orthophotoquad is produced from the orthophotograph by bringing the latter to a defined scale, relating it to a geodetic reference system, and providing a map border (Mullen 1970; Thompson 1973; National Cartographic Information Center 1980, pp. 1-3).

By late 1974, 33,991 of 53,700 sheets at 1:24,000 scale, 6,958 of 13,650 at 1:62,500 scale (excluding Alaska), 2,336 of 2,920 of Alaska at 1:63,360 scale, and 750 of 3,600 at 1:63,360 scale of the conterminous United States were complete (UN. Dept. of Economic and Social Affairs 1976, p. 61; Cook 1976).

In about 1975, the Department of the Interior officially adopted the National Mapping Program (Lyddan 1976, p. 342). In that same year, the 1:100,000-scale series was begun and there were orthophotoquads made for those areas not previously mapped. In the mid-1970s the Bureau of Land Management and the Forest Service and state agencies in Pennsylvania, Georgia, and Colorado expressed an interest in 1:50,000- and 1:100,000-scale series. This led to the 1:50,000- and 1:100,000-scale county series and to the metric 1:100,000- and 1:25,000-scale series in the second half of the decade (Fry 1975, p. 341; Ward 1976; Sixth Western Geographic Names Conference 1982).

At that time maps at scales of 1:24,000; 1:62,500; or 1:63,360 were available for about 93 percent of the country (UN 1979, p. 60). The survey was using orthophotomaps (orthophotoquads with additional cartographic information, and in color) for areas of slight relief such as the Okefenokee Swamp, the Everglades, part of Minnesota, part of Alaska, the Florida Keys, part of Arizona, part of Wyoming, and the Great Salt Lake area; such maps are particularly effective for depicting desert and swamp (Petrie 1977, p. 67). As of June 30, 1975, 68 percent at 1:24,000 scale, 7 percent at 1:50,000 scale (the new county series begun in 1975), 22 percent at 1:62,500 scale, 2 percent at 1:100,000 scale, and 1 percent in 1:100,000 scale (county map series) were completed. Alaska was at 84 percent coverage with 1:63,360-scale sheets (UN 1979, p. 148; Thompson 1979).

USGS was looking long, hard, and carefully at digital methods throughout the 1970s, seeing this as the future for topographic map publication. The survey was therefore investigating in particular new digital data-collection input systems, interactive systems, digitally driven output systems, and cartographic software packages, thus joining the national mapping agencies of many other countries who were all working on cartographic digitization (UN 1979, p. 62). USGS was looking toward a future in which the major products would be digital data, orthophoto-quads, cartographic data, and line maps (Pan American Consultation on Cartography 1977, p. 10). At the same time, the survey was busy generating traditional cartographic formats—more than 7,700 topographic quadrangles covering about 1,227,200 square kilometers between 1973 and 1976, with a total of about 45,000 quads published to the latter date.

The survey was also occupied with changing to the new metric series, in line with the metrification of the United States. "Having firmly fixed 1:24,000 in every-body's mind the Survey is about to change the whole operation" (Seavey 1979, p. 15). The new metric topographic mapping program began with the 1:25,000-scale sheets of the New York Winter Olympics region.

Between 1970 and 1977, over 7,800 new and revised 1:24,000-scale topo-graphic quadrangles were published. In fiscal 1977, USGS and the Defense Mapping Agency agreed to co-produce a series at 1:50,000 scale, the most widely used scale for military purposes in the world. The series was targeted for completion in the early to middle 1980s (Seavey 1979, p. 15).

USGS began producing orthophotoquads in a large way in the late 1970s, primarily to solve the problem of 30 percent of the conterminous United States not yet being mapped at 1:24,000 scale. USGS intended to have, by the end of 1978, complete orthophotoquad coverage for conterminous areas not covered by 1:24,000-scale sheets (G. D. Robinson and Speiker 1978, p. 5; Pan American Con-sultation on Cartography 1977, p. 11). By the late 1970s the federal government was spending over $484 million per year to produce some 35,000 maps, totaling over 120 million copies (Seavey 1980b, p. 273). The survey facilities in Denver alone had over 60 million sheets in stock.

The mapping of Alaska continued to accelerate in the late 1970s with the advent of the oil pipeline and Alaska's increasing economic importance. USGS looked at new ways to produce maps, from Landsat imagery at 1:1,000,000 to the use of SLAR for 1:250,000-scale mapping. Of the 2,920 1:63,360-scale maps required to cover Alaska, 2,321 had been published by 1979, and 374 were in pro-cess. The survey was also starting work on a 1:25,000-scale series for urban areas of Alaska, the first to be of Cordova, Seward, Valdez, and Whittier (Seavey 1980b, p. 274).

The 1:24,000-scale series, available for 71 percent of the country (7 percent in manuscript), remained the primary map series of the National Mapping Program in 1978, and served as source material for smaller-scale products such as the 1:50,000-. 1;100,000-, and 1:250,000-scale sheets. Each year 4,000 quads were reviewed, and of that number about 1,600 sheets were revised, and the need for revision was expected to grow.

A cooperative mapping program with Massachusetts to produce new metric maps of the entire state was expected to take eight to ten years. Florida and West Virginia were completed at 1:24,000 scale as the result of cooperative programs. In fiscal year 1978, the Topographic Surveys and Mapping obligation amounted to $67.3 million, including funds from 38 states, totaling $6.6 million (United States. Geological Survey 1979, pp. 47-48, 51-52).

All of this was going on in a time of staff reduction and monetary inflation; USGS had gone from a staff of 2,250 persons to 1,580, with further reductions expected. The 1:24,000-scale program had at least seven years before completion, and would be 96 or 97 percent complete at the end of fiscal 1979. By the mid-1980s, the intermediate scale 1:50,000- and 1:100,000-scale series were to be completed. Fourteen states were completely mapped at 1:24,000; all were states that had worked cooperatively with USGS over the years. The entire 1:24,000-scale program seems to have been "a twenty-year plan since 1920" ("ASP-ACSM" 1979, p. 3).

In 1979, with Virginia, Pennsylvania, Ohio, Indiana, Maryland, the District of Columbia, New Jersey, Florida, Georgia, Delaware, Massachusetts, Connecticut, Rhode Island, Kentucky (geologic 1:24,000-scale sheets also completed, again due to cooperative efforts), West Virginia and Tennessee covered by 1:24,000-scale sheets, and with four-fifths of the nation as a whole covered at that scale, the Geological Survey quietly celebrated its centennial ("Topographic mapping completed for Florida" 1979, pp. 5-6; Kluge 1979).

USGS began 1980 by completing orthophoto coverage of the remaining unmapped areas, and by working toward "creating and maintaining a national digital cartographic data base" (Southard 1980, p. 399; Sixth Western Geographic Names Conference 1982). This was done despite a 1980/81 budget 3.3 percent lower than the previous year (while inflation was running at 13.3 percent); 32.7 percent ($205,284,000) of the total budget ($627,682,000) was committed to mapping projects (Seavey 1980, p. 62). In September of 1980 USGS announced a major reorganization—the establishment of a National Mapping Division. This division was designed to carry out the functions formerly performed by three separate units—the Topographic Division, the Publications Division, and the Geography Program of Land Information and Analysis Program (see: *Federal register* 45 FR 58415).

By the end of fiscal 1981 sixteen states were covered at 1:24,000 scale, overall coverage at 1:24,000 scale stood at 77.2 percent and 1:100,000 scale at 65 percent (United States. Geological Survey 1982, pp. 31, 33). Kansas was one of the states finished in late 1981 ("Kansas" 1982, pp. 9-11). Even with all of the automation being integrated into the system it was still taking around four years and $10,000-$15,000 to produce a quad.

In 1981 USGS put together a plan for the issuance of provisional maps (p-maps) as substitutes for the standard quads, largely as a move to complete 1:24,000-scale coverage by some reasonable date, that is, between 1987 and 1989. P-maps were to be prepared for most remaining unmapped 7.5-minute quadrangle areas, including areas currently covered by 15-minute maps, and all unmapped Alaska 15-minute areas. These maps were to be published on a standard 7.5- x 7.5-minute format, at 1:24,000 or 1:25,000 scale (in accordance with agreements already made with states), and in color. The sheets would have a brown rather than a black "collar" of information, some hand lettering, roads in black, and no building symbols. Pre-field procedures would enable the survey to cut field work by 25 percent, there would be no rescribing, and editing would be at 70 percent, meaning that a sheet could be finished two or even three years earlier than with normal procedures and would cost 25 percent less ("Provisional mapping program" 1981, pp. 5-6). Any sheet not finished as of October 1, 1981, would follow the p-map schedule. In 1982 the first p-map (of Banner, Illinois) rolled off the presses. USGS had about 10,000 or 11,000 quads to complete by the end of the decade; it would use the p-map procedure and an increasing use of automation and electronic data processing to attempt to complete all quds. The first USGS computer-generated topographic map (of Birch Tree, Missouri) at 1:24,000 scale was produced in 1982 (Roney 1982).

Mary Rabbitt is writing a monumental history of the Geological Survey; see Rabbitt 1979 and 1980 for volumes 1 and 2.

Map of North and Central America:
Topographic Mapping, 1900-1970
(1:250,000 and more detailed)

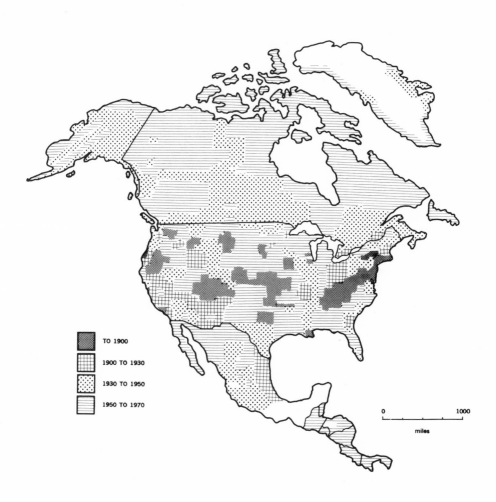

TO 1900

1900 TO 1930

1930 TO 1950

1950 TO 1970

0   1000

miles

NOTE: U. S. coverage greatly generalized. Base map: Aitoff's Equal Area Projection.

(Sources for map on page 110.)

Sources for Map of North and Central America
Topographic Mapping, 1900-1970
(1:250,000 and more detailed)

Greenland

Denmark. Geodetic Institute 1975, p. 38.

Karo 1955, plate II.

Platt 1945, map following p. 180.

UN. Dept. of Social Affairs 1949, map following p. 19.

Canada

Edinburgh Geographical Institute 1922, plate I.

Great Britain. War Office 1920, index map XII.

Platt 1945, map following p. 180.

Sebert 1970, p. 22.

UN. Dept of Economic and Social Affairs 1970, p. 95.

Central America and Mexico

Barrantes Ferrero 1967, pp. 43-44.

Guzmán 1967, pp. 58-59.

Núñez 1967, p. 78.

Pan American Union (all for Central America).

"Topographic map of Mexico" 1914, map following p. 434.

United States

"Cartography in the United States of America" 1951, pp. 88-89.

Mahoney 1950, p. 22.

United States. Dept. of the Interior 1901, map.

United States. Federal Mapping Task Force 1973, p. 69.

United States. National Resources Board 1934, map facing p. 76.

"Unmapped U.S." 1922, p. 24.

Zelinsky 1951, p. 66.

Part V
BIBLIOGRAPHY

BIBLIOGRAPHY

Bibliography is the geography of the book world.

—Pierce Butler

The bibliography that follows lists those works which the author found to be most valuable to the study of topographic mapping in the Americas, Australia, and New Zealand. Each item in this bibliography has been cited in the text in the appropriate discussion(s).

Several basic bibliographical tools were invaluable in assembling this bibliography. The *Bibliography of Cartography*, maintained by the Geography and Map Division of the Library of Congress and reproduced in book form in 1973 by G. K. Hall, with two-volume 1980 supplement, covers the pre-1980 time period very well. *Bibliographica cartographica* (and its predecessor *Biblioteca cartographica*, 1957-1973), Section VIII: Topographic and Landscape Cartography, 1974-1978, is another basic source, as is *Geo-Abstracts* (1970-1978), especially Section G: Remote Sensing and Cartography (1974-1982). *Reader's Guide* (1900-1909; 1915-1924), *Reader's Guide Supplement* (1907-1910), and *Poole* (1897-1906) were also searched.

Many periodicals have been included in this bibliography. The authority used to verify periodical names is:

> Harris, Chauncy D., and Fellman, Jerome D. 1980. *International list of geographic series.* 3rd ed. Chicago: Department of Geography, University of Chicago.

The form followed in this bibliography is as follows:

Book

> Author's last name, Author's first name. date. *Title.* Place: Publisher. (Series author. *Series title* no.)

Chapter or section of a book

> Author's last name, Author's first name. date. "Title." pp. ____ in: Author's last name, Author's first name (if different from section's author). *Title.* Place: Publisher.

Periodical article or symposium/conference article

a) journal title—no author given:

"Title of article." date. *Journal title* vol.:pp.

b) journal title—author given:

Author's last name, Author's first name. date. "Title." Journal author (if any). *Journal title* vol.:pp.

Month is given only if the volume or year of a periodical does not use consecutive numbering for all pages in a year, and thus the issue number or the month is required to find the article.

A mention of the idiosyncrasies of this bibliography may be helpful. Acronyms are placed at the beginning of letter groupings. The abbreviations "s.l." ("sine loco") and "s.n." ("sine nomine") are used to indicate "no place given" and "no publisher given" respectively. When any element in an entry is in doubt this is indicated by a parenthetical question mark.

Cross referencing has been kept to a minimum but there are a few—for example , at the abbreviation "UN" the reader is directed to "United Nations."

When reference to the bibliography entries is made in the text an abbreviated citation has been used—in most cases only the first one or two words of the full citation. Enough of the full citation has been given that the reader can easily locate the entry and avoid confusion among similar entries.

Names beginning with "de"—for example *de Mattos*—can be found alphabetized by the first word following the "de"—in the case of de Mattos, therefore, under "M."

It is all too easy for errors to creep into a bibliography. The author would appreciate notification of any errors discovered.

AGS. See: American Geographical Society of New York.

"ASP-ACSM Rocky Mountain Region meeting spotlights role of private sector." 1979. *Photogrammetric coyote* (March) 2(1):3, 10.

"Activities in the field of cartography in various countries 1964-1968 (reports by national organizations)." 1969. *Internationales Jahrbuch für Kartographie* 9:74-194.

Adams, Cyrus Cornelius. 1907. "Unexplored regions of the earth." *Harper's magazine* 114:305-11.

Adams, Kenneth T. 1941. "Federal surveys and maps." *American year book 1940:* 286-90.

Advisory Committee on Commonwealth Mapping. 1969. "Annual report to the Institute on Commonwealth mapping activities." *Australian surveyor* 22(6): 480-83.

Aero Service. 1982a. *Geodetic surveying.* Houston, TX.

Aero Service. 1982b. *SAR, synthetic aperture radar.* Houston, TX.

"Air mapping." 1956. *Military engineer* 48(323):227-28.

Akovetskiy, V. I. 1968. "Review of the status of radar aerial surveys abroad." *Geodesy and aerophotography* no. 4:276-79.

Alaskan Science Conference (3rd; Mt. Mckinley National Park, 1952). 1953. "Alaska mapping programs and needs, a symposium." *Surveying and mapping* 13(2):189-219.

Alcock, F. I. 1950. "Cartography in Canada since 1938." International Geographical Congress (16th; Lisbon, 1949). *Comptes rendus* 1:203-4.

Altenhofen, Robert E. 1971. "Small-scale mapping on a national level." *Canadian surveyor* 25(1):4-27.

Alvarado, Julio. 1900(?) *The Geographical and Exploring Commission of the Mexican republic.* Buffalo, NY(?): Gies & Co.

American Congress on Surveying and Mapping. Cartographic Division. 1972. "United States national cartographic report for 1969-1972." *Surveying and mapping* 32(3):369-91.

American Geographical Society of New York. 1930. *A catalogue of maps of Hispanic America, including maps in scientific periodicals and books, and sheet and atlas maps, with articles on the cartography of the several countries, and maps showing the extent and character of existing surveys. vol. 1. Maps of Mexico, Central America and the West Indies.* Map of Hispanic America, pub. no. 3. New York: AGS.

American Geographical Society of New York. 1932a. *A catalogue of maps of Hispanic America, including maps in scientific periodicals and books, and sheet and atlas maps, with articles on the cartography of the several countries, and maps showing the extent and character of existing surveys. vol. 2. Maps of South America, Colombia, Ecuador, Peru, and Bolivia.* Map of Hispanic America, pub. no. 3. New York: AGS.

American Geographical Society of New York. 1932b. *A catalogue of maps of Hispanic America, including maps in scientific periodicals and books, and sheet and atlas maps, with articles on the cartography of the several countries, and maps showing the extent and character of existing surveys. vol. 4. Maps of the Argentine Republic, Chile and Uruguay.* Map of Hispanic America, pub. no. 3. New York: AGS.

American Geographical Society of New York. 1933. *A catalogue of maps of Hispanic America, including maps in scientific periodicals and books, and sheet and atlas maps, with articles on the cartography of the several countries, and maps showing the extent and character of existing surveys. vol. 3. Maps of Venezuela, Guianas, Brazil, and Paraguay.* Map of Hispanic America, pub. no. 3. New York: AGS.

American Society of Civil Engineers. Surveying and Mapping Division. Task Committee on Status of Surveying and Mapping. 1958. "The status of surveying and mapping in the United States." *Surveying and mapping* 18(4):431-37.

Andregg, Charles H. 1976. "Status of federal mapping in 1976." American Congress on Surveying and Mapping. *Proceedings* 36:385-88.

Anguiano, Angel. 1913-14. "Cartografía mexicana." Sociedad Mexicana de Geografía y Estadística. *Boletin* 6(2):539-44; 7(3):139-48; 7(4):168-92.

Antioquía (Prov.), Colombia. Departamento Administrativo de Planeación. 1969. *Índice cartográfico de Antioquía.* Medellín, Colombia.

Arce, Arturo Ayalá. 1967. "Report on Chile." *World cartography* 8:13-16.

Arden-Close, Charles Frederick. 1905. "The ideal topographic map." *Geographical journal* 25(6):633-47.

Argentine Republic. Instituto Geográfico Militar. 1927. *Catálogo del material cartográfico.* Buenos Aires: Talleres gráficos del Instituto Geográfico Militar.

Argentine Republic. Instituto Geográfico Militar. 1940. *Catálogo de las publicaciones editadas por el Instituto Geográfico Militar.* Buenos Aires: Talleres Gráficos del Instituto Geográfico Militar.

Argentine Republic. Instituto Geográfico Militar. 1943. *Catálogo del material cartográfico.* Buenos Aires: Talleres Gráficos del Instituto Geográfico Militar.

Argentine Republic. Instituto Geográfico Militar. 1947. *Catálogo de publicaciones cartográficas.* 1st ed. Buenos Aires.

Argentine Republic. Instituto Geográfico Militar. 1955. *Memoria sobre los trabajos geodésico-topográficos y cartográficos realizados en el lapso 1°. de enero de 1944-31 de diciembre 1954; ... VI Asamblea General del I.P.G.H., Mexico, 1955.* Buenos Aires.

Argentine Republic. Instituto Geográfico Militar. 1956. "La carta topográfica del país: A. Labor cientifica del I.G.M.B. Reseña histórica." *Atlas, órgano official* 3(3):34-38, 59-60.

Arjona Esponda, Belizario. 1952. *How to complete the geographical map and cadastral survey of Colombia in a reasonable time.* St. Louis, MO: US Aeronautical Chart and Information Center.

Arredondo, José María. 1957. "La carta de la República Argentina." Academia Argentina de Geografía. *Anales* 1:90-95.

Asanachinta, Phoon Phon. 1974. "Topographic mapping of humid tropical Asia." pp. 13-26 in: *Natural resources of humid tropical Asia.* Paris: Unesco. (Unesco natural resources research 12.)

Australia. Division of National Mapping. 1971. *Report on work completed during the period 1945-1970.* Canberra.

Australia. National Library. 1966. *Index atlas to maps in series in the Map Collection, National Library of Australia.* Canberra.

Australia. National Mapping Office. 1954. "National Mapping Office." *Cartography* 1:20-24.

Australia. National Mapping Office. 1955a. *Map catalogue.* 1st ed. Canberra.

Australia. National Mapping Office. 1955b. "Topographic mapping in Australia." *World cartography* 3:41-47.

Australian maps. 1968- . Canberra: National Library of Australia.

"Availability of maps." 1949. *New Zealand survey draughtsmen's journal* 1(4): 143-44. See also: *New Zealand geographer,* October 1946.

Avery, Thomas Eugene. 1968. *Interpretation of aerial photographs.* 2nd ed. Minneapolis: Burgess.

Bailey, Jean. 1970. "Mapping the Americas: a summary." *Military engineer* 62(410):399-400.

Baker, J. N. L. 1967. *A history of geographical discovery and exploration.* 4th ed. New York: Cooper Square.

Baldock, E. Douglas. 1971. "Cartographic relief portrayal." *Internationales Jahrbuch für Kartographie* 11:75-78.

Ballew, G. I., and Lyon, R. J. P. 1977. "The display of Landsat data at large scales by matrix printer." *Photogrammetric engineering and remote sensing* 43(9): 1147-50.

Barrantes Ferrero, Mario. 1954. "El Instituto Geográfico de Costa Rica." *Revista cartográfica* 3(3):151-57.

Barrantes Ferrero, Mario. 1967. "Progress report on cartographic activities in Costa Rica." *World cartography* 8:40-44.

Barrett, Eric Charles, and Curtis, Leonard. 1977. *Environmental remote sensing 2: practices and problems; papers presented at the Second Bristol Symposium on Remote Sensing, Department of Geography, University of Bristol.* New York: Crane Russak.

Barriga, Guillermo. 1972. "El levantamiento de la carta nacional." Sociedad Geográfica de Lima. *Boletín* 91:49-53.

Bartholomew, John George. 1891. "The mapping of the world. Part IV—North America." *Scottish geographical magazine* 7:586-611.

Barton, Phillip L. 1977. "A bibliography of material relating to surveying and mapping of New Zealand." Special Libraries Association. Geography and Map Division. *Bulletin* no. 109:24-32. See also: *The globe* no. 8:14-22.

Barton, Phillip L. 1978a. "New Zealand metric topographical maps." Association of Canadian Map Libraries. *Bulletin* 27:8-10.

Barton, Phillip L. 1978b. "New Zealand topographical maps, a status report." Western Association of Map Libraries. *Information bulletin* 9(3):219-21.

Barton, Phillip L. 1980. "The history of the mapping of New Zealand." *Map collector* (June) 11:28-35.

Barton, Phillip L. 1981."Map collections & map librarianship in New Zealand: a synopsis." *Library trends* 29(3):537-46.

Baskin, C. R. 1970. "State agency topographic mapping responsibilities in Texas." ACSM-ASP Technical Convention (Denver, 1970). *Papers*. pp. 1-6.

Baskin, C. R. 1980. *Modern topographic mapping of Texas: an historical sketch.* Austin: Texas Dept. of Water Resources. (Texas Dept. of Water Resources. *Report* 247.)

Baudoin, Alain. 1980. "Utilisation des images SPOT pour la cartographie topographique des pays industriels et des pays neufs." *International archives of photogrammetry* 23(B4):56-65.

Baughman, Robert W. 1961. *Kansas in maps.* Topeka: Kansas State Historical Society.

Bechert, Charles H. 1956. "Indiana's new mapping program." *Surveying and mapping* 16(4):467-71.

Beck, Francis J. 1979. "USGS digital cartographic pilot projects." American Congress on Surveying and Mapping (39th; 1979). *Proceedings*, pp. 300-5.

Bennett, Charles F. 1968. "Notes on Latin American cartography and geography." Special Libraries Association. Geography and Map Division. *Bulletin* no. 74:7-14.

Bergquist, Wenonah E. et al. 1978. *Worldwide directory of national earth-science agencies.* Washington, DC: US Government Printing Office. (US Geological Survey. *Circular* 771.)

Bergquist, Wenonah E. et al. 1981. *Worldwide directory of national earth science agencies and related international organizations.* Washington, DC: US Government Printing Office. (US Geological Survey. *Circular* 834.)

Berry, Ralph Moore. 1976. "History of geodetic leveling in the United States." *Surveying and mapping* 36(2):137-53.

Bertrand, Alejandro. 1915. "La cartographie officielle au Chili en 1913." International Geographical Congress (10th; Rome, 1913). *Proceedings*, pp. 662-65.

Bettex, Albert. 1960. *The discovery of the world.* London: Thames and Hudson.

"Bibliografía y cartografía centro-americanas." 1913. *Centro-America* 5:182-96.

"Bibliografía y cartografía de Nicaragua." 1914. *Centro-America* 6:548-61.

Biddle, D. S.; Milne, A. K.; and Shortle, D. A. 1974. *The language of topographic maps.* Milton, Queensland: Jacaranda Press.

Birch, Thomas William. 1964. *Maps, topographical and statistical.* 2nd ed. Oxford: Clarendon Press.

Boaga, Giovanni. 1952. "Geografìa e cartografìa a grande scala." Sociedad Geográfica, Madrid. *Boletín* 89(1,2,3): 85-93. Also in: Società geogràfica italiana. *Bollettino*, ser. 8 5(fasc. 5):369-75.

Bock, Alan. 1979. "Mark Hurd—pioneers in high-altitude photography." *Photogrammetric coyote* 2(1):6-7.

Bocksette, W. 1965. "Bench marks and levelling in Western Australia." *Cartographers bulletin* (March), p. 408.

Bogotá. Biblioteca Nacional. 1923."Catálogo topográfico de de los mapas, planos... de la Biblioteca Nacional." *Revista de la Biblioteca Nacional* 1:170-75, 190-205.

Böhme, R. 1971. "The status of world topographic mapping." *Kartographische Nachrichten* 21(4):156-58.

Bomford, A. G. 1960-61. "Surveying in northern Australia." *Chartered surveyor* 93:321-24, 509-10.

Borgerding, L. H. 1966. "Planning the National Map Revision Program." *Surveying and mapping* 26(2):247-51.

Bowie, William. 1936. "No maps in a mapping age." *Photogrammetric engineering* 2(1):36-39. Also in: *Civil engineering* 6(2):88-90.

Bowie, William. 1938. "Taking stock of national mapping." *Civil engineering* 8(4): 266-67.

Boyer, Marc. 1953. "Panel on Arctic mapping: opening remarks." *Photogrammetric engineering* 19(3):375-80.

Bradford, James Edward Stratton. 1952. *The geodetic triangulation and trigonmetrical survey of Southern Rhodesia, 1897-1952.* Salisbury: [s.n.]

Brandenberger, Arthur J. 1970. "World-wide mapping survey." *Photogrammetric engineering* 36(4):355-59.

Brandenberger, Arthur J. 1976. "Study on the status of world cartography." *World cartography* 14:71-96.

Brasseur, Gerard. 1974. "La cartographie de la Guyane française." Comité français de cartographie. *Bulletin* 60(2):56-58.

Brazil. Commissão da Carta Geral do Imperio. 1877. *Estudios acêrca da organizacão da Carta geografica e da história físca e política do Brazil.* Rio de Janeiro: Typografía Nacional.

Brazil. Conselho Nacional de Geografía. 1951. "Cartography in Brazil." *World cartography* 1:61-68.

Brazil. Conselho Nacional de Geografía. Divisão de Cartografía. 1957. *Trabalhos técnicos da Divisão de Cartografía.* Rio de Janeiro.

Brazil. Diretoria do Serviço Geográfico do Exército. 1954. *Catálogo das cartas e obras diversas.* Rio de Janeiro (?).

Brazil. Superintendência do Desenvolvimento do Nordeste. Divisão de Cartografía. 1965. *Bibliografía cartográfica do Nordeste.* Recife: Divisão de Documentação.

Brocklebank, R. A. 1966. "The use of photogrammetry in integrated surveys." *Canadian surveyor* 20(2):66-72.

Brown, Edward B. 1955. "On duty with the Inter-American Geodetic Survey." *Journal of the Coast and Geodetic Survey* no. 6:57-64.

Brown, Lloyd Arnold. 1949. *The story of maps.* Boston: Little, Brown.

Brown, Lloyd Arnold. 1953. "Maps—a necessary medium to world progress." *Surveying and mapping* 13(3):276-85.

Brunner, Frederico. 1939. "Historia de la fotogrammetría en Chile." Chile. Ejército. *Memoria* 7:301-15.

Bubberman, Ir. F. C. et al. 1973. *Links with the past: the history of cartography of Surniam 1500-1971.* Amsterdam: Theatrum Orbis Terrarum B. V.

Buhler, F. W. 1948. "Topographical surveys." pp. 298-308 in: Boyd, Louise A. et al. *The coast of northeast Greenland with hydrographic studies on the Greenland Sea, the Louise A. Boyd Arctic Expeditions of 1937 and 1938.* New York: American Geographical Society. (American Geographical Society of New York. *Special publication* 30.)

Burnside, Clifford Donald. 1979. *Mapping from aerial photographs.* New York: Halsted Press.

Caceres, Carlos Rivera. 1967. "Report on cartographic activities in Honduras." *World cartography* 8:60-62.

Calver, James L. 1974. "New directions in topographic mapping." pp. 46-48 in: *Earth science in the public service: a symposium presented during the dedication ceremonies, U.S. Geological Survey National Center, Reston, Virginia, July 10-13, 1974.* Washington, DC: US Government Printing Office. (US Geological Survey. *Professional paper* 921.)

Calvo, Carlos A. 1952. "El Instituto Panamericano de Geografía e Historia." *Revista cartográfica* 1:281.

Calvo, Carlos A. 1956. "Como se hace una carta." Argentine Republic. Instituto Geográfico Militar. *Atlas, órgano oficial* 3(3):26-27.

Canada. Archives. 1912. *Catalogue of maps, plans and charts in the Map Room of the Dominion Archives ...* Ottawa: Government Printing Bureau. (*Publications of the Canadian Archives* 8.)

Canada. Board on Geographical Names. 1922. *Catalogue of the maps in the collection of the Geographic Board.* Ottawa: F. A. Acland.

Canada. Bureau of Geology and Topography. 1931. *Published maps (1917-1930 inclusive).* Ottawa: F. A. Acland.

Canada. Bureau of Geology and Topography. 1945. *Published maps (1917-1945 inclusive).* Ottawa: Bureau of Geology and Topography, Mines and Geology Branch.

Canada. Dept. of Energy, Mines, and Resources. 1976. *How a topographic map is made.* Ottawa: Information Canada (?) (M52-41/1975).

Canada. Dept. of the Interior. 1916. *Geographical publications of the Department of the Interior.* Ottawa: Government Printing Bureau.

Canada. Geographic Board. 1918. *Catalogue of maps in the collection of the Geographic Board.* Ottawa.

Canada. Geological Survey. 1909. *Annual report.* Ottawa.

Canada. Surveys and Engineering Branch. 1939. *Catalogue of maps, plans, and publications* ... 7th ed. Ottawa: J. O. Patenaude.

Canada. Surveys and Mapping Branch. 1951. "Cartography in Canada." *World cartography* 1:69-80.

Canada. Surveys and Mapping Branch. 1957. "Surveying and mapping activities by the Federal government." *Canadian surveyor* 13(9):571-76.

Canada. Surveys and Mapping Branch. 1966(?) *Sequence of mapping operations.* Ottawa.

Canada. Surveys and Mapping Branch. 1982a. *1:50 000 digital mapping five year program = cartographie numérique, plan quinquennal.* Ottawa.

Canada. Surveys and Mapping Branch. 1982b. *1:50,000 topographic data in digital form-données topographique sous forme numérique.* Ottawa.

Canada. Surveys Branch. 1917. *List of maps and publications issued by the Topographical Surveys Branch and available for distribution.* Ottawa: J. de L. Taché.

Canada. Surveys Branch. 1930. *Catalogue of maps, plans and publications of the Topographical Survey.* 5th ed. Ottawa: F. A. Acland.

Canada. Topographical Survey. 1903-04. *Report.* Ottawa.

Canada. Topographical Survey. 1925. *Maps, plans and publications of the Topographical Survey of Canada.* 3rd ed. Ottawa: F. A. Acland.

Canadian map makers. 1975. Montreal: Dept. of Energy, Mines, and Resources.

Carbonnell, Maurice. 1965. "Photographies aériennes et cartes topographiques." *Science et nature* no. 71:25-37.

Cardoze, Nydia M., and Tempone, Consuelo. 1978. *Guía para investigadores de Panamá.* Mexico City(?): Pan American Institute of Geography and History. (Pan American Institute of Geography and History. *Publication* 341.)

Carlberg, Berthold. 1931. "Die Kartierung der Vereinigten Staaten von Amerika." *Petermanns Mitteilungen* 77:229.

Carlberg, Berthold. 1935. "Die Karte von Uruguay in 1:50,000." *Petermanns Mitteilungen* 81:190.

Carlton, E. W. 1949. "United States needs large-scale mapping program to meet postwar demands." *Civil engineering* 19(5):37-39.

Carmichael, L. D. 1969. "The relief of map making." *Cartographic journal* 6(1): 18-20.

Caro Molina, Fernando. 1954. *De Agustín Codazzi a Manuel María Paz.* Calí, Colombia: Editorial La Voz Católica.

Carroll, John. 1945. "Canadian trimetrogon photography." US Army Map Service. *Bulletin* 20:2-10.

Carroll, John.1947. "Photogrammetric mapping operations in Canada." *Canadian surveyor* 9(6):7-17.

"Cartas geográficas publicadas en Chile (1951-1954)." 1958. *Informaciones geográficas* 4(1):102-9.

"Cartografía chilena." 1955. *Revista geográfica de Chile* no. 13:25-31.

"Cartografía extranjera: Bolivia. Austria. Hungary." 1913. Argentine Republic. Instituto Geográfico Militar. *Anuario* 2:23-56.

"Cartography in Argentina." 1953. *World cartography* 2:43-61.

"Cartography in the Americas." 1951. *World cartography* 1:49-59.

"Cartography in the United States of America." 1951. *World cartography* 1:81-97.

Cartography in western Australia. 1946. Perth: Institute of Cartographers of Western Australia.

Castelnuovo-Tedesco, Giovanni. 1965. "Nota sullo sviluppo della cartografìa e dell' aerofotogrammetrìa nei paesi dell' America Latina." Associazione italiana di cartografìa. *Bollettino* no. 5:20-22.

Castro, Cristovão Leite de. 1940. "Atualidade de cartografía brasileira." *Revista brasileira de geografía* 2:462-70.

Castro, Christovem Leite de. 1945. "Cartography in Brazil." *Surveying and mapping* 5:8-13.

Chapman, Edward Francis. 1895. "The triangulation of Africa." *Geographical journal* 5:467-70.

Cheesman, A. J. "The 1:10,000 Pentateuch." *Cartography* 11(4):223-27.

Chile. Instituto Geográfico Militar. 19–. *Anuario.* Santiago de Chile.

Chile. Instituto Geográfico Militar. 19–. *Catálogo de mapas y cartas para la venta.* Santiago de Chile.

Chile. Instituto Geográfico Militar. 1950. "Breve exposición de los trabajos geodésicos y topográficos del Instituto Geográfico Militar." *Revista geográfica de Chile* no. 4:97-110.

Chile. Instituto Geográfico Militar. 1955. *Informe nacional a la VIII Reunion Panamericana de Consulta sobre Cartografía y Geografía e Historia.* Mexico City.

Chile. Instituto Geográfico Militar. 1975. "Mapas y levantamientos a escala media y grande y mapas y levantamientos catastrales." Chile. Institute Geográfico Militar. *Boletín informativo* no. 3:3-23.

Chile. Instituto Geográfico Militar. 1978. *Guía para investigadores de Chile.* Mexico City: Pan American Institute of Geography and History.

Chipman, Kenneth G.; and Hanson, George. 1944. "Mapping by the Bureau of Geology and Topography." Canadian Institute of Mining and Metallurgy. *Transactions* 47:99-113.

Close, Charles Frederick Arden. See: Arden-Close, Charles Frederick.

Cluerg, George. 1933. "The cartography of the Mexico-Vera Cruz regions." Geographical Society of Philadelphia. *Bulletin* 21(1):115-22.

Cobb, David Allen. 1971. *Vermont maps prior to 1900; an annotated cartobibliography.* Burlington, VT: Vermont Historical Society.

Colbert, Leo Otis. 1947. "Maps and the needs of our national welfare." *Surveying and mapping* (Jan.-June) 7:5-9.

"Collaborative mapping in Chile." 1956. *Military engineer* 48(322):139-40.

"Collaborative mapping in Costa Rica." 1956. *Military engineer* 48(325):385-86.

"Collaborative mapping in Guatemala." 1957. *Military engineer* 49(328):126-27.

"Collaborative mapping in Nicaragua." 1957. *Military engineer* 49(329):215-16.

"Collaborative mapping in Peru." 1957. *Military engineer* 49(330):290-95.

Collier, Heloise. 1972. "A short history of Ordnance Survey contouring with particular reference to Scotland." *Cartographic journal* 9(1):55-58.

Collins, Arthur. 1951. "High flying helicopters aid mapping in Yukon." *Canadian aviation* 24:16-18, 42, 44.

Colombia. Instituto Geográfico "Agustín Codazzi." 1955. *Informe de progreso de las actividades cartográficas de Colombia a la VI Asamblea General del Instituto Panamericana de Geografía e Historía (VII Reunion de Consulta sobre Cartografía).* Bogotá.

Colombia. Instituto Geográfico "Agustín Codazzi." 1964. *Informe estudios recursos básicos, Colombia (detallado) enero a septiembre 1964.* Bogotá.

Colombia. Oficina de Longitudes y Fronteras. 1921. *Coordenadas geográficas deter-minadas por la Oficina de Longitudes (República de Colombia).* Bogotá: Imprenta del Estado Mayor General.

"Completion of the topographic map of the alluvial valley of the Mississippi." 1934. *Geographical review* 24:651-52.

Conferencia Argentina de Coordinación Cartográfica (1st; Buenos Aires, 1936). 1937. *Primera Conferencia Argentina de Coordinación Cartográfica, Buenos Aires, 1936.* Buenos Aires: Imprenta y Casa Editorial "Conti."

Congreso Nacional de Cartografía. 1951-. *Memoria.* Buenos Aires.

Conley, Robert Leslie. 1956. "Men who measure the earth; surveyors from 18 new world nations invade trackless jungles and climb snow peaks to map Latin America." *National geographic magazine* 109(3):335-62.

Consultation on Geodesy, Aeronautical Charts and Topographic Maps (1st; Washington, DC, 1943). 1945. *Primera Reunion de Consulta sobre Geodesía, Cartas Aeronáuticas y Mapas Topográficos.* Mexico City: Pan American Institute of Geography and History. (Pan American Institute of Geography and History. *Publication* 76.)

Consultation on Geodesy, Aeronautical Charts and Topographic Maps (4th; Buenos Aires, 1948). 1950. *Anales.* Buenos Aires: [s.n.]

"Contemporary cartography: Department of Lands and Survey." 1958. *Cartography* 2:105-7.

"Contemporary cartography: Royal Australian Survey Corps." 1956. *Cartography* 1(4):151-60.

Cook, Reuben D. 1976. "Problems, shortfalls, and needs of topographic mapping." American Congress on Surveying and Mapping. *Proceedings* 36:420-30.

Corrêa Filho, Virgílio. 1957. "Exposicão cartográfico." *Boletín geográfica* 15: 717-19.

Costa Rica. Instituto Geográfico Nacional. 1954. *Mapas topográficos del territorio nacional.* [S.l.]

Couzinet, Marceau. 1949. "Le problème de l'uniformisation des signes conventionnels sur les cartes topographiques." International Geographical Congress (16th; Lisbon, 1949). *Proceedings* 1:189-94.

Crocker, W. T. 1975. "Mapping Australia." *Australian library journal* 24:106-10.

Crone, Gerald Roe. 1948. Early map makers of Switzerland and the Netherlands." *Geographical journal* 112:227-28.

Crone, Gerald Roe. 1953. *Maps and their makers; an introduction to the history of cartography.* London: Hutchinson University Library.

Crone, Gerald Roe. 1968. *Maps and their makers, an introduction to the history of cartography.* 4th rev. ed. London: Hutchinson University Library.

Cumberland, Kenneth B. 1946. "The status of topographic mapping in new Zealand." *Geographical review* 36:135-36.

Curnow, Irene J. 1929. "Some contrasts in standard topographic maps of Great Britain and the United States of America." *Geography* 15:274-81.

Curnow, Irene J. 1930. *The world mapped; being a short history of attempts to map the world from antiquity to the twentieth century.* London: S. Praed.

Curran, J. P. 1967. "Cartographic relief portrayal." *Cartographer* 4(1):28-38.

Dainville, Francois de. 1962. "De la profundeur à l'altitude; des origines marines de l'expression cartographique du relief terrestre par cotes et çourbes de niveau." *Internationales Jahrbuch für Kartographie* 2:151-62. Also in: *Surveying and mapping* 30(3):389-403, 1970 (see Dainville 1970), and in: International Colloquium of Maritime History (2nd; 1957). *Travaux.*

Dainville, François de. 1964. *Le langage des géographes: terms, signes, couleurs des cartes anciennes, 1500-1800.* Paris: A. J. Picard.

Dainville, François de. 1970. "From the depths to the heights." *Surveying and mapping* 30(3):389-403.

Dake, C. Laurence. 1925. *Interpretation of topographic and geologic maps with special reference to determination of structure.* New York: McGraw-Hill.

"Danish topographical maps of Greenland." 1956. *Polar record* 8(52):39-42.

Davis, William Morris. 1922. "Topographical maps of the United States." *Scientific monthly* 15:557-60.

Davis, William Morris. 1924. "Shaded topographic maps." *Science* 60:325-27.

De la Barra, Ignacio L. 1935. "Breve reseña sobre la cartografía mexicana." Sociedad Mexicana de Geografía y Estadística. *Boletín* 44(9):357-68.

Debenham, Frank. 1960. *Discovery and exploration, an atlas-history of man's wanderings.* Garden City, NY: Doubleday.

Defense Mapping Agency. Topographic Center. 1973. *Glossary of mapping, charting, and geodetic terms.* Washington, DC: US Government Printing Office.

Denmark. Geodetic Institute. 1975(?) *Maps of Denmark.* Copenhagen.

DeVries, B. F. 1974. "The colonial surveyors of New Zealand—1800-76; an overview." *New Zealand surveyor* 37(5):509-17.

Dianderas, Gerardo. 1936. "Servicio Geográfico del Ejército y la carta nacional del Perú." Sociedad Geográfica de Lima. *Boletín* 53:42-61.

Doyle, Frederick J. 1972. "Can satellite photography contribute to topographic mapping?" *World cartography* 12:32-42. Also in: US Geological Survey. *Journal of research* 1(3):315-25. See also: pp. 153-60 in: Holz, R. K. 1973. *The surveillant science: remote sensing of the environment.* Boston: Houghton Mifflin.

Ebner, Herwig. 1975. "1:50,000 mapping in Canada." *Bildmessung und Luftbildwesen* 43(2):78-79.

Edinburgh Geographical Institute. 1922. *The Times survey atlas of the world.* London: The Times.

Ehrenberg, Ralph. 1977. "Taking the measure of the land." *Prologue* (3):128-50.

Ehrenberg, Ralph. 1982. *Archives & manuscripts: maps and architectural drawings.* Chicago: Society of American Archivists. *(SAA basic manual series)*

El Salvador. Dirección General de Cartografía. 1963. *Índice de publicaciones.* San Salvador.

El Salvador. Instituto Geográfico Nacional "Ingeniero Pablo Arnoldo Guzmán." 1977. *Guía para investigadores, República de El Salvador.* Mexico City(?): Pan American Institute of Geography and History.

El Salvador. Sección Nacional del Instituto Panamericano de Geografía e Historia. Comisión de Cartografía. 1961(?) *Informe de progreso de las actividades cartográficas de la República de El Salvador ...* San Salvador.

Émanaud, M. 1938. "Revue de topographie." *Revue générale des sciences* 49(17): 456-67.

Escoria Marín, Walter. 1972. "Importancia y necesidad de una carta topográfica nacional de Colombia." Sociedad Geográfica de Colombia. *Boletín* 27(104): 374-80.

Espenshade, Edward B., and Schytt, S. Valter. 1956. *Problems in mapping snow cover.* Wilmette IL: US Army Corps of Engineers. (US Army Corps of Engineers. Snow, Ice, and Permafrost Research Establishment. *Research report* 27.)

Ewing, Karen J., and Marcus, Melvin G. 1966. "Cartographic representation and symbolization in glacier mapping." *Canadian journal of earth sciences* 3(6): 761-69.

Falk, A. L., and Miller, K. L. 1975. *Worldwide directory of national earth-science agencies.* Washington, DC: US Government Printing Office. (US Geological Survey. *Circular* 716.)

Federal Map Users' Conference on National Topographic Program (Washington, DC, 1964). 1965(?). *Proceedings.* Washington, DC: [s.n.]

"Federal mapping and government reorganization." 1938. *Journal of geomorphology* 1:244-46.

Feild, Lance. 1982. *Map user's sourcebook.* New York: Oceana.

Fennell, Earle J. 1954. "Planning for national map coverage." *Surveying and mapping* 14(3):277-82.

Field, Richard M., and Stetson, Harlan T. 1942. *Map reading and navigation, an introduction.* New York: Van Nostrand.

Filchner, Wilhelm; Przybyllok, Erich; and Hagen, Toni. 1957. *Route-mapping and position-locating in unexplored regions.* New York: Academic Press.

Finch, James Kip. 1920. *Topographic maps and sketch mapping.* New York: Wiley.

Finch, James Kip. 1925. "Our indebtedness to the old surveyors." *Military engineer* 17(94):320-25.

FitzGerald, Gerald. 1945. "Surveying and mapping in the Americas." *Surveying and mapping* 1:26-29.

FitzGerald, Gerald. 1949. *Modern mapping methods.* Washington, DC(?): [s.n.]

FitzGerald, Gerald. 1951a. *Surveying and mapping in Alaska.* Washington, DC: US Government Printing Office. (US Geological Survey. *Circular* 101.)

FitzGerald, Gerald. 1951b. *Surveying and mapping in peace and war.* Washington, DC(?): [s.n.]

FitzGerald, Gerald. 1952. "New reconnaissance maps of Alaska." *Surveying and mapping* 12(4):376-81.

FitzGerald, Gerald. 1953. "Mapping in the Arctic." *Photogrammetric engineering* 19(3):406-8.

FitzGerald, Gerald. 1956. "The national mapping program—a review of progress." *Surveying and mapping* 16(4):447-58.

FitzGerald, Gerald. 1957. "New tools for mapping in Arctic Alaska." *Canadian surveyor* 13(8):484-90.

FitzGerald, Gerald. 1960. "New maps of Arctic Alaska." *Geographical review* 50(1):108-9.

FitzGerald, Lawrence. 1948. "Mapping a continent." *Australian geographical magazine* 14(10):8-15.

FitzGerald, Lawrence. 1951a. "An approach to national mapping, with due regard to the factors of developments in technique and manpower potential." Australian and New Zealand Association for the Advancement of Science (28th; Brisbane, 1951). *Report* pp. 124-30.

FitzGerald, Lawrence. 1951b. "National mapping with due regard to the factors of developments in techniques and man power potential." *Australian geographer* 5(9):242-49.

FitzGerald, Lawrence. 1980. *Lebanon to Labuan: a story of mapping by the Australian Survey Corps, World War II (1939 to 1945).* Melbourne, Australia: J. G. Holmes Ltd.

Fleming, E. A. 1971. "Photo maps at 1:50,000 for northern Canada." *Canadian surveyor* 25(4):378-88.

Fleming, E. A., 1975. "Canada sits for its portrait: maps, photomaps, a recent development in cartography, add new and useful detail to the country's profile." *Geoscope* pp. 5-7.

Fleming, Elizabeth. 1978. "Photomapping in review: progress in geometry, reproduction and enhancement." *American cartographer* 5(2):141-48.

Fletcher, L. N. 1968. "Integration of surveys." *Australian surveyor* 22(4):311-17.

Flötner, H. A. 1963. "Der gegenwartige Stand der Kartographie in Kanada." *Kartographische Nachrichten* 13(5):125-36.

Flotte de Roquevaire, René de. 1909. *Cinq mois de triangulation au Maroc.* Alger: Typ. A. Jourdan.

Fontanges, G. de. 1948. *Topographie.* Paris: A. Colin.

Forster, B. C. 1978. "Priorities for mapping in a developing country." *Australian surveyor* 29(1):37-48.

Fox, James W. 1978. "Topographic maps as national images." *The globe* no. 9:58-64.

Fraguela, Ernesto Medina. 1909. "Monografía de la Carta Militar de Chile." American Scientific Congress (1st; Santiago de Chile, 1908). *Proceedings* 6:90-122.

France. Armée. Service géographique. 1931. *La carte de l'empire colonial français.* Paris: G. Lang.

France. Institut géographique national. 1950. *La nouvelle carte de France au 20.000ᵉ; son utilité, son execution.* Paris.

Francis, D. G. 1964. "The organization of mapping activities." *New Zealand Geographical Society record* no. 37:8-11.

Francis, D. G. 1966. "Topographical mapping." *New Zealand Geographical Society record* no. 38:11-13.

Freeman, P. H.; Peacock, H. L.; and Weil, P. J. 1963. "An inventory of Latin American mapping." Special Libraries Association. Geography and Map Division. *Bulletin* no. 53:3-5.

Frenzel, Konrad. 1958. "Kartographie in Australien." *Nachrichten aus dem Karten- und Vermessungswesen* no. 6:5-33.

Frenzel, Konrad. 1962. "Mapas topográficos." *Boletim geográfico* 20(168):295-96.

Friis, Herman Ralph. 1952. *Geographical exploration and topographical mapping by the United States government, 1777-1902, as reflected in official records.* Washington, DC: National Archives. Also in: *Revista geográfica* 14:107-11 (in Spanish: "Exploración geográfica y levantamiento de cartas topográficos del gobierno de los Estados Unidos de America de 1777 a 1902."), 1954.

Friis, Herman Ralph. 1976. "Organization and reorganization of Federal mapping activities, a brief history: 1774-1976." American Congress on Surveying and Mapping. *Proceedings* 36:358.

Fry, Clifton J. 1975. "National mapping requirements—status and goals." American Congress on Surveying and Mapping (Fall Convention). *Proceedings*, 1975, pp. 338-46.

Fuechsel, Charles F. 1944. "Status of topographic mapping in Alaska." American Congress on Surveying and Mapping. *Bulletin* 4(3):13-16.

Fuechsel, Charles F. 1949. "Cartographic activities of the U.S. Geological Survey." *Surveying and mapping* 9(3):174-82.

Fuechsel, Charles F. 1953. "Some current trends in cartography in the United States of America." *World cartography* 3:17-24.

Fuechsel, Charles F. 1967. "Current trends of cartography in the United States." American Society of Cartographers. *Bulletin* 2(2):3-5, 8-10.

Gamble, S. G. 1957. "Mapping the island of Newfoundland." *Canadian surveyor* 13:333-36.

Gamble, S. G. 1964. "Aerial photographic coverage of Canada." *Photogrammetric engineering* 30(4):573-78.

Gannett, Henry. 1892a. "The mapping of the United States." *Scottish geographical magazine* 8:150-53.

Gannett, Henry. 1892b. "The mother maps of the United States." *National geographic magazine* 4:101-16.

Gannett, Henry. 1898. "The aims and methods of cartography, with especial reference to the topographic maps now under construction in Maryland by the United States Geological Survey, in co-operation with the Maryland Geological Survey." Maryland. Geological Survey. *Special publication* 2(3a): 245-335.

García, A. Montano. 1967. "Brief report on the state of cartography in Bolivia." *World cartography* 8:1-2.

García, Benjamin Aparicio. 1913. *La carte de la République Argentina; mémoire présenté au xeme Congrés international de géographie, Rome, 27 mars-4 avril 1913* ... Buenos Aires: Établissement graphique de l'Institut géographique militaire. (Argentine Republic. Instituto Geográfico Militar. *Publicaciones*).

Gardini, Marilia Junia de Almeida. 1979. "Brazilian map sources." Society of University Cartographers. *Bulletin* 13(1):42-51. Also in: *Revista da Escola de Biblioteconomia da Universidade Federal de Minas Gerais* 6(1):45-66, March 1977 (in Portuguese: "Fontes de informação cartográfica na Brazil").

Gast, Pablo. 1922. "Aerofotogrametría." Argentine Republic. Instituto Geográfico Militar. *Anuario* 4:99-115.

Geomorfología, aerofotointerpretación, hidrología y climatología, cartografía y nombres geográficos, metodología geográfica. 1967(?) v. 3 of: International Geographical Union. Conferencia Regional Latino-americana (Mexico, 1966). *Proceedings.* Mexico City(?): Sociedad Mexicana de Geografía y Estadística.

Gertsen, W. M. 1970. "Danish topographic mapping." *Cartographic journal* 7(2): 113- 21.

Gill, William H. 1945. "Key to a better understanding of maps." *Military engineer* 37:58-60, 102-4, 402-5.

Goetzmann, William H. 1959. *Army exploration in the American West, 1803-1863.* New Haven: Yale University Press.

Goetzmann, William H. 1966. *Exploration and empire: the explorer and the scientist in the winning of the American West.* New York: Alfred A. Knopf.

Goodrick, B. E. 1975. "Contemporary cartography: National map series 1:100,000." *Cartography* 9(1):35-38.

Goodrick, B. E. 1976. "The national topographic map series at 1:250,000 scale." *Cartography* 9(4):231-35.

Granados Garay, Rigoberto. 1977. *Guía para investigadores de Honduras.* Mexico City: Instituto Panamericana de Geografía e Historia. (Pan American Institute of Geography and History. *Publication* 344.)

Great Britain. Colonial Office. 1946. *Central organization for geodetic and topographical surveys in the colonial empire.* London: HMSO. (Great Britain. Colonial Office. *Colonial* 200.)

Great Britain. Colonial Survey Committee. 1928. *Report, 1927.* London: HMSO. (Great Britain. Colonial Office. *Colonial* 1383.)

Great Britain. Ordnance Survey. 1949. *A description of Ordnance Survey medium scale maps.* Chessington.

Great Britain. Ordnance Survey. 1954. *A description of Ordnance Survey large scale plans.* Chessington.

Great Britain. War Office. General Staff. Geographical Section. 1920. *Catalogue of maps.* London.

Greene, J. J. 1971. "The 1:250,000 map of Canada: its history and its future." *Canadian surveyor* 25(3):269-72.

Greenhood, David. 1964. *Mapping.* Rev. ed. Chicago: University of Chicago Press.

Gregory, Alan F. 1971. "Earth-observation satellites: a potential impetus for economic and social development." *World cartography* 11:1-15.

Greve, Ernesto. 1950. "Breve resumen de la historia de la cartografía nacional." *Revista geográfica de Chile* no. 4:9-21.

Gribben, H. Robert et al. 1971. "Side-looking radar: state of the art." *World cartography* 11:33-67.

Griffith, Shirley V. 1957. "The national mapping program." *Cartography* 2:46-51. Also in: *Surveying and mapping* 17(1):49-54, 1957.

Griffith, Shirley V. 1962. "Surveying and mapping in the United States of America. National report to F.I.G. Commission III. Tenth International Congress of Surveyors, Vienna, Austria, 1962." *Surveying and mapping* 22(3):385-96.

Groenningsaeter, Asgeir. 1976. "La production automatique des cartes topographiques." Societé belge de photogrammetrie. *Bulletin trimestral* 121/122:5-19.

Guatemala. Dirección General de Cartografía. 1958(?)-. *Memoria.* Guatemala.

Guatemala. Instituto Geográfico Nacional. 1978. *Guía geográfica de Guatemala para investigadores; research guide of Guatemala.* Mexico City(?): Pan American Institute of Geography and History. (Pan American Institute of Geography and History. *Publication* 319.)

Gurtner, Martin. 1972. "Unusual? A comment on N.Z. mapping." *New Zealand cartographic journal* 2(4):8-9.

Guzmán, Rolando R. 1967. "Summary of cartographic activities in Guatemala." *World cartography* 8:52-59.

Haddon, J. A. 1979. "Ontario basic mapping." Association of Canadian Map Libraries. *Bulletin* no. 32:30-33.

Hagen, Carlos B. 1977. "Map libraries in the 1970s and the University of California." Western Association of Map Libraries. *Information bulletin* 8:200-29.

Hagen, Carlos B. 1979. "The new mapping of Mexico." Western Association of Map Libraries. *Information bulletin* 10(2):108-15.

Hammer, James E. 1963. "Mapping operations in Central and South America." *Surveying and mapping* 23(4):603-6.

Hammond, Allen L. 1977. "Remote sensing (II): Brazil explores its Amazon wilderness." *Science* 196(4289):513-15.

Handbook of Latin American studies. 1935-. Gainesville, FL: University of Florida Press. See section on "Cartography."

Hargett, Janet L. 1971. *List of selected maps of states and territories.* Washington, DC: US National Archives and Records Service. (US National Archives and Records Service. *Special list* 29.)

Harley, John Brian. 1975. *Ordnance Survey maps, a descriptive manual.* Southampton: British Ordnance Survey.

Harris, Lewis John. 1960. "Hillshading for relief depiction in topographical maps, with some recent applications." *Scottish geographical magazine* 76(1):14-20.

Harris, Lewis John. 1970. "Effect of user needs on topographic mapping programs." *Surveying and mapping* 30(1):103-9.

Harris, Lewis John. 1971. "An approach to automatic cartography for topographic mapping in Canada." *Canadian cartographer* 8(2):90-95.

Harris, Lewis John. 1972a. "Automated cartography in federal mapping in Canada." *Canadian cartographer* 9(1):50-60.

Harris, Lewis John. 1972b. "Mapping the land of Canada." *Geographical journal* 138(2):131-38.

Harris, Lewis John. 1973. "Automated cartography in federal mapping in Canada." pp. 16-22 in: *Computer cartography in Canada.* Toronto: York University, B.V. Gutsell. (*Cartographica monograph* no. 9; *Supplement* no. 3 to *Canadian cartographer*)

Harris, Lewis John et al. 1964. "British map making and cartographic activities." *Geographical journal* 130(2):226-40.

Harvey, P. D. A. 1980. *The history of topographical maps; symbols, pictures and surveys.* London: Thames & Hudson.

Hawkins, R. S. 1966. "A survey tour down under." *Royal engineers journal* 80(3): 252-59.

Hay, J. C., and Davidson, R. D. 1951. "A brief history of mapping in Canada." *Canadian surveyor* 10(9):24-29.

Helk, Jørgen V. 1961a. "The mapping of Greenland by the Danish Geodetic Institute." International Geographical Congress. *Proceedings; physical geography,* pp. 128-50.

Helk, Jørgen V. 1961b. "Some questions on the ice-topography on the Greenland maps made by the Danish Geodetic Institute." International Geographical Congress. *Proceedings; physical geography,* pp. 131-32.

Helk, Jørgen V. 1966. "Glacier mapping in Greenland." *Canadian journal of earth sciences* 3(6):771-74.

Henoch, W. E. S. 1969. "Topographic maps of Canada in glaciological research." *Canadian cartographer* 6(2):118-28.

Henoch, W. E. S., and Croizet, J. L. 1976. "The Peyto Glacier map, a three-dimensional depiction of mountain relief." *Canadian cartographer* 13(1):69-86.

Herrera, Horacio. 1945. "Las cartas geográficas y su evolución." Sociedad Mexicana de Geografía y Estadística. *Boletín* 60:597-619.

Hinks, Arthur Robert. 1925. "The science and art of map-making." *Scottish geographical magazine* 41:321-36.

Hinks, Arthur Robert. 1944. *Maps and survey.* 5th ed. Cambridge, England: Cambridge University Press.

Hoar, Gregory J. 1982. *Satellite surveying: theory—geodesy, map projections; applications—equipment, operations.* Torrance, CA: Magnavox Advanced Products and Systems Company.

Hocking, Dave. 1976. "National mapping." *The globe* 1(5/6):16-17.

Hodgkiss, A. G. 1981. *Understanding maps: a systematic history of their use and development.* Folkestone, Kent, England: Dawson.

Hoehn, R. Philip. 1977. "A union list of map series: Mexico and Central America, held by the libraries of the University of California and Stanford University." Western Association of Map Libraries. *Information bulletin* 8:188-96.

Honduras cartográfica. 196 (?)-.

Honduras. Instituto Geográfico Nacional. 1967, 1969a-71. *Informe anual.* Tegucigalpa.

Honduras. Instituto Geográfico Nacional. 1969b. *Perfil geográfico, cartográfico, histórico, económico, nuestra patria, la República de Honduras.* Tegucigalpa.

Hotine, Martin. 1956. "Forty years on." *Canadian surveyor* 13(5):268-73.

Huber, Ernst. 1962. "Die Landeskarten der Schweiz." *Internationales Jahrbuch für Kartographie* 2:130-55.

Hudson, N. O., and Johnson, William G. 1972. "Field surveys in Minnesota northwoods; an adventure in wilderness mapping." American Congress on Surveying and Mapping (32nd annual meeting). *Proceedings* 337-43.

Huggett, G. R. 1981. "Two-colour terrameter." *Tectonophysics* 71(1-4):29-39.

Hughes, Thomas T. 1971. "Mapping remote areas of eastern Honduras." *Surveying and mapping* 31(2):307, 310.

Hurault, Jean. 1949. "La cartographie des regions plates et très boisées en zone equatoriale; example: La Guyane française." Association des ingénieurs géographes. *Bulletin* 4(9):60-70. Also in: International Geographical Congress (16th; Lisbon, 1949). *Proceedings* 1:147-57.

Hurault, Jean. 1963. *Applications de la photographie aérienne aux recherches de sciences humaines dans les régions tropicales.* Paris: Impr. de l'Institut géographique national. (*Mémoires de photo-interpretation* 1.)

"IAGS mapping experts aid the Americas." 1970. American Society of Cartographers. *Bulletin* 5(3):1-3.

Imhof, Eduard. 1951. *Terrain et carte.* Erlenbach-Zurich: Éditions Eugen Rentsch.

Imhof, Eduard. 1958. *Problems of the cartographic terrain representation.* Chicago: Rand McNally. Also pp. 9-30 in: International Cartographic Conference (2nd; Chicago, 1958). *Informations* [sic] *relative to cartography and geodesy. Series II: German contributions in a foreign language.* Frankfurt am Main: Institut für Angewandte Geodäise.

Imhof, Eduard. 1964. "Beiträge zur Geschichte der topographischen Kartographie." *Internationales Jahrbuch für Kartographie* 4:129-53.

Imhof, Eduard. 1982. *Cartographic relief presentation.* Berlin NY: De Gruyter.

Ingleton, Geoffrey Chapman. 1958. "Maps and mapping of Australia." *Australian encyclopedia* 5:485-90. East Lansing: Michigan State University Press.

"Inter American Geodetic Survey." 1970. *Military engineer* 62(407):192.

Israel. Mahleket ha-medidot. 1970. *Atlas of Israel.* 2nd ed. Jerusalem.

Jack, E. M. 1930. "National surveys; address to Section E.—Geography." British Association for the Advancement of Science. *Report of the ninety-seventh meeting (ninety-ninth year), South Africa, 1929, July 22-August 3,* pp. 100-18.

James, Preston E. 1972. *All possible worlds, a history of geographical ideas.* Indianapolis: Odyssey.

Janicot, R. 1969. "General organization, execution and cost of cartographic work." *World cartography* 9:66-74.

Jáuregui, Ernesto O. 1968. *Mapas y planos contemporáneos de Mexico.* Mexico City: Universidad Nacional Autónoma de Mexico.

Jenks, George F. et al. 1971. "Illustrating the concepts of the contour symbol, interval and spacing via 3-D maps." *Journal of geography* 70(5):280-88.

Jensen, Homer et al. 1977. "Side-looking airborne radar." *Scientific American* 237(4):84-95.

Jensen, J. Granville. 1977. "Some important cartographic agencies and available maps of Mexico." Western Association of Map Libraries. *Bulletin* 8(2): 107-14.

Jerie, H. G. 1972. "New concepts of topographic mapping in developing countries." *World cartography* 12:3-20.

Jervis, Walter Willson. 1938. *The world in maps; a study in map evolution.* 2nd ed. London: G. Philip.

Joerg, Wolfgang Louis Gottfried. 1912. "Development and state of progress of the United States portion of the International Map of the World." American Geographical Society. *Bulletin* 44:838-44.

Joerg, Wolfgang Louis Gottfried. 1935. "Geography and national land planning." *Geographical review* 35(2):177-208.

Joerg, Wolfgang Louis Gottfried. 1940. "Federal surveys and maps." *American year book, 1939,* pp. 274-78.

Joerg, Wolfgang Louis Gottfried. 1951. "175 years of the official mapping of the United States." *Surveying and mapping* 11(3):271-76.

Johnston, Duncan. 1909. "Topographical surveys and maps." *Scottish geographical magazine* 25(10):505-19.

Johnston, Frederick Marshall. 1948. *Report on mapping activities in Australia, as of 30 June 1948.* Canberra: Dept. of the Interior.

Johnston, Frederick Marshall. 1949a. "Australian organization for (a) cadastral surveys; (b) topographical mapping." *Australian surveyor* 12(1-2):63-71.

Johnston, Frederick Marshall. 1949b. *Mapping activities in Australia.* New York: United Nations. (E/1322/Add.l.o.J.)

Jones, A. D. 1978. "Technological changes in topographic map making and the map librarian." *The globe* no. 9:69-76.

Jones, Yolande. 1974. "Aspects of relief portrayal on nineteenth century British military maps." *Cartographic journal* 11(1):19-33.

Kakisita, Seizo. 1963. "La cartographie au Japon." Comité française de cartographie. *Bulletin* 25(3):191-95.

Kanow, Hermann. 1967. "Kartenindexe der lateinamerikanischen Länder." *Kartographischen Nachrichten* 17(6):213-15.

"Kansas topographic mapping completed." 1982. *The journal, Kansas Geological Survey* 4(2):9-11.

Karo, H. Arnold. 1955. *World mapping.* Washington, DC: Industrial College of the Armed Forces.

Karo, H. Arnold. 1956. "World mapping." *Surveying and mapping* 16(4):421-30.

Keates, John S. 1962. "The small-scale representation of the landscape in color." *Internationales Jahrbuch für Kartographie* 2:76-83.

Keates, John S. 1972. "Symbols and meaning in topographic maps. *Internationales Jahrbuch für Kartographie* 12:168-81.

Kennedy, Edward. 1981. *Trends in provincial mapping in Canada.* Unpublished paper presented at Western Association of Map Libraries meeting, Edmonton, Alberta, October 1981.

Kennedy, G. H. C. 1962. "The development of standard mapping in South Australia." *Australian surveyor* 19:107-10.

Kennedy, G. H. C. 1976. "South Australian mapping." *The globe* 1(5-6):11-16.

Key, Charles Edward. 1938. *The story of twentieth-century exploration.* New York: Alfred A. Knopf.

Kihl, T. H. 1977. "Automated production 1:50 000 topographic maps." *New Zealand cartographic journal* 7(1):21-24.

Kilmartin, J. O. 1951. "Federal surveys and maps." *American year book, 1950,* pp. 222-35.

King, J. E. 1951. "Topographic map revision and maintenance." *Surveying and mapping* 11(3):285-87.

Kish, George. 1976. "Early thematic mapping: the work of Philippe Buache." *Imago mundi* 28:129-36.

Kish, George. 1980. *La carte, image des civilisation.* Paris: Seuil.

Klawe, Janusz J. 1955. "The role of photography in Canadian mapping." *Canadian geographical journal* 51(5):190-97.

Klawe, Janusz J. 1965. "The future of Canadian cartography." *Canadian surveyor* 19(4):331-37.

Klawe, Janusz J. 1971. "Kartografia topograficzna Kanady." *Polski przeglad kartograficzny* 3:116-23.

Kluge, P. F. 1979. "Those who chart our vast lands explore vital new frontiers." *Smithsonian* 9(12):40-55.

Knowles, R., and Stowe, P. W. 1976. *North America in maps: topographical studies of Canada and the USA.* London: Longman.

Knox, Robert W. 1955. "Mapping the earth." *Journal of the Coast and Geodetic Survey* 6:65-74.

Koch, Lauge. 1940. *Survey of North Greenland.* Kφbenhaven: C. A. Reitzels (*Meddelelser om Grφnland* 130:1-364.)

Koeman, Irene Cornelis. 1973. *Bibliography of printed maps of Suriname 1671-1971.* Amsterdam: Theatrum Orbis Terrarum.

Kölbl, O. 1973. "Combined restitution of aerial and satellite photographs for topographic mapping." British Interplanetary Society. *Journal* 26:677-87.

Krauss, Georg. 1965. "Difficulties in maintaining topographic maps and possibilities of overcoming them." *Internationales Jahrbuch für Kartographie* 5:51-65.

"Labor ejecutada por el Instituto Geográfico Militar a propósito de su trigesino primer aniversario." *Revista geográfica de Chile* no. 10:5-8.

Lambert, B. P. 1969. "Geodetic survey and topographic mapping in Australia." *Australian surveyor* 22(7):515-28.

Lambert, B. P. 1973. "The impact of satellites on mapping." *Australian surveyor* 25(4):303-15.

Larned, C. W. 1907. "History of mapmaking and topography." *Scientific American supplement* 64:116-18, 132-34.

Lasche, R. H. 1937. "Modern maps for Colombia by aerial methods." *Photogrammetric engineering* 3(2):35-37.

Lawrence, G. R. P. 1971. *Cartographic methods*. London: Methuen.

Lawson, James M. 1957. *Altimetry in topographic mapping*. Salt Lake City: University of Utah. (University of Utah. *Bulletin* 48(13).) Also in: University of Utah. Engineering Experiment Station. 1957. *Bulletin* no. 85:48-75.

Leikis, C. E. 1954. "Brief outline of map history." *New Zealand survey draughtsmen's journal* 2:98-100.

Leppert, K. L. 1973. "Geodesy in Australia, 1956-72." Australian Survey Congress (16th). *Proceedings*, p. 10.

Lewis, A. D. 1938. "Topographical mapping in the Union of South Africa." *South African geographical journal* 20:3-11.

Lewis, A. J. 1976. "Geoscience applications of imaging radar systems." *Remote sensing of the electromagnetic spectrum* 3(3).

Lillesand, Thomas M., and Kiefer, Ralph W. 1979. *Remote sensing and image interpretation*. New York: Wiley.

Lillestrand, Robert L., and Johnson, Gerald W. 1971. "Cartography of north Greenland." *Surveying and mapping* 31(2):233-50.

Lines, J. D. 1967. "Control surveys for 1:100,000 mapping." *Cartography* 6(3): 133-40.

Lobeck, A. K. 1945. "Cartography." *Scientific monthly* (June) pp. 417-25.

Lock, Clara Beatrice Muriel. 1969. *Modern maps and atlases, an outline guide to twentieth century production*. Hamden, CT: Archon.

Loewe, F. 1933. "Eine neue Karte von Grönland." Gesellschaft für Erdkunde, Berlin. *Zeitschrift* pp. 218-20.

"The longest triangulation arc." 1943, 1944. American Congress on Surveying and Mapping. *Bulletin* 3(4):13; 4(4):48.

Low, Julian Williams. 1952. *Plane table mapping.* New York: Harper.

Luna, Julio A. 1973. "La cartografía en el Perú." Sociedad Geográfica de Lima. *Boletín* 92:31-33.

Luxardo de Castro, Julio F. B. 1952. "Historia de la cartografía argentina." Primer Congreso Nacional de Cartografía. *Memoria* pp. 84-88.

Lyddan, R. H. 1974. "USGS Antarctic cartography and Doppler program." *Antarctic journal of the United States* 9(5):247-49.

Lyddan, R. H. 1976. "The national mapping program of the United States." American Congress on Surveying and Mapping. *Proceedings* 36:342-51.

Lynn, Bill. 1979. "USGS centennial." *Photogrammetric engineering and remote sensing* 45(3):338-39.

Lyons, Herbert George. 1911. "The colouring of relief maps." *Geographical journal* 37:428-30.

Lyons, Herbert George. 1914. "Relief in cartography." *Geographical journal* 43(3): 233-48, 395-407.

Lyubkov, A. N. 1971. *Survey of major modern methods of relief map preparation– translation.* Rockville MD: National Technical Information Service. (AD-772 422) Originally published in Russian: *Geodeziya i kartografiya* no. 12:53-57. 1971.

McBryde, Felix Webster. 1969. *Geografía cultural e histórica de suroeste de Guatemala.* Guatemala: Editorial José de Pineda Ibarra. (Smithsonian Institute of Social Anthropology. *Publication* 4.)

MacDonald, D. 1953. "Development of photogrammetry in Australia. Period up to June, 1949." *Australian surveyor* 14:252-56.

McDonald, Frederick N. 1935. "Mapping for national planning." *Civil engineering* 5:171-73.

MacDonald, William R. 1974. "New space technology advances knowledge of the remote polar regions." pp. 1011-22 in: Symposium on Earth Resources Technology Satellite-1, (3rd; Washington, DC, 1973). *Technical presentations, section B.* vol. 1. Washington, DC: US Government Printing Office. (United States. National Aeronautics and Space Administration. *NASA-SP* 351.)

MacFadden, Clifford Herbert. 1941. *A bibliography of Pacific area maps.* San Francisco: American Council Institute of Pacific Relations. (*Studies of the Pacific* 6.)

Mackay, Donald. 1934. "The Mackay aerial survey expedition, central Australia, May-June 1930." *Geographical journal* 84(6):511-14.

McKenzie, Morris L. 1973. "Photoimages for map bases." United States. Geological Survey. *Journal of research* 1(3):327-40.

Magnan, George A. 1973. "Defense Mapping Agency charts the world." *Engineering graphics* 13(3):6-11.

Mahoney, J. R. 1950. *A program to strengthen the scientific foundation in natural resources.* Washington, DC: US Government Printing Office. (United States. 81st Congress, 2nd session. *House document* 706; *Serial set* 11419.)

Manning, Thomas G. 1967. *Government in science; the U. S. Geological Survey, 1867-1894.* Lexington: University of Kentucky Press.

"Map of the Donald Mackay aerial reconnaissance survey expedition." 1938. *Australian geographer* 3(4):22.

"Mapeamento topografico na Amazônia." 1973. *Revista brasiliera de geografía* 35(1):142.

"Mapping." 1964. *Canadian surveyor* 18(4):313-15.

"Mapping in Ecuador." 1949. *Military engineer* 41(282):295.

"Mapping progress in Brazil." 1958. *Military engineer* 40(336):290-91.

"Mapping the northland." 1947. *Canadian weekly bulletin* 2(2):2-3.

"Mapping with the squeeze of a bulb." 1920. *Scientific American* 122:34, 47.

"Maps and mapping." 1968. *Earth-science review* 4(4):A232-35.

"Maps and mapping agencies in Mexico." 1950. *Map research bulletin* MB-13:1-7.

"Maps of North America." 1892. *Goldthwaite's geographical magazine* 3:34-36.

"Maps of the Northwest Territories." 1952. *Arctic circular* 5(4):44.

Margerison, T. A. 1976. *Computers and the renaissance of cartography.* London: Natural Environment Research Council, Experimental Cartography Unit, Royal College of Art.

Margerison, T. A. 1977. "Computer-aided map making." *Endeavour* 1(3-4):139-42. Also in *New scientist* 77(1094):716-18. 1978.

Marschner, F. J. 1943. "Maps and a mapping program for the United States." Association of American Geographers. *Annals* 33(4):199-219.

Marshall, Brian. 1977. "Map production and map collecting in New Zealand." Special Libraries Association. Geography and Map Division. *Bulletin* no. 110: 25-29.

Martin, F. O. 1929. "Exploration in Colombia." *Geographical review* 19:621-37.

Martinson, Tom L. 1975. *Research guide to Colombia.* Mexico City(?): Pan American Institute of Geography and History. (Pan American Institute of Geography and History. *Publication* 341.)

Martonne, Emmanuel de. 1947. *Géographie aérienne.* Paris: Éditions Albin Michel.

Masry, S. E., and McLaren, R. A. 1979. "Digital map revision." *Photogrammetric engineering and remote sensing* 45(2):193-200.

Mathieson, John. 1926. "Geodesy: a brief historical sketch." *Scottish geographical magazine* 42:328-47.

Mato, Silvestre. 1917. *Cartografía nacional; conferencia dada el día 9 de junio de 1917.* Montevideo: Talleres El Siglo, la Razón y el Telégrafo.

Matthes, Francois Emile. 1908. "The mapping of landforms." *Science* 27:893-94.

Mattos, Allyrio H. de. 1944. "Cartography in Brazil." American Congress on Surveying and Mapping. *Bulletin* 4(1):20-25.

Mattos, René de. 1967. "Progress report of Brazil." *World cartography* 8:3-12.

Maugenest, J. 1950. "La représentation du relief sur les cartes." International Geographical Congress (16th; Lisbon, 1949). *Proceedings* pp. 128-35.

Medina Peralta, Manuel. 1944. "Program of the geodetic and topographic work in Mexico, from March, 1943, to date." *Eos* pt. 2:259-63.

Medina Peralta, Manuel. 1950. *The cartographic situation in Mexico.* [S.l.: s.n.]

Medina Ruiz, Antonio. 1954-55. "Comisión Nacional de Cartografía de Bolivia." *Revista cartográfica* 3(3):255-61, 4(4):155.

Meine, Karl-Heinz. 1951. "Notizen zur Kartographie in den USA." *Kartographische Nachrichten* 9(1):22-25.

Meine, Karl-Heinz. 1972. "Considerations on the state of development with regard to topographical maps of the different countries of the earth." *Internationales Jahrbuch für Kartographie* 12:182-200.

Merideth, Robert W. 1980. "Remote sensing overview." *Wisconsin mapping bulletin* 6(4):1-6.

Merrill, F. J. H. 1906. "Maps of Mexico." American Geographical Society of New York. *Bulletin* 38:281-87.

Meux, A. H. 1960. *Reading topographical maps.* 2nd ed. London: University of London Press.

Mexico. Comisión Cartográfica Militar. 1953. "Dos años más de vida." Mexico. Comisión Cartográfica Militar. *Boletín* no. 2:7-8.

Mexico. Comisión Geográfica-Exploradora. 1893. *Catálogo de los objetos que componen el contingente de la Comisión, precedido de algunas notas sobre su organización y trabajos.* Xalapa: Enriquez.

Mexico. Comisión Geográfica-Exploradora. 1974. *La Comisión Geográfico-Exploradora del Ministerio de Fomento y la Carta general de la República Mexicana a la 100 000a 1877-1914.* Mexico City: SAG-DGGM.

Mexico. Dirección de Estudios Geográficos y Climatológicos. 1931. *Acta de la Sexta sesión del Consejo Directivo de los levantamientos topográficos de la República, 27 de noviembre de 1930.* Tacubaya.

Mexico. Dirección de Geografía, Meterología e Hidrología. 1945 *Cinco anos de cartografía en Mexico; guía de las cartas que componen la exposición cartográfica con los datos referentes a los mapas terminados en el período de 1941 a 1945 expuestos en la Sociedad de Geografía y Estadística.* Mexico City.

Mexico. Dirección de Geografía, Meteorología e Hidrología. 1950, 1961, 1965. *Catálogo de publicaciones.* Mexico City.

Mexico. Dirección General de Estudios del Territorio Nacional. 1980. *Inventario de información geográfica.* Mexico City. (enero, no. 1.)

Middleton, C. E. 1955. "Aspects and trends of photogrammetry in Australia." *Cartography* 1:56-65.

Miller, Ralph Leroy. 1951. "Developments in Alaska in 1950." American Association of Petroleum Geologists. *Bulletin* 35:1369-79.

Miller, W. H. 1951. "Organization of surveys, mapping and charting in Canada." *Surveying and mapping* 11(3):281-84.

Mitchell, Guy Elliott. 1925. "Heroes of mapmaking." *Scientific American* 133: 221-23.

Moffat, Riley Moore. 1981. *Printed maps of Utah to 1900: an annotated carto-bibliography.* Santa Cruz CA: Western Association of Map Libraries. (Western Association of Map Libraries. *Occasional paper* 8.)

Mohn, Michel. 1968. "La cartographie au Venezuela." *Cahiers d'Outre-mer* 21(84): 424-30.

Mohn, Michel. 1969. "Los mapas venezolanos." Bogotá. Universidad de los Andes. *Revista geográfica* 9(20):43-55.

Montagano, G. A. 1970. *Automated cartography development at the Surveys and Mapping Branch.* Ottawa: Surveys and Mapping Branch. (Canada. Surveys and Mapping Branch. *Technical report* 70-11.)

Montagnes, James. 1929. "Charting Canada's wilderness from the air." *Scientific American* 141:214-15.

Monteiro, Palmyra V. M. 1967a. *A catalogue of Latin American flat maps, 1926-1964.* vol. I. *Mexico, Central America, West Indies.* Austin: University of Texas, Institute of Latin American Studies. (University of Texas. Institute of Latin American Studies. *Guides and bibliographies series* 2.)

Monteiro, Palmyra V. M. 1967b. *A catalogue of Latin American flat maps, 1926-64.* vol. II. *South America, Falkland (Malvinas) Islands and the Guianas.* Austin: University of Texas, Institute of Latin American Studies. (University of Texas. Institute of Latin American Studies. *Guides and bibliographies series* 2.)

Montgomery, R. B. 1928. "On the need for a topographical survey of Australia." *Australian surveyor* 1:51-56.

Mori, Attilio. 1914. "La cartografia della repubblica Argentina." *Rivista geogràfica italiana* 21:102-8.

Morison, Samuel Eliot. 1978. *The great explorers: the European discovery of America.* New York: Oxford University Press.

Mrowka, Jack. 1978. Personal interview. Eugene, OR: University of Oregon. Dept. of Geography.

Mullen, Roy R. 1970. "Current status of orthophotomapping in the U.S.G.S." American Society of Photogrammetry. *Papers* 36:670-76.

National Academy of Sciences. 1878. *Surveys of the territories.* Washington, DC: US Government Printing Office. (United States. Congress. House. *Miscellaneous document* 5; *Serial set* 1861.)

National Cartographic Information Center. 1980. *Digital terrain tapes.* 2nd ed. Reston, VA.

National Cartographic Information Center. 1981. *Intermediate-scale base maps.* Reston, VA.

National Cartographic Information Center. Rocky Mountain Affiliate Network. "Orthophotoquads - orthophotomaps." National Cartographic Information Center. Rocky Mountain Affiliate Network. *Newsletter* (October) p. 1-3.

National Mapping Council of Australia. 1970. *Statement of activities for the period 1 January 1969 - 12 December 1969.* Canberra(?)

National Mapping Council of Australia. 1976. *Report on work completed during the period 1945-1975.* Canberra. (NMP/75/014)

Nelson, Clifford M. 1979. "Topographic maps." *Geotimes* 24(3):30-31.

Neubauer, Hermann G. 1978. "Beiträge zur digitalen photogrammetrischen Messung für die Herstellung topographischer Karten." *Nachrichten aus dem Karten- und Vermessungswesen. Reihe I,* no. 76:5-122.

"New map of Mexico." 1950. *Military engineer* 42(287):226.

"New mapping of western North America." 1977. Western Association of Map Libraries. *Information bulletin* 8(3):178.

New Zealand. Dept. of Lands and Survey. 1925-. *Records of the Survey of New Zealand.* Wellington.

New Zealand. Dept. of Lands and Survey. various. *Report on the Department of Lands and Surveys.* Wellington.

New Zealand. Dept. of Lands and Survey. 1959-1969. *Catalogue of maps.* Wellington: R. E. Owen.

New Zealand. Dept. of Lands and Survey. 197-(?). *Maps.* 5th ed. Wellington.

New Zealand. Dept. of Lands and Survey. 1973. *New maps by Department of Lands and Survey: a brief description of new metric series to be published by the Department.* Wellington.

New Zealand. Dept. of Lands and Survey. 1975. *Catalogue of maps.* Wellington: A. R. Shearer.

New Zealand. Dept. of Lands and Survey. 1976. *Topographical maps & route finding.* 1st ed. Wellington: A. R. Shearer. (NZMS 235)

New Zealand. Dept. of Lands and Survey. 1977. *Maps of New Zealand.* 7th ed. Wellington. (NZMS 197/1)

New Zealand. Dept. of Lands and Survey. 1980. *Report on cartographic activities of New Zealand 1977-1980.* Wellington(?)

New Zealand Geographical Society. 1964. "Department of Lands and Survey." New Zealand Geographical Society. *Record* no. 37:8-11.

New Zealand in maps. 1977. New York: Holmes & Meier.

"New Zealand topographic maps and air photographs." 1946. *New Zealand geographer* 2(2):370-71.

Newcombe, S. F. 1920. "The practical limits of aeroplane photography for mapping." *Geographical journal* 56:201-6.

Nicaragua. Instituto Geográfico. 1977. *Guía de recursos básicos contemporáneos para estudios de desarrollo en Nicaragua.* Managua. (Pan American Institute of Geography and History. *Publication* 343.)

Nicholson, Norman L., and Sebert, Lou M. 1981. *Maps of Canada: a guide to official Canadian maps, charts, atlases, and gazetteers.* Hamden, CT: Archon.

Nørlund, N. E. 1939. "The survey work of the Danish Geodetic Institute in Greenland and Iceland." *Polar record* 3(17):38-42.

"Notes on the application of satellite imagery to topographic, bathymetric and land use mapping in Australia." 1973. *Cartography* 19(4):217-33.

Nowicki, Albert L. "U.S. mapping in the Arctic and sub-Arctic regions of the Western Hemisphere." *Photogrammetric engineering* 19(3):408-10.

Núñez de las Cuevas, Rodolfo. 1967. "Color in topographic maps." *Internationales Jahrbuch für Kartographie* 7:43-49.

O'Brien, Charles Ian Milward. 1970. "The place of large scale mapping in the cartographic programmes of developing countries." *Internationales Jahrbuch für Kartographie* 10:154-60.

Ogrissek, R. 1966. "Zum Stand der Kartographie in Australien." *Vermessungstechnik* 14:355-59.

Oliveira, Cêurio de. 1952. "Ebôço histórico de desenho de mapas." *Revista brasileira de geografía* 14(2):213-22.

Olsen, Marilyn. 1971. "Aspects of the mapping of southern Ontario." Association of Canadian Map Libraries (5th annual conference). *Proceedings* pp. 30-40.

Olson, Everett Claire, and Whitmarsh, Agnes. 1944. *Foreign maps.* New York: Harper.

1:250,000 Unified Hemispheric Mapping Series, newsletter. number 1- , 198-(?)-

Oost, L. van. 1935. "Établissement des cartes topographiques par photographie aérienne au Canada." Societé royale belge de géographie. *Bulletin* 59 (4): 44-49.

Outhwaite, Leonard. 1938. *Unrolling the map, the story of exploration.* New York: Reynal and Hitchcock.

PAIGH See: Pan American Institute of Geography and History.

Palma, Andrés. 1957. "Apuntes sobre la cartografía de Honduras." Honduras. Dirección General de Cartografía. *Boletín* 1(3):34.

Palmer, P. E. 1957. "Cartography, 20th-century." *Encyclopedia Canadiana* 2: 265-68. Ottawa: Canadiana Company Ltd.

Palmerlee, Albert E. 1945. *Maps of Costa Rica; an annotated cartobibliography*. Lawrence: University of Kansas Libraries.

Pan American Consultation on Cartography. 1948. *Actas*. Buenos Aires.

Pan American Consultation on Cartography. 1950. *Anales*. Buenos Aires.

Pan American Consultation on Cartography. 1954. *Resoluciones sobre cartas topográficas y aerofotogrametría, dirigidas a los gobiernos; a la Comisión de Cartografía; al PAIGH*. [S.l.: s.n.]

Pan American Consultation on Cartography. 1977. *Actas*. [S.l.: s.n.]

Pan American Consultation on Cartography. Delegación de Venezuela. 1955. *Informe que presenta la Delegación de Venezuela a la VII Reunion Panamericana de Consulta sobre Cartografía*. Caracas.

Pan American Institute of Geography and History. 1954. *The Pan American Institute of Geography and History, its creation, development and current program 1929-1964; a quarter century of service to its member governments*. Mexico City.

Pan American Institute of Geography and History. 1978. *User survey for the 1:250,000 scale unified hemispheric topographic mapping program*. Mexico City.

Pan American Institute of Geography and History. Centro de Entretenamiento para la Evaluación de Recursos Naturales. Comisión de Expertos. 1952-54. *Los estudios de los recursos naturales en las Americas*. Mexico City: Pan American Institute of Geography and History. (Proyecto 29 del programa de cooperación técnica de la Organización de los Estados Americanos).

    1952.   Tomo   I.   *Guatemala, Honduras, El Salvador, Nicaragua, Costa Rica, Panamá y Zona del Canal.*

    1953a. Tomo II.   *Colombia y Venezuela.*

    1953b. Tomo IV. *México.*

    1954.   Tomo V.   *Mapas.*

Pan American Institute of Geography and History. Commission on Cartography. 1965. *Status of topographic mapping in the Americas as of December 1964.* Washington, DC(?).

Pan American Institute of Geography and History. Commission on Cartography. 1982.(?) *Program unificado de Cartografía Hemisférica 1:250 000 = 1:250 000 unified hemispheric mapping program.* Mexico City.

Pan American Institute of Geography and History. Sección Nacional Argentina. 1955. *Informe nacional presentado a la VI Asamblea General del Instituto Panamericano de Geografía e Historia.* Buenos Aires.

Pan American Institute of Geography and History. Sección Nacional de Honduras. 1969. *Informe de la Sección Nacional de Honduras: IX Asamblea General, Washington, D.C., 30 de Mayo al 19 de Junio, 1969.* Tegucigalpa.

Pan American Union. Department of Economic Affairs. 1963. *Colombia: Indice anotado de los trabajos aerofotográficos y los mapas topográficos y de recursos naturales realizados en los paises de la América Latina miembros de la OEA; annotated index of aerial photographic coverage and mapping of topography and natural resources undertaken in the Latin American member countries of the OAS.* Washington, DC: Pan American Union.

Pan American Union. Department of Economic Affairs. 1964a. *Bolivia: Indice anotado de los trabajos aerofotográficos y los mapas topográficos y de recursos naturales realizados en los paises de la América Latina miembros de la OEA; annotated index of aerial photographic coverage and mapping of topography and natural resources undertaken in the Latin American member countries of the OAS.* Washington, DC: Pan American Union.

Pan American Union. Department of Economic Affairs. 1964b. *Chile: Indice anotado de los trabajos aerofotográficos y los mapas topográficos y de recursos naturales realizados en los paises de la América Latina miembros de la OEA; annotated index of aerial photographic coverage and mapping of topography and natural resources undertaken in the Latin American member countries of the OAS.* Washington, DC: Pan American Union.

Pan American Union. Department of Economic Affairs. 1964c. *Ecuador: Indice anotado de los trabajos aerofotográficos y los mapas topográficos y de recursos naturales realizados en los paises de la América Latina miembros de la OEA; annotated index of aerial photographic coverage and mapping of topography and natural resources undertaken in the Latin American member countries of the OAS.* Washington, DC: Pan American Union.

Pan American Union. Department of Economic Affairs. 1964d. *Paraguay: Indice anotado de los trabajos aerofotográficos y los mapas topográficos y de recursos naturales realizados en los paises de la América Latina miembros de la OEA; annotated index of aerial photographic coverage and mapping of topography and natural resources undertaken in the Latin American member countries of the OAS.* Washington, DC: Pan American Union.

Pan American Union. Department of Economic Affairs. 1964e. *Peru: Indice anotado de los trabajos aerofotográficos y los mapas topográficos y de recursos naturales realizados en los paises de la América Latina miembros de la OEA; annotated index of aerial photographic coverage and mapping of topography and natural resources undertaken in the Latin American member countries of the OAS.* Washington, DC: Pan American Union.

Pan American Union. Department of Economic Affairs. 1965a. *Argentina: Indice anotado de los trabajos aerofotográficos y los mapas topográficos y de recursos naturales realizados en los paises de la América Latina miembros de la OEA; annotated index of aerial photographic coverage and mapping of topography and natural resources undertaken in the Latin American member countries of the OAS.* Washington, DC: Pan American Union.

Pan American Union. Department of Economic Affairs. 1965b. *Brazil: Indice anotado de los trabajos aerofotográficos y los mapas topográficos y de recursos naturales realizados en los paises de la América Latina miembros de la OEA; annotated index of aerial photographic coverage and mapping of topography and natural resources undertaken in the Latin American member countries of the OAS.* Washington, DC: Pan American Union.

Pan American Union. Department of Economic Affairs. 1965c. *Costa Rica: Indice anotado de los trabajos aerofotográficos y los mapas topográficos y de recursos naturales realizados en los paises de la América Latina miembros de la OEA; annotated index of aerial photographic coverage and mapping of topography and natural resources undertaken in the Latin American member countries of the OAS.* Washington, DC: Pan American Union.

Pan American Union. Department of Economic Affairs. 1965d. *El Salvador: Indice anotado de los trabajos aerofotográficos y los mapas topográficos y de recursos naturales realizados en los paises de la América Latina miembros de la OEA; annotated index of aerial photographic coverage and mapping of topography and natural resources undertaken in the Latin American member countries of the OAS.* Washington, DC: Pan American Union.

Pan American Union. Department of Economic Affairs. 1965e. *Guatemala: Indice anotado de los trabajos aerofotográficos y los mapas topográficos y de recursos naturales realizados en los paises de la América Latina miembros de la OEA; annotated index of aerial photographic coverage and mapping of topography and natural resources undertaken in the Latin American member countries of the OAS.* Washington, DC: Pan American Union.

Pan American Union. Department of Economic Affairs. 1965f. *Honduras: Indice anotado de los trabajos aerofotográficos y los mapas topográficos y de recursos naturales realizados en los paises de la América Latina miembros de la OEA; annotated index of aerial photographic coverage and mapping of topography and natural resources undertaken in the Latin American member countries of the OAS.* Washington, DC: Pan American Union.

Pan American Union. Department of Economic Affairs. 1965g. *Mexico: Indice anotado de los trabajos aerofotográficos y los mapas topográficos y de recursos naturales realizados en los paises de la América Latina miembros de la OEA; annotated index of aerial photographic coverage and mapping of topography and natural resources undertaken in the Latin American member countries of the OAS.* Washington, DC: Pan American Union.

Pan American Union. Department of Economic Affairs. 1965h. *Nicaragua: Indice anotado de los trabajos aerofotográficos y los mapas topográficos y de recursos naturales realizados en los paises de la América Latina miembros de la OEA; annotated index of aerial photographic coverage and mapping of topography and natural resources undertaken in the Latin American member countries of the OAS.* Washington, DC: Pan American Union.

Pan American Union. Department of Economic Affairs. 1965i. *Panama: Indice anotado de los trabajos aerofotográficos y los mapas topográficos y de recursos naturales realizados en los paises de la América Latina miembros de la OEA; annotated index of aerial photographic coverage and mapping of topography and natural resources undertaken in the Latin American member countries of the OAS.* Washington, DC: Pan American Union.

Pan American Union. Department of Economic Affairs. 1966. *Colombia: Indice anotado de los trabajos aerofotográficos y los mapas topográficos y de recursos naturales realizados en los paises de la América Latina miembros de la OEA; annotated index of aerial photographic coverage and mapping of topography and natural resources undertaken in the Latin American member countries of the OAS.* Washington, DC: Pan American Union.

"Panel discussion on the Canadian 1:250 000 series." 1975. Association of Canadian Map Libraries (9th annual conference). *Proceedings* pp. 27-31.

Pannekoek, A. J. 1949. "Some rules of representation of land forms on small scale maps." International Geographical Congress (16th; Lisbon, 1949). *Proceedings* 1:136-42.

Paris. Université. Institut des hautes études de l'Amérique Latine. Centre de documentation. 1967. *Relevé des cartes latino-américaines à moyenne et grande échelle disponibles à Paris.* Paris.

Patterson, Bradford R. 1980(?) *The surveying & mapping of Wellington province 1840-76.* Wellington, New Zealand: Alexander Turnbull Library.

Patterson, James A. 1951. "New concepts needed for topographic mapping." *Surveying and mapping* 11:344-49.

Pearson, D. F. 1974. "An historical outline of mapping in British Columbia." *Canadian cartographer* 11:114-24.

Pendleton, Thomas P. 1944. "Topographic mapping in the Americas." *Surveying and mapping* (January) 4:18-19.

Pendleton, Thomas P, and Hall, C. L. 1928. "Topographic mapping in the Americas." American Society of Civil Engineers. *Proceedings, 1927* 54:339-43.

Penrose, Boies. 1955. *Travel and discovery in the Renaissance, 1420-1620.* Cambridge, MA: Harvard University Press.

Perrier, Georges. 1924. "La carte nationale du Perou." *La géographie* 42:485-88.

Peru. Instituto Nacional de Planificación. 1969. *Atlas histórico geográfico y de paisajes peruanos.* Lima.

Peru. National Office for the Evaluation of Natural Resources. 1979. *Guide to cartographic and natural resource information of Peru.* Mexico City: Pan American Institute of Geography and History.

Peters, F. H. 1936. "Mapping Canada." *Canadian geographical journal* 12(1):3-16.

Peters, F. H. 1943. "Surveying and mapping in Canada." *Surveying and mapping* 3(4):8-11.

Peters, F. H. 1945. "Surveying and mapping in Canada." *Surveying and mapping* 5(3):26-29.

Petrie, G. 1970. "Some considerations regarding mapping from earth satellites." *Photogrammetric record* 6:590-624.

Petrie, G. 1977. "Orthophotomaps." Institute of British Geographers. *Transactions, new ser.,* 2(1):49-70.

Phillips, A. M. L. 1915. "Mapping mountains and swamps in the wilderness." *Technical world magazine* 23:202-5, 264.

Phillips, Philip Lee. 1900. "Cartography; list of maps of Mexico from 1858 to 1898." pp. 356-74 in: United States. Bureau of American Republics. *Mexico; a geographical sketch, with special reference to economic conditions and prospects of future development.* Washington, DC: US Government Printing Office.

Piket, J. J. C. 1972. "Five European topographic maps: a contribution to the classification of topographic maps and their relation to other map types." *Geografisch tijdschrift* 6(3):266-76.

Platt, Raye Roberts. 1927. "Millionth map of Hispanic America." *Geographical review* 17:301-8.

Platt, Raye Roberts. 1930. "Surveys in Hispanic America; notes on a new map showing the extent and character of surveys in Hispanic America." *Geographical review* 20:138-42.

Platt, Raye Roberts. 1933. "Catalogue of maps of Hispanic America." *Geographical review* 23:660-63.

Platt, Raye Roberts. 1943. "Milestones in American cartography." American Scientific Congress (8th; Washington, DC, 1940). *Proceedings* 10:55-63.

Platt, Raye Roberts. 1945. "Official topographical maps; a world index." *Geographical review* 35:175-81.

Poletayeva, S. S. 1967. "Hypsometric and physical maps." *Geodesy and aerophotography* no. 2:120-22.

Polezhayev, A. P. 1962. "Cartography in the U.S.S.R." *Canadian surveyor* 16: 73-79.

Posada, Eduardo. 1937-42. "Cartografía colombiana." Sociedad Geográfica de Colombia. *Boletín* 4:206-20, 5:34-52, 147-56, 255-67; 6:30-37, 121-32, 215-22, 310-19; 7(1, 2):25-34, 164-76.

Potash, Lawrence M., and Jeffrey, Thomas E. 1978. *Factors in design of hardcopy topographic maps.* Alexandria, VA: US Army Research Institute for the Behavioral and Social Sciences. (United States. Army Research Institute for the Behavioral and Social Sciences. *Technical paper* 284.)

Pousardien, Stephen F. 1975. "Mapping for the energy crisis." *Surveying and mapping* 35(3):207-15.

"Preparation of geological and topographical maps." 1953. *Australian surveyor* 14: 260-61.

"El primer symposium cartográfico nacional." 1972. Chile. Instituto Geográfico Militar. *Boletín informativo* no. 3:44.

"O programa da Divisão de Cartografía." 1963. *Revista brasileira de geografía* 25(1):105-18.

"Progress in the work of mapping the United States." 1921. *Science* 54:165-66.

"Progress report on the cartographic activities of the United States for the period ... for presentation to the ... Pan American Consultation on Cartography ... various. Washington, DC: various federal agencies.

"Proposed map of Brazil on the scale of one to a million." 1919. *Science* 49: 259-60.

"Provisional mapping program." 1981. *biblio* no. 3:5-6.

Queensland. Surveying and Mapping Advisory Council. 1981. *Pictorial index of survey and mapping activities.* [S.l.]

Quijada, Ernesto Salazar. 1967. "National cartography in Venezuela during the period 1935-1965." *World cartography* 8:106-8.

"50° [i.e., quincuagésimo] aniversario del Instutito Geográfico Nacional." 1972. Sociedad Geográfica de Lima. *Boletín* 91:72-74.

Quinn, A. O. 1957. "Recent developments and capabilities of photogrammetry in answering the needs for up-to-date maps." University of Utah. *Bulletin* 48(13):21-28.

Rabbitt, John C., and Rabbitt, Mary C. 1954. "The U. S. Geological Survey, 75 years of service to the nation, 1879-1954." *Science* 119:741-58.

Rabbitt, Mary C. 1979. *Minerals, lands, and geology for the common defence and general welfare.* vol. 1. *Before 1879.* Washington, DC: US Government Printing Office.

Rabbitt, Mary C. 1980. *Minerals, lands, and geology for the common defence and general welfare.* vol. 2. *1879-1904.* Washington, DC: US Government Printing Office.

"Radar's 'magic eye' surveys a continent." 1948. *Civil engineering* 18(2):65.

Radlinski, William A. 1978. *Federal mapping and charting in the United States.* [S.l.: s.n.]

Raisz, Erwin Josephus. 1931. "Physiographic method of representing scenery on maps." *Geographical review* 21(2):297-304.

Raisz, Erwin Josephus. 1937. "Outline of the history of American cartography." *Isis* 26(72):373-89.

Raisz, Erwin Josephus. 1956. *Mapping the world.* New York: Abelard-Schuman.

Raju, A. V., and Parthasarathi, E. V. R. 1977. "Stereoscopic viewing of Landsat imagery." *Photogrammetric engineering and remote sensing* 43:1243.

Randall, Robert H. 1944. "Consultation on Cartography." *Surveying and mapping* 4(1):2-10.

Randall, Robert H. 1945. "Second Pan American Consultation on Geography and Cartography." *Surveying and mapping* 5(1):2-7.

Randall, Robert H. 1946. "Co-ordinating and administering federal surveying and mapping activities." *Surveying and mapping* 6(3):235-38.

Randall, Robert H. 1948. "The national mapping program." *Photogrammetric engineering* 14(1):7-10.

Randall, Robert H. 1958. "Federal surveys: Coast and Geodetic, Geological, etc." *Surveying and mapping* 18(2):207-12.

Reeves, Edward Ayearst. 1917. "The mapping of the earth—past, present, and future." British Association for the Advancement of Science. *Report of the eighty-sixth meeting* ... Newcastle-on-Tyne, 1916 (September 5-9) pp. 421-34. Also in: *Geographical journal* 48(4):331-46, 1961; and a summary as "Progress in the mapping of the earth." in *Scientific monthly* 3:515-20, 1916.

Research and development in topographic mapping. 1974. Reston, VA: US Geological Survey. (PB-232 451)

Resources for the twenty-first century: proceedings of the International Centennial Symposium of the United States Geological Survey, held at Reston, Virginia, October 14-19, 1979. 1982. Washington, DC: US Government Printing Office. (US Geological Survey. *Professional paper* 1193.)

Richardus, P. 1973. "The precision of contour lines and contour intervals of large- and medium-scale maps." *Photogrammetria* 29(3):81-107.

Rio de Janeiro. Universidade do Brasil. Centro de Pesquisas de Geografía do Brasil. 1951- . *Bibliografía cartográfica do Brasil.* Rio de Janeiro. (*Serie bibliográfica., publicacão* 1- .)

Roberts, James A. 1962. "The topographic map in a world of computers." *Professional geographer* 14(6):12-13.

Roberts, Joseph K., and Bloomer, Robert O. 1939. *Catalogue of topographic and geologic maps of Virginia.* Richmond, VA: Dietz.

Roberts, Leo Bond. 1924. *Topographic mapping.* Washington, DC: Society of American Military Engineers.

Robertson, Robert T. 1955. "Accomplishments of the Inter American Geodetic Survey." *Surveying and mapping* 15(4):449-52.

Robinson, Arthur H. 1946. "A method for producing shaded relief from aerial slope data." Association of American Geographers. *Annals* 36(4):248-52.

Robinson, Arthur H. 1956. "Mapping the land." *Scientific monthly* 82:294-303.

Robinson, Arthur H. 1982. *Early thematic mapping in the history of cartography.* Chicago: University of Chicago Press.

Robinson, G. D., and Spieker, Andrew M. 1978. *"Nature to be commanded...", earth-science maps applied to land and water management.* Washington, DC: US Government Printing Office. (US Geological Survey. *Professional paper* 950.)

Robinson, John Lewis. 1954a. "Changes in Canadian Arctic maps." *Polar record* 7(47):67-68.

Robinson, John Lewis. 1954b. "Mapping in the North American Arctic." *Geographical review* 44(2):290-92.

Robles Ramos, Ramiro, and Ortiz Santos, Gabriel. 1950. "Informe sobre las labores del Comité Coordinador del Levantamiento de la Carta de la República Mexicana." Sociedad Mexicana de Geografía y Estadística. *Boletín* 69(1, 2): 191-215.

Romer, Eugene. 1930. "Hachure in recent cartography." International Geographical Congress (Cambridge, 1928). *Proceedings* pp. 149-52.

Romero, Adolfo C. 1964. "El estado actual de la cartografía en Venezuela." Academia de Ciencias Físicas, Matemáticas y Naturales, Caracas. *Boletín* 24(66): 65-72.

Ronchetti, Julio J. J. 1954. "Nuevo método de preparación de originales para cartografía a escala 1:100,000." Argentine Republic. Instituto Geográfico Militar. *Atlas, órgano official* 1(2):37.

Roney, John I. 1982. *U.S. Geological Survey provisional edition maps.* Reston, VA: US Geological Survey.

Rozo M., Dario. 1952. "Historia de la cartografía de Colombia." Sociedad Geográfica de Colombia. *Boletín* 10(4):179-87.

Rueger, J. M. 1980. "Recent developments in electronic distance measurements." *Australian surveyor* 30(3):170-77.

Ruge, Sophus. 1883. "List of topographic maps." in his: "Map." *Encyclopedia Britannica* 15:529-30. 9th ed.

Ruiz Moreno, Adrian. 1917. *Formación de la carta general de la Republica Argentina; trabajo presentado al 1er Congreso Nacional de Ingeniera, en 1916, en homenaje.* Buenos Aires: Talleres Gráficos del Estado Major del Ejército.

Saavedra Rojas, Eduardo. 1939. "Levantamientos aerofotogramétricos." Chile. Ejército. *Memoria técnico* 7(27):141-49.

Saenz, José A. 1969. *Informe, presentado a la: XI Reunion Panamericana de Consultación sobre Cartografía.* Panama. Instituto Geográfico Nacional "Tommy Guardia."

Sanchez Lamego, Miguel A. 1949. "Servicio Geográfico del Ejército." Mexico. Ejército. *Revista del Ejército* 5(6):4-13.

Sanchez Lamego, Miguel A. 1952. "La cartografía en México." *Surveying and mapping* 12(2):238-46.

Santiago de Chile. Universidad Católica. Instituto de Geografía. 1978. *Guía para investigadores de Chile.* Mexico City: Pan American Institute of Geography and History.

Santiso, Florencio. 1944. *Informe acerca de la cartografía de Guatemala presentado por el delegado Ingeniero Florencio Santiso ante de la II Reunion Panamerican de Consulta sobre Geografía y Cartografía.* Guatemala: Tipografía Nacional.

Sargent, R. H. 1912. "Progress of Alaskan topographic survey." American Geographical Society of New York. *Bulletin* 44:481-92.

Satzinger, Walter. 1973. "Costs and procedures of official and private mapping." *Internationales Jahrbuch für Kartographie* 13:144-53.

Saubers, Rodney W. 1969. "Inter-American Geodetic Survey; mapping in Honduras." *Military engineer* 61(401):210.

Schierhout, B. 1938. "A note on the trigonometrical survey of Southern Rhodesia." *Empire survey review* 4:267-72.

Schulz, B. 1938. "Neue Karten von Grönland und Svalbard." *Annalen der hydrographie und maritimen Meteorologie* 66:201-4.

Schulz, Wilhelm. 1951. "Geschichte und Stand der Argentinischen Landesaufnahme und Kartographie." *Die Erde* no. 2:180-85.

Schulz, Wilhelm. 1962. "Karten- und Vermessungswesen in Argentinien." *Allegemeine Vermessungs-Nachrichten* 69:66-71.

Schulz, Wilhelm. 1963. "Das Karten- und Vermessungswesen in Argentinien." *Kartographische Nachrichten* 13(3):61-66.

Scientific Council for Africa South of the Sahara. 1955. *Topographic maps of Africa south of the Sahara.* Bukavu. (Scientific Council for Africa South of the Sahara. *Publication* 15.)

Seavey, Charles A. 1979. "Mapnews." *Dttp* 7(1):15-16.

Seavey, Charles A. 1980a. "Exploration and mapping of the Grand Canyon, 1859-1903." Special Libraries Association. Geography and Map Division. *Bulletin* no. 119:4-15.

Seavey, Charles A. 1980b. "Mapnews." *Dttp* 8(6):273-74.

Sebert, Lou M. 1967. "The three-mile sectional maps of the Canadian West." *Cartographer* 4:112-19.

Sebert, Lou M. 1970a. *Every square inch, the story of Canadian topographic mapping.* Ottawa: Information Canada.

Sebert, Lou M. 1970b. "The history of the 1:250 000 map of Canada." *Canadian cartographer* 7(1):15-26.

Sebert, Lou M. 1973. "The continuous revision of a large topographic map series." American Congress on Surveying and Mapping. *Proceedings* 33:371-74.

Sebert, Lou M. 1974. "The 1:50,000 monochrome series of the National Topographic System." *Canadian cartographer* 11(2):167-74.

Sebert, Lou M. 1975. "The 1:25,000 series of the National Topographic Mapping Program." *Canadian cartographer* 12(1):68-79.

Sebert, Lou M. 1976. "The one inch to one mile series of the National Mapping Program." *Canadian cartographer* 13(2):123-31.

Sebert, Lou M. 1979(?) *The work of the Commission on Cartography of the Pan American Institute of Geography and History.* [S.l.: s.n.]

Sebert, Lou M. 1981. *Federal maps and charts.* Ottawa(?): Canadian Surveying and Mapping Branch(?)

Serviços Aerofotogrametricos Cruzeiro do sul, S. A. 1962. *Tendencias modernas para a produção de mapas en escalas 1:50,000 e menores.* [S.l.]

Short, Nicholas M. 1982. *Landsat tutorial workbook; basics of satellite remote sensing.* Washington, DC: US Government Printing Office. (*NASA Reference* 1078.)

Sibert, Winston. 1972. "Role of Federal agencies in large-scale mapping." *Photogrammetric engineering* 38(3):239-42.

Silley, P. T. 1955. *Topographical maps and photographic interpretation.* London: G. Philip.

Simon, K. H. 1978. "Amazonien: Kartographierung mit Radar und Landsat." *Naturwissenschaftliche Rundschau* 31(1).

Simonpietri, Andre C. 1943. "Cartography in Latin America." American Congress on Surveying and Mapping. *Bulletin* 3(3):24-26.

Simonpietri, Andre C. 1947. "The future of mapping in the Americas." *Photogrammetric engineering* 13(1):85-91.

Sixth Western Geographic Names Conference, Denver, October 14-15, 1982. *Proceedings.* unpublished.

Skelton, Raleigh Ashlin. 1952. *Decorative printed maps of the 15th to 18th centuries.* Rev. ed. of: *Old decorative maps and charts,* by A. L. Humphreys. London: Staples Press.

Skelton, Raleigh Ashlin. 1961. "The cartographic record of the discovery of North America: some problems and paradoxes." Congresso Internacional de Historia dos Descobrimentos, Lisbon, 1960. *Actas* 2:343-63.

Skidanenko, K. K. 1969. "Problems of relief generalization in large-scale topographic surveys." *Geodesy and aerophotography* 6:377-80.

Skop, Jacob. 1947. "The new 1:250,000 scale map of the Army Map Service." *Surveying and mapping* 7(3-4):161-64.

Smit, G. Sicco. 1975. "Will the road to Green Hell be paved with SLAR?" *ITC journal* no. 2:245-66.

Smith, C. H. 1951. "The problem of control for topographic mapping in northern Canada." *Surveying and mapping* 11(4):368-73.

Smith, Glenn S. 1924. "A review of topographic mapping." *Military engineer* 16:108-15.

Smith, Henry Nash. 1947. "Clarence King, John Wesley Powell, and the establishment of the United States Geological Survey." *Mississippi Valley historical review* 34:37-58.

Smith, Thomas R. 1977. *The mapping of Ohio.* Kent, OH: Kent State University Press.

Snyder, John Parr. 1973. *The mapping of New Jersey; the men and the art.* New Brunswick, NJ: Rutgers University Press.

Sociedad Mexicana de Geografía y Estadística. 1955. *Informe sobre los trabajos cartográficos, geofísicos, hidrométricos y meteorológicos, estudios de suelos, trabajos demográficos, la enseñanza y labor editorial en geografía y las actividades de la Sociedad Mexicana de Geografía y Estadística, 1° de julio de 1952-30 junio de 1955.* Mexico City.

Southard, Rupert B. 1969. "An analysis of the national topographic program." American Congress on Surveying and Mapping (29th; 1969). *Papers* pp. 72-81.

Southard, Rupert B. 1978. *Development of a digital cartographic capability in the National Mapping Program.* Reston, VA(?): US Geological Survey(?)

Southard, Rupert B. 1980. "The changing scene in surveying and mapping." *Surveying and mapping* 40(4):397-403.

Southard, Rupert B., and MacDonald, William R. 1974. "Cartographic and scientific application of ERTS 1 imagery in polar regions." pp. 373-86 in: Symposium on Approaches to Earth Survey Problems through Use of Space Techniques (Constance, Federal Republic of Germany, 1973). *Proceedings.* Berlin: Akademie Verlag.

Steele, Robert C. 1980. *Modern topographic drawing.* Houston, TX: Gulf Publishing Company.

Stephenson, Robert C. 1949. *Topographic maps.* Harrisburg, PA: Topographic and Geologic Survey. (Pennsylvania. Bureau of Topographic and Geological Survey. *Progress report* 132.)

Stewart, R. A. 1964. "Aerotriangulation procedures for national mapping of Canada." *Photogrammetric engineering* 30(1):130-33.

Stiefel, Alfred C. 1953. "Ten thousand maps at your service." *Surveying and mapping* 13(2):162-67.

Stirling, Ian F. 1976. "Trends in New Zealand and overseas mapping." *New Zealand cartographic journal* 6(1):13-26.

Stoneman, Walter G. 1951. "International cooperation in mapping Latin America." *Surveying and mapping* 11(2):149-58.

Strunkel, Kenneth R. 1965. "A chronicle of mapping." *Military engineer* 57(375): 1-5, (376):110-15.

Stubbe, David G. 1970. "Mapping challenge in northern Alaska." ACSM-ASP Technical Conference (Denver, 1970). *Papers* pp. 428-34.

Styles, Showell. 1970. *The forbidden frontiers; the Survey of India from 1765 to 1949.* London: Hamish Hamilton.

"Summary of surveying and mapping activities by Dominion and Provincial governments." 1955. *Canadian surveyor* 12(9):592-606.

"Summary of surveying and mapping activities by Dominion and Provincial governments." 1956. *Canadian surveyor* 13(4):215-32.

"Surveying and mapping activities in the provinces." 1957. *Canadian surveyor* 8(9): 577-85.

Sylvester, Dorothy. 1952. *Map and landscape*. London: G. Philip.

Symposium on Glacier Mapping (Ottawa, 1965). 1966. *Proceedings and papers. Canadian journal of earth sciences* 3(6).

Tamayo, Jorge L. 1962. "Chapter III: Cartografïa." 1:43-96 in his: *Geografïa general de Mexico*. 2nd ed. Mexico City: Instituto Mexicano de Investagaciones Económicas.

Tanaka, Kitiro. 1974. "Relief methods of representing cartography on maps." *Chizu* 12(3):i-xviii, 1-15.

Taylor, E. G. R. 1928. "A regional map of the early sixteenth century." *Geographical journal* 71:474-79.

Taylor, E. G. R. 1929. "The plane-table in the sixteenth century." *Scottish geographical magazine* 45:205-11.

Teledyne, Inc. 1978. *Teledyne report first quarter 1978: Aerial mapping; faster and better with computer techniques*. Los Angeles.

Temple, Ella Dunbar. 1964a. "La cartografïa peruana actual." Sociedad Geográfica de Lima. *Boletín* 83:13-60.

"Les tendances cartographiques aux Etats-Unis." 1959. Comité français de techniques cartographiques. *Bulletin* no. 4:24-31.

Tennessee Valley Authority. 1979. *How topographic maps are made*. 5th ed. Chattanooga(?)

"Terrain analysis program." 1979. *AAG newsletter* 14(9):15.

Thiele, Walter. 1938. *Official map publications, a historical sketch, and a bibliographical handbook of current maps and mapping services in the United States, Canada, Latin America, France, Great Britain, Germany, and certain other countries*. Chicago: American Library Association.

Thompson, Morris M. 1973. "Trends in map revision." *South African journal of photogrammetry* 5(1):22-31.

Thompson, Morris M. 1977. "Automation in surveying and mapping: present and future." American Society of Civil Engineers. Surveying and Mapping Division. *Journal* 103:15-24. (Paper no. 13206.)

Thompson, Morris M. 1979. *Maps for America*. Washington, DC: US Government Printing Office.

Thompson, Morris M., and Speert, Julius L. 1964. "Mapping the surface of the earth." *Natural history* 73(8):30-37.

Thomson, Don W. 1967a. "The history of surveying and mapping in Canada." *Surveying and mapping* 27(1):67-72.

Thomson, Don W. 1967b. *Men and meridians; the history of surveying and mapping in Canada*. vol. II. *1867 to 1917*. Ottawa: Roger Duhamel.

Thomson, Don W. 1969. *Men and meridians; the history of surveying and mapping in Canada*. vol. III. *1817 to 1947*. Ottawa: Roger Duhamel.

Thomson, Don W. 1975. *Skyview Canada; the story of aerial photography in Canada*. Ottawa: Canadian Dept. of Energy, Mines, and Resources.

Thomson, W. A. 1980. "Maintenance of the Australian 1:100 000 national topographic map series." *International archives of photogrammetry* 23(B4): 715-21.

Thrower, Norman Joseph William. 1972. *Maps & man, an examination of cartography in relation to culture and civilization*. Englewood Cliffs, NJ: Prentice-Hall.

Toniolo, Sandro. 1972. "Grönland." Società geogràfica italiana. *Bollettino* 1-3: 155-56.

Tooley, Ronald Vere. 1961. *Maps and map-makers*. New York: Bonanza.

Tooley, Ronald Vere. 1979. *The mapping of Australia*. London: Holland.

"The topographic map of Mexico." 1914. American Geographical Society of New York. *Bulletin* 46:433-36.

"Topographic map series of Mexico." 1950. *Map research bulletin* MB-18:15.

"Topographic mapping completed for Florida." 1979. *biblio* no. 4:5-6.

"Topographic mapping in Australia." 1962. *Surveying and mapping* 22(4):574.

"Topographic maps of the U. S. Geological Survey." 1946. *Surveying and mapping* 6(2):161-63, map following p. 176.

"Topographical maps." 1931. *Science* 74:478-79.

"Topographical maps of Australia." 1935. *Geographical journal* 85(6):575.

"Topographical survey of New Zealand." 1920. *Geographical journal* 55:55-56.

Troxel, Bennie W. 1960. "Maps used in mineral investigations." California. Division of Mines. *Mineral information service* 13(2):1-13.

Turco Greco, Carlos A. 1967. *Catálogo cartográfico de la República Argentina.* Buenos Aires: Editorial Universitaria de Buenos Aires.

Turco Greco, Carlos A. 1968. *Los mapas; breve historia del mundo y su imagen.* Buenos Aires: Editorial Universitaria de Buenos Aires.

Tuttle, A. C. 1961. "The aeroplane and Canadian mapping." *Scottish geographical magazine* 77(1):44-47.

Twenty years of mapping the Americas, 1946-1966. 1966. Quito, Ecuador: Instituto Geográfico Militar.

Tyson, Basil Trevor. 1965(?) *The topographical map series of Australia.* Melbourne(?): Division of National Mapping(?)

UN. See: United Nations.

US. See: United States.

USGS. See: United States. Geological Survey.

U.S. Geological Survey orthophotoquads and orthophotomaps. 198-(?) Denver, CO: National Cartographic Information Center.

United Nations.* 1956. *Report of the United Nations Regional Cartographic Conference for Asia and the Far East, 1st, Mussorie, India, 1955. vol. I: Report* (E/CONF.18/6). New York: United Nations.

United Nations. 1957. *Report of the United Nations Regional Cartographic Conference for Asia and the Far East, 1st, Mussorie, India, 1955. vol. II: Proceedings and technical papers* (E/CONF.18/7). New York: United Nations.

United Nations. 1959. *Report of the United Nations Regional Cartographic Conference for Asia and the Far East, 2nd, Tokyo, 1958. vol. I: Report* (E/CONF. 25/3). New York: United Nations.

---

*When UN documents are cataloged, libraries index these items in the card catalog under their complete authorship: United Nations Regional Cartographic Conference for.... However, for ease of citation in the text, the author is cited here as "United Nations."

United Nations. 1961. *Report of the United Nations Regional Cartographic Conference for Asia and the Far East, 2nd, Tokyo, 1958. vol. II: Proceedings and technical papers* (E/CONF.25/4). New York: United Nations.

United Nations. 1962. *Report of the United Nations Regional Cartographic Conference for Asia and the Far East, 3rd, Bangkok, 1961. vol. I. Report.* (E/CONF.36/2). New York: United Nations.

United Nations. 1963a. *Report of the Conference on the Application of Science and Technology for the Benefit of the Less Developed Areas. vol. II. Natural Resources.* (E/CONF.39/1). New York: United Nations.

United Nations. 1963b. *Report of the United Nations Regional Cartographic Conference for Africa, 1st, Nairobi, 1963. vol. I. Report.* (E/CN.14/INR/40; E/CONF.43/105). New York: United Nations.

United Nations. 1965a. *Report of the United Nations Regional Cartographic Conference for Asia and the Far East, 3rd, Bangkok, 1961. vol. II. Proceedings.* (E/CONF.36/3). New York: United Nations.

United Nations. 1965b. *Report of the United Nations Regional Cartographic Conference for Asia and the Far East, 4th, Manila, 1964. vol. I. Report.* (E/CONF.50/4). New York: United Nations.

United Nations. 1966a. *Report of the United Nations Regional Cartographic Conference for Africa, 1st, Nairobi, 1963. vol. II. Proceedings and technical papers.* (E/CONF.43/106). New York: United Nations.

United Nations. 1966b. *Report of the United Nations Regional Cartographic Conference for Asia and the Far East, 4th, Manila, 1964. vol. II. Proceedings and technical papers.* (E/CONF.50/5). New York: United Nations.

United Nations. 1967a. *Report of the United Nations Regional Cartographic Conference for Africa, 2nd, Tunis, 1966. vol. I. Report.* (E/CN.14/CART/240/Rev. 1). New York: United Nations.

United Nations. 1967b. *Report of the United Nations Regional Cartographic Conference for Africa, 2nd, Tunis, 1966. vol. II. Proceedings and technical papers.* (E/CN.14/CART/242). New York: United Nations.

United Nations. 1967c. *Report of the United Nations Regional Cartographic Conference for Asia and the Far East, 5th, Canberra, 1967. vol. I. Report.* (E/CONF.52/4). New York: United Nations.

United Nations. 1968. *Report of the United Nations Regional Cartographic Conference for Asia and the Far East, 5th, Canberra, 1967. vol. II. Proceedings and technical papers.* (E/CONF.52/5). New York: United Nations.

United Nations. 1974a. *Report of the United Nations Conference on the Standard-ization of Geographical Names, 2nd, London, 1972. vol. II. Technical papers.* (E/CONF.61/4/add.1). New York: United Nations.

United Nations. 1974b. *Report of the United Nations Regional Cartographic Con-ference for Asia and the Far East, 6th, Tehran, 1970. vol. II. Technical papers.* (E/CONF.57/3). New York: United Nations.

United Nations. 1976a. *Report of the United Nations Regional Cartographic Con-ference for Asia and the Far East, 7th, Tokyo, 1973. vol I. Report.* (E/CONF. 62/3). New York: United Nations.

United Nations. 1976b. *Report of the United Nations Regional Cartographic Con-ference for Asia and the Far East, 7th, Tokyo, 1973. vol. II. Technical papers.* (E/CONF.62/40. New York: United Nations.

United Nations. 1977a. *Report of the United Nations Regional Cartographic Con-ference for the Americas, 1st, Panama, 1976. vol. I. Report.* (E/CONF.67/3). New York: United Nations.

United Nations. 1977b. *Report of the United Nations Regional Cartographic Con-ference for Asia and the Far East, 8th, Bangkok, 1977. vol. I. Report.* (E/ CONF.68/3). New York: United Nations.

United Nations. 1979. *Report of the United Nations Regional Cartographic Con-ference for the Americas, 1st, Panama, 1976. vol. II. Technical papers.* (E/ CONF.67/3/add.1). New York: United Nations.

United Nations. 1980. *Report of the United Nations Regional Cartographic Con-ference for Asia and the Far East, 8th, Bangkok, 1977. vol. II. Technical papers.* (E/CONF.68/3/add.1). New York: United Nations.

United Nations. Dept. of Economic and Social Affairs. 1970. "The status of world topographic mapping." *World cartography* 10:1-96.

United Nations. Dept. of Economic and Social Affairs. 1976. "The status of world topographic mapping." *World cartography* 14:3-70.

United Nations. Dept. of Social Affairs. 1949. *Modern Cartography; base maps for world needs.* Lake Success, NY.

United Nations. Secretariat. 1957. "A preliminary survey of world topographical mapping." *World cartography* 5:3-26.

United States. 1888. *Statutes at large* 25:505, 526. Washington, DC.

United States. Army. Inter-American Geodetic Survey, Fort Clayton, Canal Zone. 1967. *Mapping and geodesy goals in Latin America.* [S.l.: s.n.]

United States. Army Map Service. 1954a. *Alaska and Canada Arctic regions map catalog.* Washington, DC.

United States. Army Map Service. 1954b. *Asia, Australia, and the Pacific map catalog*. Washington, DC.

United States. Army Map Service. 1954c. *Central and South America, Caribbean map catalog*. Washington, DC.

United States. Army Map Service. 1966. "Modern quality control in the production of topographic maps." *Revista cartográfica* 15(15):215-21.

United States. Congress. House. 1878. *Geological and geographical surveys*. Washington, DC: US Government Printing Office. (United States. 45th Congress, 2nd session. House. *Executive document* 80 and 81; *Serial set* 1809.)

United States. Congress. House. 1950. *Accelerated program for surveying and mapping of the United States and its territories and possessions*. Washington, DC: US Government Printing Office. (United States. Congress. House. *House report* 2587; *Serial set* 11382.)

United States. Congress. Joint Commission on the Governmental Scientific Bureaus. 1886. *Testimony before the Joint Commission to consider the present organization* ... Washington, DC: US Government Printing Office. (United States. 49th Congress, 1st Session. Senate. *Miscellaneous document* 82; *Serial set* 2345.)

United States. Dept. of State. Office of Research and Intelligence. 1946. *Some Brazilian maps and map sources* ... Washington, DC (No. 3614).

United States. Dept. of the Army. 1956. *Foreign maps*. Washington, DC. (United States. Dept. of the Army. *Technical manual* TM5-248.)

United States. Dept. of the Army. 1963. *Foreign maps*. Washington, DC. (United States. Dept. of the Army. *Technical manual* TM5-248.)

United States. Dept. of the Army. 1970. *Cartographic aerial photography*. Washington, DC. (United States. Dept. of the Army. *Technical manual* TM5-243.)

United States. Dept. of the Interior. 1901. *Annual report*. Washington, DC: US Government Printing Office.

United States. Federal Mapping Task Force on Mapping, Charting, Geodesy, and Surveying. 1973. *Report*. Washington, DC: US Government Printing Office.

United States. General Accounting Office. 1968. *Opportunity to reduce expenditures for map revision and accelerate mapping through changes in map revision practices; report to the Congress—Geological Survey*. Washington, DC.

United States. Geological Survey. 1911. *Topographic maps and folios and geologic folios published by the United States Geological Survey.* Washington, DC.

United States. Geological Survey. 1926. *Topographic instructions of the United States Geological Survey.* Washington, DC. (US Geological Survey. *Bulletin* 788).

United States. Geological Survey. 1930. *Annual report.* Washington, DC.

United States Geological Survey. 1952. *Announcement to map users.* Washington, DC.

United States. Geological Survey. 1958. "U. S. Geological Survey." *Cartography* 2:151-58.

United States. Geological Survey. 1979. *United States Geological Survey yearbook, fiscal year 1978.* Washington, DC: US Government Printing Office.

United States. Geological Survey. 1982. *U.S. Geological Survey activities, fiscal year 1981.* Washington, DC: US Government Printing Office. (US Geological Survey. *Circular* 875.)

United States. Geological Survey. Alaska Branch. 1926. *Mineral industry of Alaska in 1924 and administrative report.* Washington, DC: US Government Printing Office. (US Geological Survey. *Bulletin* 783-A.)

United States. Geological Survey. Topographic Branch. 1947, 1950. *Status of topographic mapping as reported* ... Washington, DC (3rd ed., 1947; Map A, 2nd ed., 1950).

United States. Library of Congress. 1904. *Maps published by foreign governments (Great Britain excepted) in the Library of Congress.* Washington, DC: US Government Printing Office.

United States. Library of Congress. Map Division. 1918. *List of atlases and maps applicable to world war.* Washington, DC: US Government Printing Office.

United States. Map Information Office. various. *Federal surveys and maps; accomplishments.* Washington, DC.

United States. Map Information Office. 1950. *Maps of Alaska.* Washington, DC.

United States National Archives. 1952. *Geographical exploration and topographical mapping by the United States government, 1777-1952; catalog.* Washington, DC: US Government Printing Office. (United States. National Archives. *Publication* 53-2.)

United States. National Resources Board. 1934. *A report on national planning and public works in relation to natural resources and including land use and water resources with finding and recommendations.* Washington, DC: US Government Printing Office.

United States. President (Roosevelt, Franklin Delano, 1933-1945). 1942. *Executive order 9094; abolishing the Board of Surveys and Maps and authorizing the Director of the Bureau of the Budget to perform its functions.* Washington, DC: US Government Printing Office.

United States. Science Advisory Board. 1935. *Report, September 1, 1934 to August 31, 1935.* Washington, DC: US Government Printing Office.

United States. Treaties, etc. 1955. *Brazil aerial mapping program agreement effected by exchange of notes signed at Rio de Janeiro June 2, 1952; entered into force June 2, 1952.* Washington, DC: US Government Printing Office. (TIAS 2656)

United States. Treaties, etc. 1957. *Aerial mapping; cooperative photographing and mapping project; agreement between the United States of America and Venezuela.* Washington, DC: US Government Printing Office. (TIAS 3915)

United States. Treaties, etc. 1959. *Aerial mapping of New Zealand coastal area; agreement between the United States of America and New Zealand ...* Washington, DC: US Government Printing Office. (TIAS 4364)

"Unmapped United States." 1922. *Literary digest* (May 13) 73:24.

Unno, Kazutaka. 1978. *The origin of the cartographical symbol representing desert areas.* [S.l.: s.n.]

Upton, William B. 1970. *Landforms and topographic maps.* New York: Wiley.

Urban, Frank. 1977. "Cartography at the crossroads." *Cartography* 10(1):18-20.

"Uruguay." 1912. Argentine Republic. Instituto Geográfico Militar. *Anuario* 1: 71-73.

Vahala, Matti E. 1978. *Computer assisted cartography in basic map production (1:20,000).* [S.l.: s.n.]

Van Ornum, John Lane. 1896. *Topographical surveys, their methods and value.* Madison: University of Wisconsin. (University of Wisconsin. Engineering Experiment Station. *Bulletin,* v. 1, no. 10)

Venezuela. Ministerio de Obras Públicas. 1938. "Dirección de Cartografía Nacional." Venezuela. Ministerio de Obras Públicas. *Memoria de obras públicas* 1:1-54E, 4:1-100E.

Viglietti, Yamandú Arumey. 1967. "Cartographic activities in Uruguay." *World cartography* 8:103-5.

Viksne, A.; Lister, T. C.; and Sapp, C. D. 1969. "SLR reconnaissance of Panama." *Geophysics* 34:54-64.

Walker, C. Lester. 1953. "Map the world." *Harper's magazine* 206:71-76.

Walling, Henry F. 1884. "Cooperation between national and state governments in topographical surveys." *Van Nostrand's engineering magazine* 31:331-42.

Walling, Henry F. 1886. "Topographic surveys of states." *Van Nostrand's engineering magazine* 34:334-43.

Wallis, Helen. 1976. *Map-making to 1900, an historical glossary of cartographic innovations and their diffusion; preliminary study, presented on the occasion of the Eighth International Conference on Cartography, Moscow, USSR, 3-10 August 1976.* London: The Royal Society.

Walter, W. 1908. "Topographische Karte und Klassenausflug." *Geographischer Anzeiger* 9:33-34, 55-58.

Ward, J. Leroy. 1976. "Intermediate scale mapping." United States. Geological Survey. *Journal of research* 4(3):253-54.

Waugh, B. W. 1953. "Arctic mapping." *Photogrammetric engineering* 19(3):404-6.

Webb, Harry W. 1978. *Topographic maps of Virginia.* Charlottesville: Virginia Division of Mineral Resources. (Virginia. Division of Mineral Resources. *Publication 7: Contributions to Virginia geology*—III.)

Weber, Peter. 1967. "Die amtliche Peruanische Kartographie." *Kartographische Nachrichten* 17(5):176-82.

Weibrecht, O. 1975. "Map revision by orthophotography." Societé française de photogrammetrie. *Bulletin* 58:45-47.

West, J. A. H. 1959. "Military survey in Iraq, 1956-58." *Royal engineers journal* 73:272-81.

Wheat, Carl Irving. 1957. *Mapping the Trans-Mississippi West, 1540-1861.* San Francisco: Institute of Historical Cartography.

Wheeler, George Montague. 1885. *Report upon the Third International Geographical Congress and Exhibition at Venice, Italy, 1881, accompanied by data concerning the principal government land and marine surveys of the world.* Washington, DC: US Government Printing Office. (United States. 48th Congress. 2nd Session. House. *Executive document* 270; *Serial set* 2293.)

Wilby, F. B. 1935. "National mapping plan of the Board of Surveys and Maps of the Federal government." *Civil engineering* 5(2):125-27.

Williams, Joseph E. 1953. "The relief map." *Journal of geography* 5(5):7-11.

Williams, Nora. 1976. "The conference as kaleidoscope." Association of Canadian Map Libraries. *Bulletin* no. 22:13-14.

Wilson, H. M. 1907. "Topographic surveys in the United States." American Geographical Society of New York. *Bulletin* 39:13-24.

Wing, Robert L. 1949. "The topographic mapping program in California." *Surveying and mapping* (3):204-10.

Winslow, Arthur. 1894. "The art and development of topographic mapping." *Factory and industrial management* 6:24-31.

Winterbotham, Harold St. John Lloyd. 1932. "The small-scale maps of the Ordnance Survey." *Geographical journal* 79(1):17-31.

Winterbotham, Harold St. John Lloyd. 1936. *A key to maps.* London: Blackie.

Winters, S. R. 1922. "What and why is a contour." *Scientific American* 126:253.

Witkege, Francis L. 1965. "The national topographic map series (USGS)." *Surveying and mapping* 25(4):567-72.

Wood, Dennis. 1977. "Now and then: comparisons of ordinary Americans' symbol conventions with those of past cartographers." *Prologue* 9:151-61.

Wood, Dennis. 1978. *Cultured symbols, thoughts on the cultural content of cartographic symbols.* [S.l.: s.n.]

Woodring, Harry H.; Johnson, J. M.; and Ickes, Harold L. 1939. "Surveys and mapping in the United States; a joint letter of the Secretary of War, Secretary of Commerce, and Secretary of the Interior." *Military engineer* 31(178):269-71.

Woodward, Douglas R. 1955. "The Federal government in the field of surveying and mapping." *Surveying and mapping* 15(1):144-48.

Woodward, Frances M. 1981. "Exploration and survey of the Kootenay District 1800-1918." Association of Canadian Map Libraries. *Bulletin* 38:2-26.

The world encompassed, an exhibition of the history of maps held at the Baltimore Museum of Art, October 7 to November 23, 1952. 1952. Baltimore: Trustees of the Walters Art Gallery.

"World in the flat; maps 'round the globe." 1965. *Times literary supplement* 64: 485-86.

Worton, F. J. 1982. "An oblique view of some early survey flying." *Photogrammetric record* 10(59):517-28.

Wrather, William. 1949. *National topographic mapping—status and progress.* Washington, DC: [s.n.]

Wright, David. 1975. "Maps are liars." *Geographical magazine* 47(11):674.

Wright, John Kirtland. 1924. *Early topographical maps, their geographical and historical value as illustrated by the maps of the Harrison Collection of the American Geographical Society.* New York: American Geographical Society.

Wright, John Kirtland. 1940. "The world in maps." *Geographical review* 30(1): 1-18.

Wright, John Kirtland. 1950. "Highlights in American cartography, 1939-1949." International Geographical Congress (15th; Lisbon, 1949). *Proceedings* 1:299-314.

Wyener, Robert Lee. 1953. "Geographic factors and cartographic problems in long range and regional mapping programs." *Professional geographer* 5(5):16-22.

Yoéli, Pinhas. 1959. "Relief shading." *Surveying and mapping* 19(2):229-32.

Yoéli, Pinhas. 1964. "Relief and contour." *Cartographic journal* 1(2):37-38.

Young, M. E. H. 1973. "1:50 000 mapping in Canada." *Bildmessung und Luftbildwesen* 41(6):205-12.

Zarzycki, J. M. 1972. "The use of airborne equipment in survey and mapping in Guyana." pp. 200-3 in: Conference of Commonwealth Survey Officers, 1971. *Report of proceedings.* London: HMSO.

Zaslow, Morris. 1975. *Reading the rocks: the story of the Geological Survey of Canada, 1842-1972.* Toronto: Macmillan.

Zegheru, N. 1980. "Remote sensing in map compilation and revision." *International archives of photogrammetry* 23(B4):744-81.

Zelinsky, Wilbur. 1951. "New 1:250,000 map of the United States." *Geographical review* 41:662-64.

Zuylen, L. van. 1978. "The use of remote sensing for the updating of maps." *ITC journal* 78:333-46.

Zuylen, L. van. 1980. "Map revision." *ITC journal* no. 1:130-39.

INDEX

A map series, 86
Aerial photography
  in Australia, 35-36, 37
  beginnings of, 23
  in Canada, 86, 87, 88
  in Central America, 57-58, 61
  disadvantages of, 25
  in Greenland, 83
  in Latin America, 50, 51
  in Mexico, 54
  in New Zealand, 42
  for relief depiction, 12
  and satellite imagery, 29
  in South America, 63, 65, 66, 67,
    68, 69, 70, 71, 72, 73, 74,
    75, 76
  in the twentieth century, 24, 25,
    26, 27, 31
  in US., 99, 103
Aerial surveys. *See* Aerial photography
Aeronautical charts, 87
Aerotriangulation. *See* Triangulation
Africa, 20
AGS. *See* American Geographical
    Society
Airborne Profile Recorder, 26
Alabama, 94, 95
Alaska
  1800s mapping of, 96
  1900s mapping of, 97, 98, 99, 100,
    101-2, 103, 104, 105, 106,
    107

Alberta
  aerial photography of, 87
  mapping units of, 88
  1:190,080-scale map of, 85
Alidade, 23-24
Alpine regions, 24
Altazimuth theodolite, 22
Amazon basin
  1900s mapping of, 68-69
  triangulation of, 20
American Geographical Society
    (AGS)
  and 1:1,000,000 series, 50
  and Paraguayan mapping, 74
AMS. *See* United States Army Map
    Service
Angular measurement, 20, 21
Antarctica
  Landsat imagery used in, 29
  and mapping of Chilean Antarctic
    Territory, 70
  snow and ice mapping of, 12
Antilles, 52
Arctic, Canadian
  early mapping of, 87-88
  1950s mapping of, 89
  1:50,000-scale sheets of, 90
Argentina
  and the IAGS, 51
  mapping of, 63-65
  survey sheets, 49, 50
  table of sheet issuance, 64

Arizona
    1869-1879 mapping of, 93
    1900s mapping of, 97, 98, 105
Arkansas, 95
Artillery Map, 35
Australia. *See also names of specific
        states*
    establishment of survey corps, 35
    introduction of aerial photography,
        35, 36
    Landsat station in, 29, 39-40
    map coverage of, 44
    mapping of, 35-40
Australian National Mapping Council,
    36, 37

Baffin Islands, 89
Barrow Island, 38
Baseline, 19, 20, 21
Belize, 57
Bolivia, 65-66
Brazil, 50
    Landsat station in, 29
    mapping of, 66-69
    sheet publication, 49
British Columbia
    contour mapping of, 86
    mapping units of, 88
    nineteenth century sheets of, 85
    1:50,000-scale sheets of, 90
    twentieth century mapping of, 87
    and work with federal government,
        91
British Directorate of Military Survey,
    57
British Directorate of Overseas Surveys
    (DOS), 57, 73
British GSGS series, 87
British Guiana. *See* Guyanas
British Honduras. *See* Belize
British Ordnance Survey, 22
    in Australia, 35, 37
    perfection of theodolite, 21
    use of contour, 17
    use of spot heights, 16
Brooks Range Project (Alaska), 103,
    104

Budgets for mapping, 95, 96, 97, 98,
    103, 107

California
    cooperative funding of, 101, 104
    1800s mapping of, 94, 95, 96
    1900s mapping of, 97, 99, 101
Canada. *See also names of specific
        provinces*
    bureaus of mapping for, 86
    and computer-assisted mapping, 31
    mapping of, 84-91
Canadian Arctic. *See* Arctic, Canadian
Canadian Department of Militia and
        Defence, 85, 86
Canadian National Topographic Sys-
        tem (NTS), 86
Cartographers, 14-18
Cascade Mountains, 92
Cave paintings, 14
Central America, 52. *See also names of
        specific republics*
    map of, 109
    mapping of, 57-62
CETENAL. *See* Comisión de Estudios
        del Territorio Nacional
Chile, 50
    mapping of, 69-70
    selection of scale, 49
CI. *See* Contour interval
Cliff drawing for relief depiction, 9,
    11, 12
Coast and Geodetic Survey. *See*
        United States Coast and
        Geodetic Survey
Coats Island, 89
Colombia
    aerial photography in, 51
    mapping of, 50, 70-71
    and Panama relationship, 61
Color relief method, 11, 17
Colorado
    1800s mapping of, 93, 94, 96
    1900s mapping of, 101, 105

Comisión de Estudios del Territorio
    Nacional (CETENAL), 55, 56
Comisión Geográfica Militar (Mexico)
    establishment of, 54
    name change for, 55
Comissão do Imperio do Brasil, 66
Compass, magnetic, 21
Computer-assisted cartography
    in Australia, 39
    in Brazil, 69
    in Canada, 90, 91
    and digitization, 26, 29, 30, 31,
        90-91, 105, 106, 107
    in U.S., 105, 106, 107, 108
Connecticut
    agreements for mapping of, 95
    1900s mapping of, 97, 99, 100, 107
Contour interval (CI)
    definition, 10
    and hypsometric tints, 11
Contours for relief depiction, 3, 4, 5,
    9, 36
    advantages and disadvantages of, 11
    definition of, 10
    eighteenth century use of, 15, 16
    for Greenland maps, 83
    and hypsometric tints, 11
    nineteenth century use of, 17
    produced from timetrogon photo-
        graphs, 88
    and relief methods, 12
    scales for best depiction of, 13
    twentieth century use of, 18
    U.S. mapping with, 93, 94
Cooperative agreements for mapping,
    95, 96, 97, 98, 99, 100, 101,
    102, 103, 104, 107
Copper engraving, 14, 23
Costa Rica
    mapping of, 57-58
    and surveying difficulties, 51
Costs of mapping, 23, 26, 27, 97, 98, 99,
    100, 101, 102, 103, 104, 107

Defense Mapping Agency (DMA), 52.
    See also United States Army
    Map Service
    issues sheets on Honduras, 60
    name change for, 51
    and the USGS, 105, 106

Delaware, 98, 99, 100, 107
Denmark
    mapping of Greenland by, 83
    use of contours, 17
Departamento Cartográfico Militar
    (Mexico)
    establishment of, 54
    series work of, 55, 56
Department of Lands and Survey,
    New Zealand, 41, 42, 43
Deserts, 35, 36
    and orthophotomaps, 105
    in relief depiction, 11, 12
DETENAL, 56
Digitization. *See under* Computer-
    assisted cartography
Dirección General de Cartografía
    (Nicaragua), 60, 61
Dirección General de Estudios del
    Territorio Nacional (DETENAL),
    56
Dirección General de Geografía y
    Meteorología (Mexico), 53, 54,
    55
Distance measurement
    with electronics, 20
    innovations in, 25
District of Columbia, 99, 100, 107
Division of National Mapping, Aus-
    tralia (NATMAP), 37, 39, 40
DMA. *See* Defense Mapping Agency
DMS, 57
DOS. *See* British Directorate of Over-
    seas Surveys
DOS map series, 57
Dufourkarte, 17
Dutch Guiana. *See* Guyanas

E map series, 57, 58, 59, 60, 61, 72
Earth Resources Technology Satellite.
    See Landsat
Ecuador, 71-72
El Salvador, 57, 58
Elevation measurement, 27
Ellesmere Island, 89
Embossing for relief depiction, 9
Emergency Mapping Scheme,
    Australia, 36
ERTS-1. *See* Landsat

F map series, 55
Florida
    cooperative program for, 103, 107
    1900s mapping of, 105, 107
Formlines for relief depiction, 9
    definition of, 10
    on maps of Belize, 57
    on sheets for Guyanas, 73
    on Tehuantepec map, 53
France, 16
    aerial photography in, 24
    and Institut geographique national,
        72, 73
    use of contours, 17
French Guiana. *See* Guyanas
Funding for mapping, 96, 97, 98, 99,
    100, 101, 103, 107

Gaspé Peninsula, 85
Geodesy, 3
    in Argentina, 63
    control in Canada, 88
    data collection in Latin America,
        50
    definition of, 19
    networks, 20
    in U.S., 93, 94, 104
Geodimeter, 26
Geographic map, 7, 15
Geographical and Geological Survey of
    the Rocky Mountain Region, 93
Geographical Survey West of the
    100th Meridian, 93
Geologic maps, 105
Geological and Geographical Survey of
    the Territories, 93
Geological Exploration of the 40th
    Parallel, 93
Georgia
    1880s mapping of, 94
    1900s mapping of, 105, 107
Germany
    computer-assisted mapping in, 31
    cost of survey in, 23
Gibson Desert (Australia), 35
Glaciers. *See* Snow and ice depiction
Grand Canyon, 95
Great Britain, 57, 85, 87
    computer-assisted mapping in, 31
    contour intervals of, 10
    use of contours, 17

Great Plains, 100
Great Sand Desert (Australia), 36
Great Trigonometrical Survey of India,
    22
Greenland
    mapping of, 83
    snow and ice mapping, 12
    triangulation, 20
Ground photography
    beginnings of, 23
    in Brazil, 66
    in Canada, 84, 86
GSGS series, 87
Guatemala
    and Central American Union, 57
    mapping of, 59
Guyana. *See* Guyanas
Guyanas, 72-73

Hachures for relief depiction, 4, 9
    on Australian sheets, 36, 38
    definition of, 10
    in eighteenth century, 16
    on Nicaraguan sheets, 61
    in nineteenth century, 17
    scales for best depiction of, 13
    in seventeenth century, 15
    on sheets for Guyanas, 73
    and spot elevations, 11
    on U.S. Wheeler survey sheets, 93
Hawaii, 99, 102, 103
Hill and mountain profiles for relief
    depiction, 9
    advantages and disadvantages of, 11
    in eighteenth century, 16
    molehills and sugarloafs, 14, 15
Hill shading for relief depiction, 9
    on Australian sheets, 36, 39
    definition of, 10
    on Greenland maps, 83
Honduras
    and the Central American Union,
        57
    mapping of, 59-60
Hypsometric tints for relief depiction,
    9
    definition of, 11
    in nineteenth century, 17
    scales for best depiction of, 13

IAGS. *See* Inter-American Geodetic Survey
IBGE, 68
IGM. *See* Instituto Geográfico Militar
Illinois
  1900s mapping of, 97
  p-map of, 108
Indiana
  and cooperative agreement with USGS, 98, 100
  1800s mapping of, 95
  funding for mapping in, 103
  1900s mapping of, 98, 107
Instituto Brasileiro de Geografía e Estatistica, 68
Instituto Geográfico e Geológico do Estado do São Paula
  first topographic map, 49
  1960s mapping, 67
  1:100,000 sheets, 66
Instituto Geográfico Militar (IGM), 63
  in Argentina, 63, 65
  in Chile, 69, 70
  in Peru, 74, 75
Inter-American Geodetic Survey (IAGS), 50, 52
  in Chile, 70
  establishment of, 51
  and Guatemalan series (E503), 59
  and Honduran series (E752), 60
  and Nicaraguan series, 60
International Boundary Commission, 100
International Map of the World
  Argentinian sheets, 63
  U.S. sheets, 101
Isobaths, 14-15
Isolines, 15. *See also* Contours for relief depiction; Isobaths
Israel, 6
Italy, 23

J map series, 75
Japan, 6
JOG, 40
Joint Operations Graphic, 40

Kansas
  1800s mapping of, 95, 96
  1900s mapping of, 107
Kelsh plotters, 26
Kentucky
  cooperative agreement with, 102
  1800s mapping of, 94, 95
  1900s mapping of, 97, 107
King, Clarence, 93, 94

Lakes Survey, 100
Landsat
  in Australia, 39-40
  in Brazil, 69
  purpose of, 28-29
  in U.S., 106
Large-scale sheets. *See* Scales for mapping
Latin America, 49-51
Layer tints for relief depiction, 18. *See also* Hypsometric tints for relief depiction
Levels and level rods, 24
Lithography
  development of, 17
  replaces copper engraving, 23
  in twentieth century, 18
Lobeck, Armin Kohl, 11

Manitoba, 85, 86, 87
Mansel Island, 89
Map printing
  nineteenth century, 23
  twentieth century, 25, 26, 27, 31, 90-91, 105, 106, 107-8
Mapa del Territorio Nacional, 60
Mapa Física y Política de Venezuela, 76
Mapa Topográfico de la República Mexicana, 53
Maryland, 98, 99, 100, 102, 107
Massachusetts
  1884 mapping of, 95
  1900s mapping of, 97, 100, 102, 107
Medium-scale. *See* Scales for mapping
Metrification, 106
Mexico, 50
  aerial photography of, 54
  mapping of, 52, 53-56

Minnesota
  1800s mapping of, 95
  1900s mapping of, 104, 105
Mississippi River flood plain, 99
Missouri
  and computer-generated sheets, 108
  cooperative agreement with, 96
  1884 mapping of, 95
Molehills. *See under* Hill and mountain
    profiles
Montana, 97
MSS. *See* Multi-spectral scanner
Multi-spectral scanner (MSS), 29, 39.
    See also Landsat

National Mapping Program, 105, 106
National Surveying and Mapping Act,
    102
National Topographic Program, 101
National Topographic System
    (Canada), 86, 87
NATMAP. *See* Division of National
    Mapping, Australia
Nebraska, 96
Netherlands Central Bureau Luckt-
    kartering, 73
Nevada, 95
New Brunswick, 85, 89
New Granada. *See* Colombia
New Hampshire
  1800s mapping of, 95, 96
  1900s mapping of, 104
New Jersey
  1800s mapping of, 95
  1900s mapping of, 97, 99, 100,
    103, 107
New Mexico, 94, 104
New South Wales, 38
  establishment of Central Mapping
    Authority, 36
  mapping of, 35, 39, 40
New York
  agreements for mapping of, 95
  1800s mapping of, 95, 96
  funding for mapping, 98
  1900s mapping of, 97, 98, 99, 100,
    102, 106
New Zealand
  mapping of, 41-43
  topographic map of, 44

New Zealand Aerial Mapping Com-
    pany, Ltd., 42
Newfoundland
  Labrador, 85, 87, 90
  mapping of, 87, 88, 89
Nicaragua, 57, 60-61
North America map, 109
North Carolina, 94, 95
North Dakota, 96
Northern Territory (Australia), 37
Nottingham Island, 89
Nova Scotia, 89
NTS, 86
NTS map series, 87
NZMS map series, 42, 43

Odometer, 21
Office of Management and Budget
    (OMB), 16, 104
Ohio, 97, 98, 99, 100, 102, 107
Oklahoma, 96
OMB. *See* Office of Management and
    Budget
Ontario, 88
  aerial photography of, 87
  expansion of mapping, 89, 91
  1912 contoured maps of, 86
Orthophotographs
  definition of, 26, 105
  Ontario's use of, 91
  USGS use of, 26, 107
Orthophotomap
  advantages of, 27
  in Australia, 39
  Canadian use of, 91
  definition of, 26
  in Nicaragua, 61
  in U.S., 105, 107
Orthophotoquad, 105, 106

Pacific Northwest, 100
PAIGH. *See* Pan American Institute
    of Geography and History
Pan American Institute of Geography
    and History (PAIGH), 50, 51, 56
Panama
  and aerial photography, 51
  mapping of, 61-62
  SLAR use in, 28
Paraguay, 73-74, 101

Paraná River (Argentina), 65
Pennsylvania
  1800s mapping of, 95, 96-97
  1900s mapping of, 97, 101, 102,
    105, 107
Peru, 50, 61
  mapping of, 74-75
  satellite photography of, 28
  sheet publication in, 49
Petén, Lake (Guatemala), 59
Petroleum companies, 104
  aerial photography by, 99
  mapping by, 66, 71
  surveys by, 76, 89
Photogrammetry, 26, 27
  in Argentina, 63, 65
  in Australia, 35
  in Brazil, 66, 67
  in Canada, 86, 91
  definition of, 24
  in Mexico, 54-55
  in Peru, 75
  replacement of plane-table, 25
Photography, aerial. *See* Aerial
    photography
Photography, ground. *See* Ground
    photography
Photolithography. *See* Lithography
Photomapping, 27
  in Australia, 36, 37
  in Canada, 84
Phototopography, 84, 85, 89
Physiographic sketching for relief
    depiction, 9, 11
Plane table, 23
  in Argentina, 63, 65
  in Canada, 88
  definition of, 21
  in Nicaragua, 60
  in Panama, 61
  replaced by photogrammetry, 25,
    55
  in U.S., 93, 99
P-maps. *See* Provisional maps
Powell, John Wesley, 93, 96
Prince Edward Island, 89
Profiles, hill and mountain. *See*
    Hill and mountain profiles
Provisional maps, 107-8
Puerto Rico, 104

Quadrant, 22
Quebec, 88
  1964 expansion of mapping of, 89
  1:50,000-scale sheets of, 90
Queensland, 37, 38
  mapping between two world wars,
    35
  1970s mapping of, 39

RADAM, 69
Raised relief depiction, 9. *See also*
    Three-dimensional relief
    methods
Raisz, Erwin Josephus, 11
Reconnaissance mapping, 49
  in Brazil, 66, 67, 68
  in the Guyanas, 73
  in the U.S., 93, 95, 97, 98, 99
Rectification, differential, 26
Relief depiction
  history of, 14-18
  methods for, 9-12
  problems of, 12-13
Remote sensing, 27
Reproduction innovation. *See* Map
    printing
Rhode Island
  agreements for mapping of, 95
  1900s mapping of, 97, 99, 100,
    102, 107
River charts, 15
Rock drawing for relief depiction, 9,
    11, 12
Rocky Mountains (Canada), 84, 85
Rocky Mountains (U.S.), 92, 93
Royal Australian Survey Corps, 35,
    39, 40
Russia, 6

São Francisco River basin, 67
Saskatchewan, 85, 86, 87
Satellite imagery, 27, 28, 29
Satellites for mapping, 26, 27, 29, 30
Scales for mapping, 6-9
Sectional Map Series
  of Canada, 85
  conversion of, 86
Serial Set (U.S.), 92
Servicio Geográfico Militar (SGM), 71
SGM, 71

Shaded relief for depiction, 4, 9, 12, 13
  in nineteenth century, 17
  in seventeenth century, 15
  in twentieth century, 18
  in U.S., 104
Sheets, definition of, 9
Shoran system, 26
Side-looking airborne radar (SLAR)
  in Brazil, 69
  in Colombia, 71
  definition of, 28
  in Panama, 61
  and remote sensing, 27
  in U.S., 106
Sierra Nevada (U.S.), 92
SLAR. *See* Side-looking airborne radar
Small-scale. *See* Scales for mapping
Snow and ice depiction, 11, 12
South America, 52. *See also names of specific republics*
  mapping of, 63-77
  1:250,000-scale sample map of, 78
South Australia, 38, 39
  beginning of mapping of, 35
  and state mapping, 36-37
South Dakota, 96
Space surveying, 30
Spot elevations for relief depiction, 4, 9, 12
  advantages of, 11
  Canadian use of, 91
  in eighteenth century, 16
  on Greenland maps, 83
  in sixteenth century, 14
Stadia principle, 22, 23, 24
Stereographic mapping, 12
Stereoplotting instruments
  Kelsh plotters, 26
  USGS research on, 99
SUDAM, 68-69
SUDENE, 68
Sugarloafs. *See under* Hill and mountain profiles
Superintendência do Desenvolvimento da Amazônia, 68-69
Superintendência do Desenvolvimento do Nordeste, 68
Surinam. *See* Guyanas
Survey Co-ordination Act of 1940, 36

Surveys, aerial. *See* Aerial photography
Switzerland, 9
  adoption of stadia system, 23
  computer-assisted cartography in, 31
  DuCarla's map of, 16
  Gyger's cantonal maps of, 15

Tasmania, 38
  formation of mapping branch, 36
  1970s mapping of, 39, 40
Tasmania Mapping Division, 40
TASMAP, 40
Tellurometer, 25
Temple Act, 98
Tennessee
  aerial photography of, 24
  mapping of, 94, 95, 107
Tennessee Valley Authority, 24
Texas
  cooperative funding for, 98, 103
  mapping of, 95, 97, 98, 100
Texas Water Planning Act, 103
Theodolites, 21, 22, 23, 24
Three-dimensional relief methods
  advantages and disadvantages of, 12
  models for, 10
  types of, 9
Topographic Atlas of the United States, 94, 99
Topographic maps, 30
  cost of surveys for, 27
  definition of, 3-6, 9
  and photogrammetry, 25
  scale delimitation of, 6-8
  system for producing, 25-26, 31
Topographic quadrangle, 94
Topographic survey
  costs, 23, 26, 27
  methodology for, 19-31
Topographical Conference, 95
Topographical Series (British Columbia), 86
Transits, 23, 24
Trans-Mississippi West, 92
Triangulation, 21, 25, 27, 31
  in Argentina, 63
  in Chile, 69, 70
  definition of, 19, 20

Triangulation (cont'd.)
in Guatemala, 59
improvements of, 22
in Latin America, 51
in New Zealand, 41
with satellites, 20
in Venezuela, 76
in U.S., 93, 99
Trimetrogon photography,
in Brazil, 67
Canadian use of, 88, 89
in Chile, 70
definition of, 25
in U.S., 101

Unified Hemispheric Mapping Series,
51-52, 56
United States, 7. *See also names of
specific states*
1800s mapping of, 92-97
hypsometric tints in, 11
negotiations with New Zealand, 42
1900s mapping of, 97-108
1700s mapping of, 92
treaty with Brazil, 67
use of contours, 17
use of stadia system, 23
treaty with Venezuela, 76
United States Air Force
and aerial photography, 54, 75
development of trimetrogon photography, 88
United States Army Corps of
Engineers, 92
aerial photography, 99
and the Inter-American Geodetic
Survey, 50
work on Panama Canal, 61
United States Army Map Service
(AMS). *See also* Defense
Mapping Agency
in Guatemala, 59
in Honduras, 60
issues series E691 for the Guyanas,
72
issues series on Mexico, 55, 56
in Panama, 61
surveys in Latin America, 51
in U.S., 101, 102, 105

United States Coast and Geodetic
Survey, 94, 95
budgets of, 96
establishment of, 93
mapping role of, 100
United States Defense Mapping
Agency. *See* Defense Mapping
Agency
United States Geological Survey
(USGS), 12, 26
and aerial photography, 24
budget of, 96, 97, 98, 99, 103
computerization of mapping, 30
and cooperative mapping funds,
97, 98-99, 100, 101
creation of, 94
mapping by, 95, 96, 97, 98, 99,
100, 101, 102, 103, 104,
105, 106, 107, 108
Uruguay, 50
and the IAGS, 51
mapping of, 75
scale selection, 49
USGS. *See* United States Geological
Survey
USSR, 6
Utah
cooperative funding for, 102
mapping of, 93, 95
orthophotomaps in, 105

Venezuela
mapping of, 76-77
petroleum companies in, 71
Vermont, 96, 103, 104
Victoria, 35, 36, 38
Virginia
1800s mapping of, 95
1900s mapping of, 97, 100, 105,
107

WAC, 54
Walcott, Charles D., 94
Washington (state), 97
West Virginia, 95
cooperative program for, 96, 107
1900s mapping of, 97, 98, 99, 100,
102, 107
Western Australia, 36, 37
1965 coverage of, 38
scales for, 39

Wilderness Line, 90
Wisconsin, 95
World Aeronautical Charts, 54
Wyoming, 105

Yucatan, 56
Yukon
    completion of mapping of, 89
    in early twentieth century, 87
    explorations of, 85
    1:50,000-scale sheets of, 90